THE
PRACTICAL
DIY
HANDBOOK

THE PRACTICAL DIY HANDBOOK

Carpentry
Plumbing · Electricity
Central Heating
& Insulation

CHANCELLOR
PRESS

Previously published in Great Britain by Octopus Books Limited,
in 4 separate volumes as follows:

CARPENTRY   Alec Limon and Paul Curtis
                             Consultant editor: Mike Trier
                             © 1983, 1984, 1987 Octopus Publishing Group Limited

ELECTRICITY   Mike Lawrence
                             Consultant editor: Richard Wiles
                             © 1984, Octopus Publishing Group Limited

PLUMBING   Alan Wakeford
                             Consultant editor: Richard Wiles
                             © 1984 Octopus Publishing Group Limited

CENTRAL HEATING   Ned Halley
& INSULATION   Consultant editor: Richard Wiles
                             © 1984 Octopus Publishing Group Limited

This omnibus edition first published in 1992 by Ivy Leaf
an imprint of Octopus Publishing Group Ltd

This edition published in 2000 by
Chancellor Press, an imprint of Bounty Books,
a division of Octopus Publishing Group Ltd,
2-4 Heron Quays, London E14 4JP

© Octopus Publishing Group Ltd 1992

ISBN 0 75370 387 4

Produced by Toppan (HK) Ltd
Printed by China

Contents

Carpentry

Alec Limon and Paul Curtis

Consultant Editor Mike Trier

Introduction

Much of the satisfaction of carpentry is measured by the quality of the end result, and this book sets about helping you to achieve a good finished product and ensure that satisfaction.

An important starting point is to buy good quality materials and make yourself aware of possible faults as, without this knowledge, the quality of a carefully constructed project can be a disappointment. Standard timber sizes vary slightly from one supplier to another, so it is as well to check those of the timber you are using before working out critical dimensions. Also bear in mind that hardwoods have greater strength than softwoods of the same section and you can therefore use smaller hardwood sections to give a less bulky appearance to your constructions.

The use of elaborate and expensive tools alone will not ensure good workmanship. The secret of success is knowing which is the right tool to use for a particular job, and how to use it. In this book you will find details of the basic tools and techniques for using them, as well as some of the more specialised tools, including some which can be home-made.

Having selected suitable materials and the necessary tools, the next important step is setting out the parts carefully and accurately, using the correct methods. Always remember to check and double check all dimensions before proceeding – a pencil line is easy to erase and reposition, but undersized pieces of timber are costly and cause frustration. A good carpenter will only use a cutting list as a guide: at each stage of the construction, he or she will measure the dimensions of the parts to fit exactly, and cut so as to leave the guideline standing.

All this information will be helpful if you are working from a set of plans and instructions. However, if you wish to design your own projects, you will need to know about different principles and methods of construction. Conventional woodworking joints and fixings, techniques for working with man-made boards and box construction are also described.

All homes need a variety of storage units designed to suit different situations, such as under the stairs or along a living-room wall. A variety of designs are covered here, including exploded drawings of some typical constructions, a selection of fittings available, and techniques for hanging a door. Do remember when fixing a unit to a wall to check first for concealed pipes and wiring. Small electronic detectors are available which make this task easy, but a general rule is never to make fixings vertically above or below electrical fittings, and to avoid the vicinity of pipe runs near plumbing appliances.

A superb finish can be the highlight of an otherwise everyday article. Different finishes are described for showing off the grain of the timber to the full or for colouring it to suit your taste. And, to enable you to put into practice some of the techniques described, you will find some excellent furniture projects with working drawings and instructional text.

> Remember that SAFETY WARNINGS and MANUFACTURERS' INSTRUCTIONS are designed for your safety and health. Use the proper equipment and wear the correct clothing – never wear a tie. Do take particular care with any electrical work, it is never trivial, and when working with chemicals. Always protect your eyes with goggles when the situation demands it. Never interfere with, or remove, safety guards on power equipment. Concentrate on safety at all times and do not rush work – it is not worth it.

Ignorance of the nature of the materials you are using can cause a project to fail. Timber is a natural material and it is necessary to know something about the way it grows in order to understand how it can best be used and how it will behave in use.

Briefly, trees grow by adding new layers round the outside of the trunk, just underneath the bark, This makes the well-known annual rings. The sap which feeds these new layers also passes through to the centre or heartwood along the medullary rays which we call the figuring when the wood has been cut into planks. This means that the first few centimetres of the tree immediately under the bark are not fully grown cells and the mature timber is found towards the middle of the tree. The actual centre is known as the pith. These distinct areas behave differently in use.

Sapwood, that is the outer, immature wood, shrinks more than the inner heartwood. It is therefore more liable to twist. As shrinkage takes place round the direction of the annual rings from the outer part of the tree towards the central heart, if the tree is simply cut straight through into wide planks they will contain more sapwood on one side than the other, and will warp away from the heart side as the sapwood dries out and shrinks more than the heartwood. The pith should be avoided for all but the least important jobs because it is the most likely to twist as it dries or seasons.

When buying timber, as well as looking for the obvious defects such as large knots, shakes and cracks, and at general appearance, look also at the end grain, as it will tell you a lot about the future movement of the wood. The best pieces have the annual-ring marks fairly vertical across the narrowest width. Square timbers should not have the rings running diagonally as this will distort the shape.

Above right *Table of commonly available sections of softwoods and hardwoods.*

Right *Cross-section through a tree showing important features.*

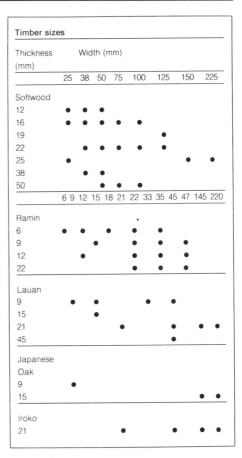

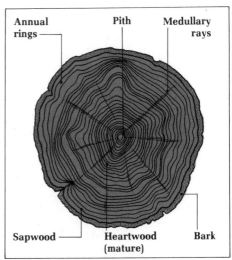

Usage of timber

Timber not only dries and shrinks but also takes up moisture and swells. Its tendency to change shape affects the choice of wood and the way it is used. For example, you should always put the timber heart side up for table tops and the tops of wooden stools, and table tops should not be fixed firmly, only buttoned or attached with slotted plates to allow for this movement.

Further, if wide boards are to be made up using a number of narrow boards edge-jointed together, it is best to arrange the boards so that they are alternately heart side up and heart side down. This will cause them to pull against each other and in this way help to hold them flat. The battens underneath, which are used to hold the boards, must be screwed through slots, not through tight screw holes. In this way the whole top can adjust itself to the atmospheric conditions.

These comments apply to both hardwoods and softwoods, although the movement of softwoods is greater than that of hardwoods. However, the movement of the latter can often have a more damaging effect because these timbers are used for furniture show-woods.

Hardwoods and softwoods

The terms hardwood and softwood are based on the structure of the wood and the characteristics of the trees. In general, softwoods are from trees with small, pointed leaves of the cone-bearing and evergreen types, while hardwoods are from trees which shed their leaves in autumn. For practical purposes, softwoods are used for general joinery and structural work while hardwoods are generally used for furniture and show woods.

Buying boards

There are three main types of manufactured wooden boards – hardboard, chipboard and plywood (including blockboard). They are sold by the square metre, hardboard and plain, standard chipboard being cheaper than veneered chipboards, ply-woods and blockboards of the same thickness.

Hardboard is shredded timber which has been pulped and remade as large sheets. It can be plain or patterned and there is an oil-tempered type which is for use externally. Hardboard is used for the base of boards finished with a woodgrain pattern or tiled finish. Fretted pattern boards are also made and these make good decorative grilles.

Chipboard is made from timber chipped into flakes and then pressed, with a resin binder, to make a large sheet of material. It is available in stock sizes of length and width, and with a range of timber-veneer or plastic facings. Special grades are available for flooring.

Plywood is made in a very wide range of sizes and thicknesses. The number of plies varies according to the thickness required which can be from about 4mm to 25mm. All kinds of facing veneers are available from plain birch to mahogany and teak. For panelling there is a planked-pattern finish as well as plain wood.

Laminated boards consist of a core of wood strips glued or laminated into one solid piece, faced with veneer. They are obtainable in similar finishes to plywood. Pine-board also comes under the general heading of laminated boards. It is made from strips of pine edge-glued together and is available in a range of widths and lengths.

Usage of boards

Hardboards and softwood-faced plywoods can be used for similar purposes. When buying them take care that the sheets are completely flat, because once they have taken up a curved or distorted shape they are difficult to straighten.

Chipboards and blockboards also have similar uses and for the same reasons care must be taken that they are flat. Both boards are stable, but as shelving, block-boards will hold greater weights over larger spans. Blockboard has a surface which will accept a finish without further work, but chipboard needs to have a decorative sur-face applied to it.

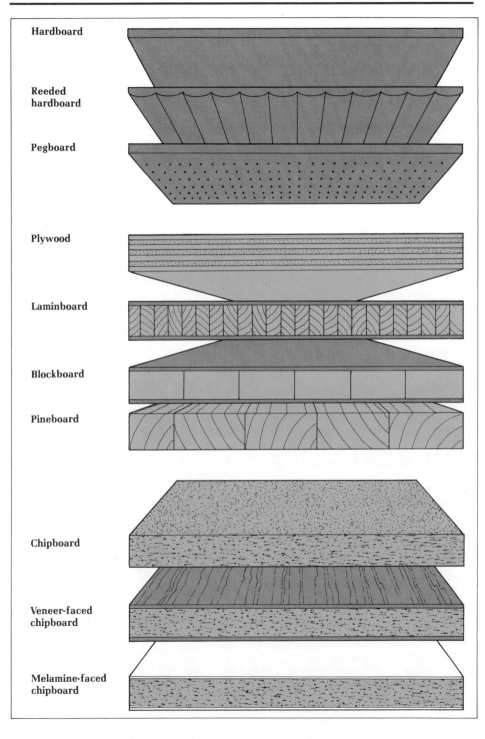

Hardboard

Reeded
hardboard

Pegboard

Plywood

Laminboard

Blockboard

Pineboard

Chipboard

Veneer-faced
chipboard

Melamine-faced
chipboard

Exactly what constitutes a basic tool kit will depend to some extent on what kind of work you intend to do.

Measuring and setting out

In furniture construction and general workshop joinery there is always measuring to be done, whatever the job. For setting out on the bench the best measuring tool is a good quality folding rule. For measuring around the house use a steel tape. A two or three metre long model will meet most requirements. Get a type which has both metric and imperial markings but be sure you only work in one or other system.

A square is needed to mark wood for cutting and although a try-square with a blade 200 or 230mm long is used for benchwork, a 300mm adjustable combination square and mitre square with a sliding blade is more useful for other work. For marking out the cutting lines you will need a setting-out, or marking, knife and a pencil sharpened to a chisel point (this is more accurate than a pointed one).

Cutting

To cut timber you will need a panel saw 500 or 550mm long with 10 teeth per 25mm. This is a suitable size for general work. For bench work you need a tenon saw. This should have 12 or 14 teeth per 25mm. When sawing, the saw should not be forced to cut but pushed evenly so that it can cut at its own speed.

Shaping

Bevel-edged chisels are the best choice for bench work, but for general purposes use a firmer chisel which has square sides and is stronger. Widths of 19 and 6mm would enable you to make a start.

There is a wide range of planes available, from small block-planes up to the long trying-planes used for obtaining straight edges. The latter is not often needed now as most timber can be bought planed straight.

Selection of basic joinery tools:
a *Firmer chisels;* **b** *Bevel-edged chisels;* **c** *Oilstone;* **d** *Steel tape;* **e** *Tenon saw;* **f** *Panel saw;* **g** *Smoothing plane;* **h** *Slotted and Supadriv screwdrivers;* **j** *Bradawl;* **k** *Auger bits;* **l** *Twist bits;* **m** *Sanding block;* **n** *Electric drill;* **p** *Mallet;* **q** *Pincers;* **r** *Claw hammer;* **s** *Warrington hammer;* **t** *Swing brace.*

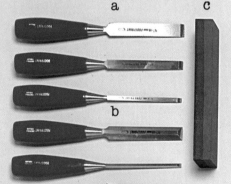

A block plane comes in very handy for rough shaping; buy one which has screw adjustment for the blade. It can be held in one hand, with the forefinger resting on the front knob of the plane, and the top of the wedge and the cutting blade in the palm of your hand. The larger, 250mm smoothing plane requires two hands to operate it successfully: one holds the handle at the back and the other holds the front knob. The hand on the knob holds the plane level at the start of the cut and raises it slightly at the end of the cut. Failure to lift the plane in this way will cause the end of the timber to be made slightly rounded as the plane drops as it reaches the end of the cut.

With both these types of plane, adjustment of the blade is made by turning a knob under the blade. This is just in front of the rear handle of the smoothing plane. Side adjustment is made by a lever fitted under the blade.

Sharpening

An oilstone is required for sharpening these tools and a medium grade provides a suitable edge for a beginner, but later you may want a finer stone in order to hone a keen edge on tools used for benchwork. The cutting edges of chisels and planes have two bevels, one at about 25 degrees made by the grindstone, and the other at about 35 degrees which is the sharpening bevel. Do not raise the handle of chisels and other blades too high when sharpening them or the cutting bevel will become too steep, reducing the ability to cut cleanly.

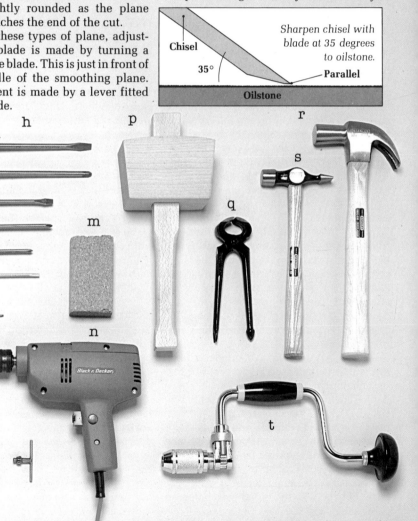

Chisel

$35°$

Sharpen chisel with blade at 35 degrees to oilstone.

Parallel

Oilstone

h

p

r

s

q

m

j

n

k

l

t

For right-handed people, hold the blade or handle firmly in the right hand, with the left hand resting on the flat blade steadying it and providing an even pressure. This is particularly important with wide plane blades as the edge must be kept square. However, the corners of the plane blades have to be rubbed off a little to prevent them digging into the wood and making marks on the surface.

Use the full width of the stone when sharpening chisels as it will otherwise wear hollow in the middle and be unable to sharpen wide blades properly.

Drilling

Drilling holes, whether for fixing or for assembling projects, is another essential part of woodwork. An electric drill is a boon for holes up to 9mm, although a simple hand-drill (or wheel brace) will do the job. For holes above this size you have a choice of using flat-bits in an electric drill or buying a carpenter's swing brace which will take a wide variety of auger bits for making deep holes of almost any size. Adjustable bits are available, and for work in confined spaces, a ratchet brace is useful.

Assembling

When it comes to assembling furniture and fittings you will need a hammer for driving nails, and a screwdriver or two. Suitable screwdriver lengths would be 150mm and 230mm. You will need tips suitable for cross-head (Supadriv) as well as the traditional slotted-head screws. A bradawl is essential for making a small hole for starting the screws.

A Warrington-pattern hammer is best for bench use and it should be about 12oz in weight. This is the type with the cross pein at the opposite side of the head to the striking face. This chisel-shaped pein is used for starting small panel-pins held between the finger and thumb. The claw hammer, much favoured by carpenters, is ideal for heavier fixings around the house and is of greater weight, about 20oz. If you have only a Warrington-pattern hammer

you will need a pair of pincers to pull out nails and tacks.

Assembling furniture made with conventional woodworking joints calls for a mallet. This tool used to be essential for use with chisels, but the modern plastic handle is able to withstand the use of a hammer. The wider head of the mallet and its softer nature makes it less likely to mark the timber when projects are being assembled. The main difference in using these tools is that the hammer is swung with a wrist action whereas the mallet is swung from the elbow.

Finishing

When projects have been completed there remains the finishing. Whether this is to be paint, varnish or polish a certain amount of preparation is necessary. Hardwoods are the most difficult to prepare because the grain may be twisted, figured or reversed and though this provides a pleasant appearance, it does take some effort to produce a good finish. When this kind of grain is to be polished or varnished it has to be scraped first.

An ordinary scraper is simply a rectangle of metal and it is sharpened with a hard steel rod by first drawing it along the edge of the scraper, square to the sides, and then tilting the rod at a slight angle and drawing it along the edge of the scraper again. This has the effect of first creating a burr on the metal then bending the burr over slightly.

The scraper is held upright with the thumbs at the back; it is pushed forward over the surface of the wood where the burr will take off very fine shavings. It takes more than a little practice to sharpen and use this tool.

The alternative is abrasive paper. There are many grades of abrasive papers and many different types of grit. Very fine ones are used for preparing wood for polish and varnish, but the coarser grades of glass-paper are all that are needed to prepare timber for painting. A comfortable sanding block either cork or cork-faced is ideal for holding these papers on flat surfaces.

If you have a workbench you will be able to fix a vice to it so that you can hold timber firmly while working on it. When it comes to assembling the parts you will need other holding devices.

Bench hook

The simplest of holding devices is the bench hook. This can be made out of a piece of 75 × 50mm timber about 225mm long. It is cut out at each side so that a 50 × 25mm block is left at each end, on opposite sides of the wood. In use, it is placed on the bench so that one of the blocks is downward and hooks against the bench top, and the other faces upward so that the timber to be cut can be held firmly against it.

An alternative form of this hook is made from a broad piece of wood approximately 150mm wide, with a block screwed to opposite sides at opposite ends. Make these blocks about 25mm shorter than the width of the board and you can cross-cut timber held against the stops and when the saw comes through the wood it will not damage the bench top.

Whether you use patent cramps, traditional cramps or home-made cramps using folding wedges, the important part of the operation is holding the members of the structure tightly until the glue has set or screws, nails or other permanent fixings have been employed.

Sash cramps

One of the most useful devices is the sash cramp of which there are patent types as well as the simple, traditional cramp. This consists of a long metal bar with a screw-adjustable jaw at one end and a movable jaw which slides along the bar. The latter is fixed at the required point by a pin which passes through holes in the bar. Two of these cramps are needed for pulling up the joints of frames, but four or even more would be ideal for furniture making if you are using traditional cabinet-making methods of construction.

Frame and web cramps

For cramping chairs, frames or other similar constructions there are frame and web cramps. The frame cramp consists of a length of strong nylon cord with four corner blocks and a cleat. The corner blocks are put in position and the cord is passed round the frame over the blocks and tightened on the cleat. This puts an even pressure on all four corners at the same time. The web cramp consists of nylon

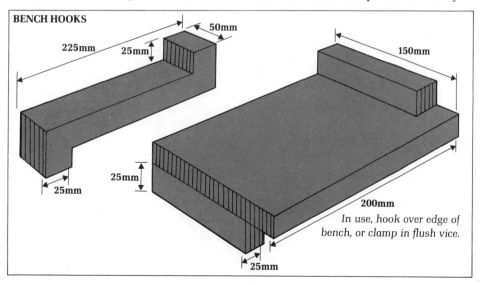

BENCH HOOKS

225mm 25mm 50mm 25mm 150mm 25mm 200mm 25mm

In use, hook over edge of bench, or clamp in flush vice.

webbing passed through a ratchet lever device which is used to tighten it. Web cramps are useful for irregular shapes.

G-cramps

Another useful tool is the G-cramp. This, as its name suggests, is in the shape of a letter G. It has a long, threaded jaw with a swivel head to grip at most angles. These cramps are made in a wide range of sizes from about 75mm to 300mm or more. Again, two would be useful, but four or more of various sizes would be the ideal.

Mitre cramps

One specialised type of cramp which is useful if you are making picture frames, or similar constructions, is the mitre cramp. This metal corner device has two screw-operated jaws which hold both pieces of wood firmly together. It has the advantage over the frame cramp that it may have a saw guide incorporated so that the mitres

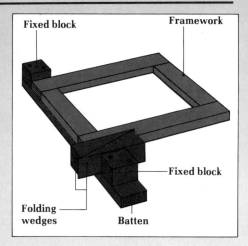

Above *Simple cramp consisting of two blocks nailed to a batten, and folding wedges to apply the pressure.*

Above right *When cramping thin wood with sash cramps, clamp battens above and below to prevent buckling.*

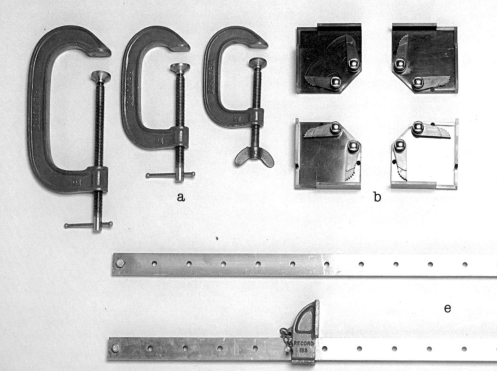

a

b

e

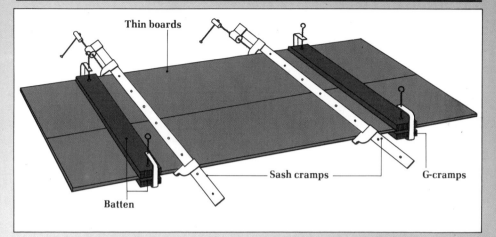

Thin boards

Batten

Sash cramps

G-cramps

Below *Selection of cramps for general-purpose and specialist uses:*
a *Three sizes of G-cramp.*
b *Set of mitre (picture-frame) cramps.*
c *Mitre-cutting cramp.*
d *Web cramp.*
e *Pair of sash cramps.*

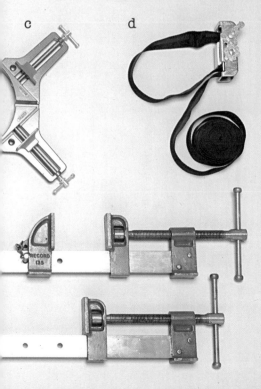

c   d

can be cut accurately while they are held in the cramp. The disadvantage is that only one corner is held at a time.

In addition to these traditional cramping devices there are other patent cramps which are designed to perform two or three different cramping actions. There are also portable workbenches which incorporate a cramping mechanism.

You can make a cramp by screwing a block to each end of a length of wood and fitting the framework to be cramped between the blocks. Then drive folding wedges between the framework and the blocks at one end.

Using cramps

Whenever cramps are used there is the danger that the edges of the timber will be marked by the pressure of the jaw, so a piece of waste wood should be placed between the jaw and the workpiece.

To overcome the tendency for frames to bend or twist under pressure, you should fit a cramp both on the top and underneath the workpiece so that they pull against each other. Frames can also be squared up by cramps. When one diagonal of the frame is longer than the other, the cramps are moved so that they are angled the same way as the frame is leaning. When the cramps are tightened it will have the effect of pulling the frame into the square position.

The start of any project, after the initial measuring up, is the setting out of the various parts. This must be done accurately if the completed work is to be satisfactory.

A wooden rule, either folding or straight, a chisel-pointed pencil, a setting-out (or marking) knife and a square are the essential tools, but others will be needed for special joints in timber.

Use the rule on its edge for greater accuracy and use the knife in place of the pencil where possible. There are in fact only five places where the pencil must be used: all rough measuring; where a cut line would be seen on the surface of the wood; for most curves; for lines which are at an angle to the grain of the wood, because a knife would tend to follow the grain; when marking out chamfers, because the cut would show as a damaged edge.

The first task on setting out is to determine which is the best side of the wood for use as the face and this should be marked so that it is easily recognisable. One edge must also be chosen as the face edge and all setting out is done from these surfaces.

Setting out dowel joints

Dowel joints, which are used a great deal when working on chipboards and blockboards, are simply marked in pencil for position. The dowel holes can be drilled by means of a jig, of which there are two or three types, providing that they are at the ends of the boards. When dowel holes are needed in the middle of the board a different approach is necessary.

Accurate measurement will provide the position of one set of holes, but to get the other set in exactly the right position to match them it is necessary to use dowel marking pins. These are simply two, short, sharp metal points separated by a ridge, like a washer. One point is pressed into

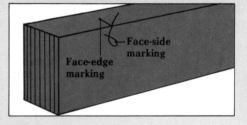

Face-side marking

Face-edge marking

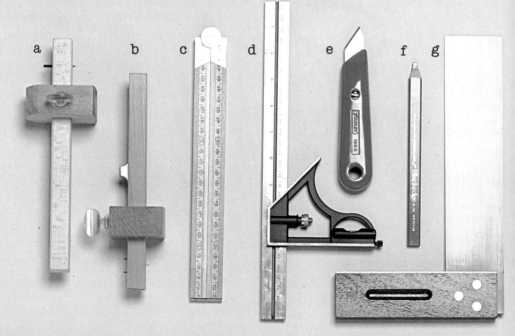

a   b   c   d   e   f   g

each marked position, then the second piece of board is placed on the points in the exact position that it is required. The points mark this piece so that when they are removed the holes can be drilled, using a vertical drill-stand, and will match each other perfectly.

Marking gauges

For accurate setting out of joints a gauge should be used where possible. A marking gauge with one spur will do for most setting out when depths of cut are being marked for halved joints and for housings and similar joints. This gauge can also be used for marking mortise and tenon joints, but because it has only one spur, when all the joints have been marked with one groove, the gauge has to be reset to mark the other side of the mortise and tenon.

Marking out these joints for furniture where there are a lot of tenons is much easier and far more accurate if a mortise gauge, which has two spurs, is used. With this gauge the two spurs are set at the mortise width first, usually by placing the

chisel to be used between the two points and adjusting them using the screw at the end of the stem. When they are correctly positioned, the stock is set on the stem so that the mortise will be marked in the required position which is usually in the centre of the wood. Whichever gauge is used, it is important that the marking is done with the stock against one face surface of the wood.

Setting out batches

Where a number of pieces of timber, for the legs of a table, for example, are to be set out the same, they should be cramped together to hold them while the edges are marked. These marks are later squared round the sides of the wood when they have been separated again. When pieces have to be set out as pairs they are placed with their face sides together and their face edges upwards and set out as before.

Where a large number of pieces of timber are required to be set out in the same way, it is often best to set out a pattern piece and cramp it to a small number of pieces. Then set them out in batches rather than try to set them all out at once. If there are complicated joints to make, they can be drawn out full size on a length of timber or plywood so that the piece for the pattern can be laid on the drawing and the joint positions marked directly on to it.

Whatever you are making, the setting out is the most important part of the job; if you don't set out accurately you cannot expect a well-fitting final product.

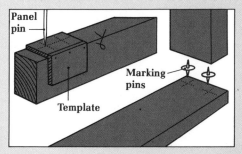

Above setting out dowel joints using template (top) and marking pins.

Left Setting-out tools:
a Marking gauge.
b Mortise gauge.
c Folding rule.
d Combination square.
e Marking knife.
f Carpenter's pencil.
g Try-square.

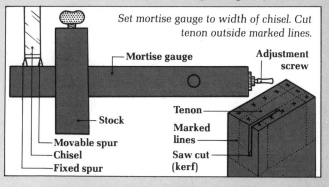

Set mortise gauge to width of chisel. Cut tenon outside marked lines.

Mortise gauge
Adjustment screw
Stock
Movable spur
Chisel
Fixed spur
Tenon
Marked lines
Saw cut (kerf)

Panel pin
Marking pins
Template

When marking out joints, as well as when cutting them, accuracy can often be aided by using special tools or jigs. Some of these aids can be bought, others you can either buy or make for yourself.

Thumb gauge

A dowelling jig has to be bought and there are various patent types to choose from, but a little gadget like a thumb gauge is easily made and is very useful. It is simply a block of wood about 50mm square and 25mm thick. A small rebate is cut in one end so that the block can be used with a pencil to make parallel lines for chamfers or rebates. If you cut a different size rebate at the opposite end of the block you will have double value from your gauge.

Mitre-box

A mitre-box is essential for cutting accurate mitres and you can buy one or make your own to whatever size you require. A box with low sides is easier to use for small mouldings than a large box, which is intended for cutting large mouldings. By making your own you can have as many and as varied sizes as you want.

Screw the side pieces of the box on to the base and mark the 45 degree mitres using a combination mitre-square. Square the lines down the sides of the box and cut carefully down them using a tenon saw. As well as mitre guides, you can make a 90 degree cut in the box so that you can cut the ends of timber square.

Pinch rod

When you are fitting shelving in an alcove, a pinch rod is very useful for measuring between the walls. It is made from two lengths of thin batten about 25mm wide and 6mm thick. Make a brass clip or strap to fit over the battens at the ends where they overlap. Screw one to the sides of the bottom batten and the other to the sides of the top batten. This enables the two battens to be extended to the length required. If you make a neat fit in the metal straps you will be able to hold the battens in the extended

a *Mitre box for 45 and 90 degree cuts.*
b *Plunging router and bits, a powered version of the router plane.*
c *Diagonal gauge.*
d *Shooting board.*
e *Thumb gauge.*
f *Hinge-recess gauge.*
g *Dovetail template.*
h *Pinch rod.*

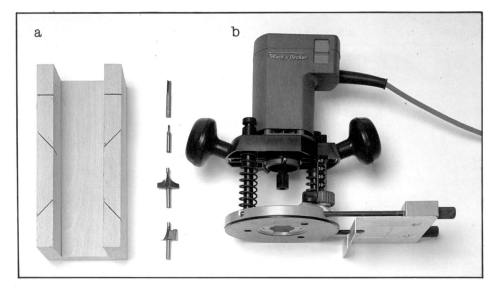

position until you have marked the timber. If the battens are a loose fit you will have to hold them with a small cramp.

Hinge-recess gauge

A countersunk-head screw driven into a 50mm square block of wood makes an ideal gauge for marking the depth of recesses for metal plates such as the leaves of hinges. Simply drive in the screw until the head is level with the plate and the head will cut a neat line in the edge of the wood.

Diagonal gauge

A thin batten pointed at one end like a chisel can be used to measure the diagonals of a frame to ensure that it is square. Push the pointed end into one corner of the frame and make a mark on the batten where the opposite corner comes. Then do the same from the remaining corners. If you put a third mark exactly halfway between the two corner marks you will have the point at which both corners will be square.

Shooting board

Mitre shooting boards can be made as well as bought. They are made from wide boards with a 50mm wide and 9mm deep rebate on one side. Two pieces of wood are

then mitred together like the corner of a picture frame, and these are screwed to the base board with the point exactly on the edge of the rebate. In use, a plane is laid on its side and slid along the rebate while the mitre is held or cramped against the mitred battens on the base board. In this way, using a very sharp and finely set plane, the mitre can be smoothed to an accurate angle.

Dovetail template

Made from thin sheet aluminium or steel, this tool should be cut to the correct angle for hardwoods or softwoods.

Router plane

If you are going to make a lot of housing joints for fitting shelves in cupboards, it is important that the housings are of an even depth, so a router plane is useful. This little plane has its cutter end at right angles to the body of the blade so that it cuts parallel with the surface of the board.

Mitre-cutting cramp

This specialised tool would only be needed by those who are cutting a lot of mitres such as for picture frames. It enables the moulding to be clamped while it is cut and incorporates 45 and 90 degree saw-guides.

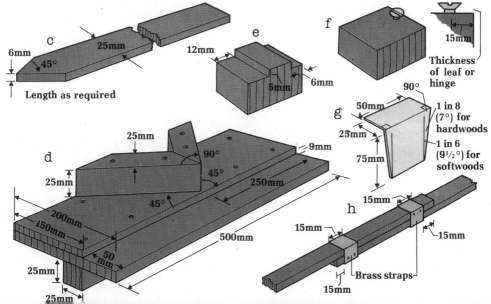

It may be thought that the use of modern resin adhesives precludes the need for traditional woodworking joints. However, there are many cases where joints such as the mortise and tenon, used for table and chair legs, are still necessary, although their strength is enhanced by a resin bond.

Mortise and tenon joint
This is used for framed-up constructions including door and cupboard frames, chairs and tables. It gives the strongest connection and the best-looking finish.

The setting out and the tools required have been described. You also need to know the correct size for the joint. A tenon should be one third the thickness of the wood and for a rigid joint it should have a shoulder all round it. If a mortise and tenon is needed at the end of a piece of wood, such as when jointing the top rails of a table to the legs, then to avoid the mortise being an open-ended slot the tenon is made only two thirds the width of the rail and a stub called a haunch is made for one third of the width. An extra 25mm of timber can be allowed on the length of the leg to avoid it splitting when the joint is assembled. This is, of course, cut off later when the glue has set.

Dowel joint
Splitting is a problem with the dowel joint, which is used as an alternative to the tenon. The dowel joint can never be as strong as the mortise and tenon joint because the size of the dowels is limited. There is no point in increasing the diameter of a dowel as this will seriously weaken the rail. A rail 25mm thick would support a dowel or tenon about 8mm thick and leave about 8mm each side to support the dowel or to form a shoulder to the tenon. If the strength of the joint needed to be increased for any reason, the tenon could be nearly doubled in thickness to 15mm, still leaving a shoulder of 5mm at each side which would provide stability to the joint. If a dowel was increased to this size there would only be 5mm at each side of the hole to support the dowel and this could prove insufficient.

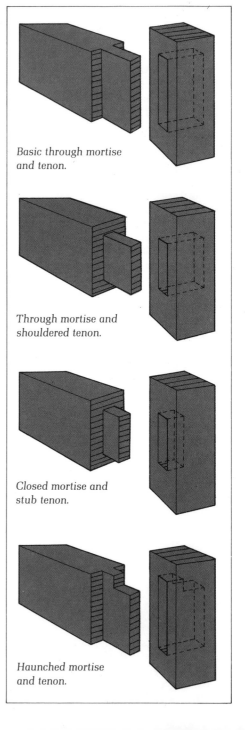

Basic through mortise and tenon.

Through mortise and shouldered tenon.

Closed mortise and stub tenon.

Haunched mortise and tenon.

This is one of the reasons for failure of the dowel joints between chair legs and rails.

Halved and lapped joint

Another strong alternative to the mortise and tenon joint is the halved and lapped joint. Usually just called a halving joint, it needs no special jig to set it out. It can be marked out using a marking gauge and cut with a fine-toothed saw, preferably a tenon saw. As its name suggests it is made by simply cutting away half the timber of each piece of wood so that the two pieces will fit together flush with each other. The joint is made in the same way even if the two pieces of wood are of different thickness. In this case the gauge is set to half the thickness of the thinner piece and both timbers are marked from the face side. The face side is left intact on the thinner piece and the back is removed. The opposite is done to the thicker piece where the joint is cut on the face side to a depth of half the thinner piece. The joint can then be assembled with the two face sides being flush with each other.

The joint is both glued and screwed. Where possible the screws are inserted from the back of the joint so that they do not show when the project is completed.

Apart from corners being halved, the joint can also be used where timbers cross each other. Such places are the diagonal cross-rails at the bottom of table legs and any form of diagonal bracing.

Housing joint

The traditional joint for shelves which are fitted into cupboards and bookcases is the housing joint. This is a groove cut into the side member and it must not be deeper than one third the thickness of the side. In solid timber the depth need only be a quarter of the thickness. In order to prevent the joint showing, the housing can be stopped about 25mm from the front edge.

Housing joints are not really suitable for chipboard because the boards are not very thick and the edges of the groove are prone to breaking away. A chipboard shelf, even though it is not suitable for heavy weights,

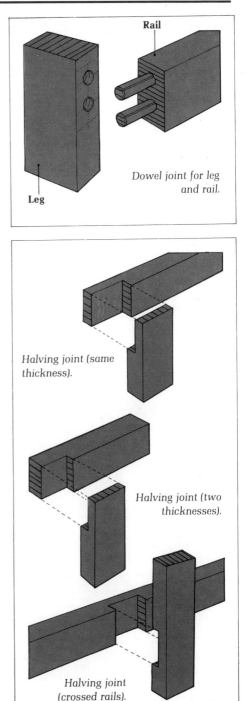

Dowel joint for leg and rail.

Halving joint (same thickness).

Halving joint (two thicknesses).

Halving joint (crossed rails).

needs better support, and this can be provided by a thin strip, or batten, of timber glued and pinned inside the cupboard.

Butt joint

Simple butt-jointed constructions, which are made by cutting the ends of boards exactly square both in width and thickness, are suitable for solid timber which can be glued and nailed or screwed at the joint. Chipboard would have to be fixed by means of a corner block.

Butt-jointing of narrow boards to make up a wide board such as a table top is done by planing the edges perfectly straight and square in thickness and then gluing the edges before cramping the boards together. They may later be given additional support by screwing battens to the underside. Again, this type of jointing process is not suitable for chipboard construction.

Reinforcing butt joints

Although they are used as a substitute for a mortise and tenon, dowels should really only be used to strengthen ordinary butt-joints. A minimum of two dowels must be used in each joint to avoid any tendency to twist. A groove or saw cut should be made along the side of the dowel to allow the air trapped at the bottom of the hole to escape; excess glue will also be released this way. The holes in each piece of timber should be slightly countersunk to make it easier to remove excess glue cleanly. Chamfering the ends of the dowels will enable them to enter the holes more easily.

Mitred joint

This is usually made in mouldings and is secured by small nails or pins. Where extra strength is needed the joint can be reinforced by veneer keys, glued and driven into

Above right *Simple horizontal, bevelled horizontal and bevelled angled notches.*

Right *Simple bird's mouth and recessed bird's mouth joints.*

Far right *Corner and through bridle joints and box joint.*

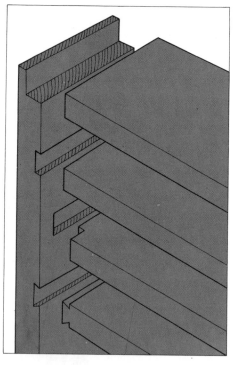

Top to bottom *Rebate; Through housing; Stopped housing; Dovetailed housing.*

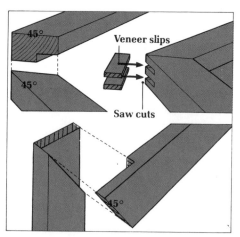

Top *Mitred joint and reinforcement*
Bottom *Mitred halving joint.*

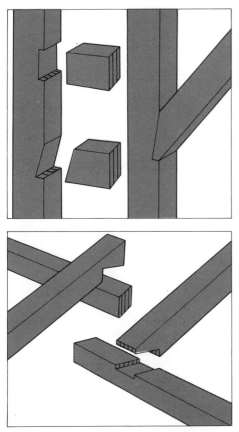

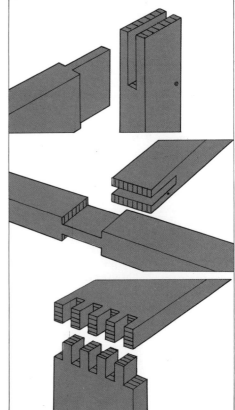

saw cuts across the point of the mitre. This is sometimes used for picture-frames.

Notching

Another simple carpentry joint is notching, which is cutting a small recess or housing in one piece of timber so that another piece can be secured in it. This is a method often used for securing the shelf-bearers where racks of shelving are being made.

Bird's mouth joint

Where an angled timber meets a horizontal timber, a bird's mouth joint is used. In this joint, a cut is made to fit the vertical face of the horizontal piece and another cut made to match the top horizontal face. The result is a right-angled v-shaped joint of a type much used in roofing work.

Bridle joint

Another carpentry joint,' used in rough woodwork instead of the mortise and tenon, is the bridle joint. In this construction, which is set out like a mortise and tenon, instead of cutting a hole for the tenon, the sides of the mortise are cut away leaving the centre solid. The end of the mating piece of timber then has what would have been the tenon cut out leaving the two sides as a forked joint which will fit over the centre web.

At a corner the bridle joint looks like a mortise and tenon which has been cut too near the end of the wood leaving one end of the mortise open to make a slot. The joint is as strong as a mortise and tenon when it is made in the middle of the rail, but when used as a corner joint it lacks stability.

The range of fixing materials and devices for timber is immense. Nails, for example, are probably the simplest of fixings available, but they come in a wide range of types and sizes, each with, if not a specific use, at least a general area where they are best employed. Most are made of iron.

Round-head wire-nails are suitable for general and outdoor work where appearance is of little importance.

Round or oval lost-head nails are often used for fixing floorboards in place of the old-fashioned cut-nail. Lost-heads do, in fact, have a slight head.

Oval wire-nails are used for the same purposes as the round-head wire-nails, but because of their oval heads they can be punched below the surface so that the small hole they make can be filled with putty or other material. They can then be painted over so that they do not show.

Panel-pins are simply small slim versions of lost-head nails and are used for fixing thin material such as panels or mouldings where, being thin, they are easily covered and hidden.

Hardboard nails are also made specially for panel fixing. They have a slightly pointed head which is supposed to allow you to drive them into hardboard without having to punch them below the surface. These nails often have square shanks and are copper finished.

Clout nails are usually short, galvanised and have large heads. They are used for fixing felt to roofs.

Nails come in all lengths from 12mm pins to 150mm constructional nails. They are made in a variety of thicknesses too, so be sure to get a type which is suitable for the job. Thick nails easily split thin wood.

Nails are also made from aluminium and copper, but there is not the same range of types and sizes. There is also a limited range of galvanised or sherardised nails.

Screws

Screws are equally prolific, although they are most freely available in a more limited range of preferred sizes. You can still get the non-preferred sizes, but you may have difficulty finding them, and they may be more expensive.

Head types

The main types of head are countersunk for all general applications, raised countersunk which are usually plated and used for fixing metal fittings, and round head which are often used for fixing flat metal and may be used in conjunction with washers. There are also pan heads which are similar to round heads but have a flatter section. Other heads are made and are often used for heavyweight coach-screw fixings.

Materials and finishes

Screws are made in steel, brass, aluminium, stainless steel or silicon bronze. There are also a number of finishes including sherardised, nickel plate, chromium plate, brass plate, bronze metal antique, dark Florentine bronze and black japanned.

The plated finishes are only suitable for interior work. For external applications the solid brass, stainless steel and sherardised screws should be used. Aluminium screws are ideal for fixing cedar as they will not

stain the surface. They are also, as are solid brass screws, suitable for fixings in kitchens and bathrooms where the damp atmosphere would soon cause ordinary steel screws to rust and stain surfaces.

Screw threads

There are two types of thread on screws. The first and most often used is the tapered thread which has a single spiral running down the shank. The other type is the chipboard screw. This has two spirals running round a parallel shank. The shorter lengths of these screws are threaded up to the head. The parallel shank reduces the tendency to split the chipboard.

Using screws

Whichever screws are being used it is always best to drill pilot holes. If these holes are the same diameter as the shank of the screw below the thread, then a full grip will be obtained without danger of the wood splitting.

The size of wood screw required for a particular application depends upon the width and thickness of the timber. The diameter of the screw should not exceed one tenth the width of the wood into which it will be inserted. You should also ensure that at least four diameters of thread, and if possible up to seven, are engaged in the wood. If the screw is fixing a piece of wood, its length should be not less than three times the thickness of the wood it passes through. If pilot holes are drilled the screws can be positioned up to 10 times the diameter from the end of the wood or five times the diameter from the edge. If pilot

holes are not drilled then the screws must be kept 20 times the diameter from the end of the wood.

If the screws are lubricated with soap, tallow, beeswax, or Vaseline, if grease stains are of no importance, you will find it easier to drive them, especially into hardwoods. They can also be removed more easily at a later date if necessary. The lubricant should be applied to the point of the screw or into the pre-drilled hole. Avoid getting any lubricant on the head of the screw as the screwdriver may slip.

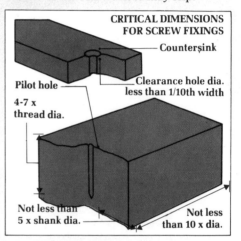

CRITICAL DIMENSIONS FOR SCREW FIXINGS

Countersink

Clearance hole dia. less than 1/10th width

Pilot hole

4-7 x thread dia.

Not less than 5 x shank dia.

Not less than 10 x dia.

Below *(left to right):*
Clout nail; Hardboard nail; Panel pin; Round-head wire-nail; Oval wire-nail; Batten-head nail; Masonry nail; Chrome-plated brass round-head woodscrew; Zinc-plated chipboard screw; Chrome-plated brass raised-head woodscrew; Four sizes of steel countersunk woodscrew.

At one time woodworking required only one type of glue – Scotch glue – which was boiled in a pot and used hot. This glue, although little used today, is still available. It has only moderate strength and it is not waterproof.

Today there are various types of adhesive which you can use. Some are in tubes and are ready for immediate use and others are in powder form and have to be mixed as required. Some of the resin glues which are waterproof are also extremely strong. A carefully made joint using these glues would not, after it had set, break along the glue line; it would be the surrounding wood which would fail under stress because of its lower strength.

Woodworking adhesives

For small woodworking projects you can use most household adhesives. The most universal is the PVA type of adhesive

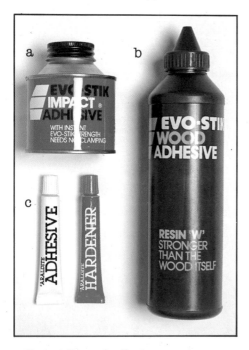

a *Contact (impact) adhesive.*
b *Resin woodworking adhesive.*
c *Two-part epoxy resin adhesive.*

which will bond many materials to wood as well as fixing wood to wood. It has the advantage that surplus glue can be wiped off the surface with a wet rag before it sets. The powdered glues which are mixed with water can also be wiped off with a wet rag. The PVA adhesives are not waterproof, so for joints which have to withstand water you must use one of the urea formaldehyde resin adhesives which have a powerful gap-filling capacity.

Contact adhesives

When veneering in wood you can still use Scotch glue or PVA, but when fixing plastic laminates to timber you have to use one of the contact adhesives. The type which gives instant grip is suitable if there is scope for finishing operations which would hide any slight error in positioning the laminate. The alternative is to use thixotropic contact adhesives which allow a slight movement before the final pressure is applied.

Epoxy resins

For extra strength there are the epoxy resins which are two-part adhesives requiring the application of a catalyst or hardener to create the required bond. With some of these glues you mix the hardener into the solution just before it is applied to the surface. There is then a time limit on assembling the parts – though this generally gives plenty of time. With the other type, the glue is applied to one part of the joint and the hardener to the other part, then when the two are brought together the necessary reaction takes place.

Such powerful adhesives are not often required for domestic woodworking and carpentry, although they could be useful for assembling furniture and projects to be used outdoors.

Finally, is there any difference between a glue and an adhesive? According to one manufacturer "No, it depends on the size of the package – some are too small to take the word adhesive and leave space for other more important information like the maker's name."

There are two main types of construction in woodwork. One is box construction in which the project is mainly composed of sheet materials which are fastened together without being attached to a framework (see page 36). The other is frame construction in which lighter panels are supported on a framework. As this framework is made rigid by the various joints which are used in its construction it is better able to support doors and is less likely to sway with the movement of the doors.

Mortise and tenon joints

The basic joint for framed construction is the mortise and tenon. This is used because the shoulders of the tenon make the frame rigid and the tenon itself enables the members to be joined without seriously weakening the timber at that point. For cupboard frames the ends of the top and bottom rails are tenoned to fit into mortises in the sides or stiles, while for door frames and window frames the joint is made the opposite way round: the sides or jambs are tenoned to fit into mortises in the head and sill.

Halved and lapped joints

These joints can be used as a substitute for the mortise and tenon, but when this is done the appearance should be preserved by allowing the stiles of the cupboard frame to run up the face of the top and bottom rails. They cannot be used for window and door frames, but a housing joint can be made in the head and sill so that the jamb can fit into it. This joint would have to be well nailed. Doors which are to be clad with hardboard or plywood can also be made with halving joints. It is best to fix the hardboard panel to the frame using an adhesive because the nails always seem to show through the paint however careful you are in punching them down and filling the hole.

Dovetail joints

Traditional box construction uses dovetail joints as these give a pleasing appearance at the corners of the furniture. This joint is

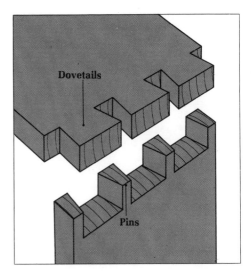

To make dovetailed bracket, cut angled notches in vertical and horizontal pieces to house bracing piece.

not used much today because of the amount of veneered chipboard which is used for furniture, and dovetails cannot be made successfully in chipboard. Some machine-made dovetails are used in quality furniture but they lack the decorative appearance of hand-made joints because the dovetails and the pins which separate them are all the same size.

However, dovetails provide a joint which will resist a lateral pulling force better than most other joints, so they are especially useful when making wooden brackets. Here the dovetail is cut in the top member, and the top end of the upright member has the cut-out for the tail to fit into. If the angled member of the bracket is let into the top and upright member, then the bracket will have considerable strength.

The correct angle for the sides of the dovetail is one in eight (7 degrees) for hardwoods and one in six ($9\frac{1}{2}$ degrees) for softwoods. If the sides are made too steeply angled the pointed corners of the tail will break and if the angle is too shallow it will have little resistance and the joint will pull apart easily.

There are fittings for almost every conceivable requirement. Hinges are available in patterns to suit any cabinet. The most popular for kitchen cabinets is the concealed type which gives the door a pivoting action so that the cabinet can be fixed close into a corner. Some of these hinges incorporate a spring so that the door locks itself into the open or closed position, doing away with the need for a separate catch.

The simplest hinge for a glass door has a pivot action. A hole is drilled about 10mm deep in the top and the bottom of the cabinet and a plastic bush is inserted. Into this bush fits the pivot of the hinge, then the glass is slid into its channel where it is held in place by grub screws.

Handles must be chosen to suit the cabinet and its location. For kitchens, robust metal channels are generally used as they will stand up to heavy use. The more decorative handles used for lounge or bedroom furniture can be in wood or metal and may screw into the face of the door or drawer or, in the case of the ring-pull types in brass, they need to be carefully let into the surface to produce a flush finish.

Magnetic catches are the easiest to fix and are neat in appearance. Some catches are of the touch-latch type which open partly at a light touch allowing the door to be fully opened. Spring operated touch latches are

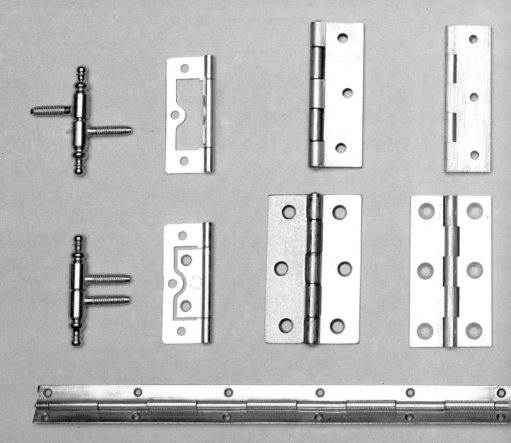

also available. In all cases fitting involves screwing the catch to the framework; recessing or drilling is not often required.

Bolts for the insides of double doors such as wardrobes and bookcases are usually in brass and are flat, not round. They may screw directly to the door or they may be let into the surface.

Adjustable shelves can be provided in bookcases by means of slotted strips screwed to the sides of the cabinet. A small clip fits into the horizontal slots to support the shelves. Four strips are required for each cabinet.

More difficult to position accurately, but less obtrusive, are shelf studs. These need carefully set out and drilled holes

into which the studs are pushed. Two columns are required at each side of the cabinet.

Sliding door gear is obtainable in all sizes from simple channels to heavy overhead rollers. It is necessary to choose from the range made for the weight and type of door which you wish to hang.

Whatever type of cabinet you are preparing to build, always ensure that the fittings of the type you need are obtainable in the sizes you require before starting work. It is best to have all the fittings to hand at the outset, otherwise you could get into problems if you look for fittings only after the work is well advanced – well thought out planning is essential.

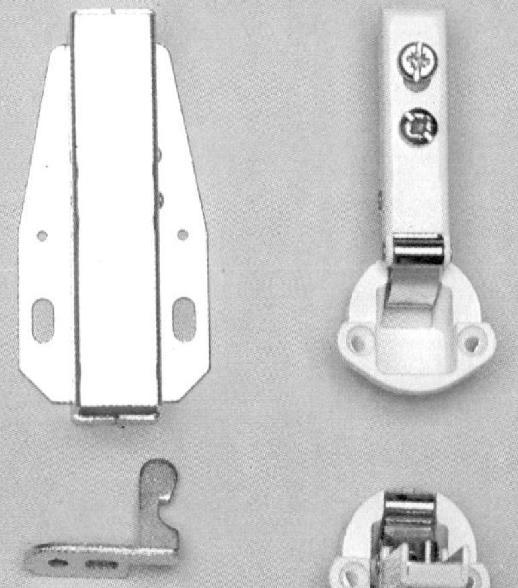

These small hinges and fittings are easy to fit and are suitable for a variety of cabinets. They include, on the opposite page (left to right): pivot hinges; flush hinges which require no recess; pressed-steel butt hinges; narrow-leaf brass butt hinges; and piano hinge (bottom). On this page: automatic touch latch (top left); concealed sprung mini hinges which need no catch (top right); mini automatic latch (bottom left); magnetic catches (bottom centre); and sliding and fixed mirror clips (bottom right).

Hanging doors calls for care and neatness if the finished job is to look acceptable. The framework must be rigid if the door is to be hung within it. You can use a piano hinge screwed directly to the edge of the door or you can use butt hinges which have to be let into the edge of the door and the cabinet side. In either case, the door must be carefully fitted into the framework so that it will show about 1.5mm joint all round when it is hung. With a piano hinge you will need to make the door equal to the width of the opening less 1.5mm and the thickness of the hinge. Butt hinges need an even joint all round as they are let into the wood.

It is obvious that to make a good job takes a little extra care and if the framework is not rigid it will move slightly when the door is hung and cause it to bind at some point.

These problems can be overcome by having the door laid on the face of the framework. It will then be cut to the same size as the outer dimensions of the cabinet with no need to plane it to an accurate joint. There are two types of lay-on hinge, one that is partly let into the door and one that simply screws into place.

The lay-on hinge is screwed to the door allowing for the thickness of the cabinet side. The door is then hung with the hinge screwed flush with the front of the cabinet. This hinge can also be used for inset doors if the hinge is screwed to the side of the cabinet set back the thickness of the door and also set back from the edge of the door the thickness of one leaf of the hinge.

The other type of hinge for lay-on doors has a round boss on one leaf that has to be let into the door. A special end mill bit is necessary for boring the blind hole. An ordinary bit has the centre point too long and it will pierce the front of the door before the hole is deep enough. The best end mills, which are 26 or 35mm diameter, have built-in depth stops to ensure that the holes are milled to exactly 12.5mm deep.

Holes are 3mm from the edge of the door which makes 20.5mm to the centre of the hole for 35mm diameter and 16mm from the edge for the 26mm diameter holes. The boss is set into the hole and screwed into place. Then the door is offered up and the cabinet marked so the base plates can be screwed into position. The door is hung by screwing the leaf of the hinge on to the plate where the correct closure of the door can be adjusted by two screws.

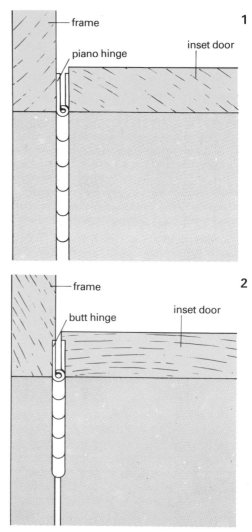

Two of the main types of hinge are illustrated here: piano and butt hinges which are suitable for the doors of furnishing cabinets, and concealed hinges which are more suitable for the doors of kitchen cabinets.

1 Piano hinges are useful for chipboard doors because they cover the raw edge and offer a large number of screw positions.

2 Butt hinges can be let into the frame and the door.

3 Both leaves of the butt hinge can also be let into the door.

4 The lay-on hinge needs no recesses.

5 The concealed hinge needs a circular recess in the door.

6 The hinge and the drill, or mill as it is called. Both these last two hinges allow doors to pivot close to a wall.

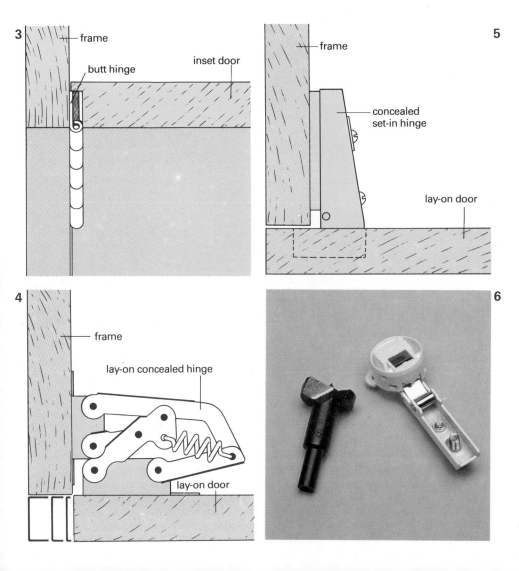

3 — frame — butt hinge — inset door

5 — frame — concealed set-in hinge — lay-on door

4 — frame — lay-on concealed hinge — lay-on door

6

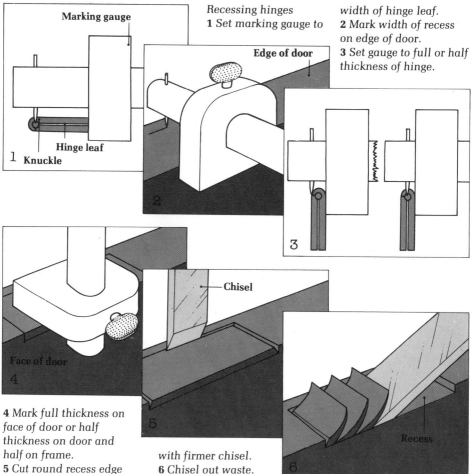

Recessing hinges
1 Set marking gauge to width of hinge leaf.
2 Mark width of recess on edge of door.
3 Set gauge to full or half thickness of hinge.

Marking gauge

Edge of door

Hinge leaf

1 **Knuckle**

Chisel

Face of door

Recess

4 Mark full thickness on face of door or half thickness on door and half on frame.
5 Cut round recess edge with firmer chisel.
6 Chisel out waste.

Doors for solid-wood cabinets made in the traditional manner are set inside the framework and not laid on the face of the cabinet as is frequently done with modern furniture made from veneered chipboard. Carpenters usually let one leaf of the hinge into the frame and the other leaf into the edge of the door, but cabinet-makers often let the whole of the hinge into the edge of the door so that the hinge does not break the neat joint line. The hinge position should be just clear of the mortise and tenon or other joint which may have been used so that the fixing screws grip into solid timber.

Fit the hinge to the door first. As this is cabinet work, there will not be a number of coats of paint to be applied. The wood will only be polished, so the door can be planed to a neat fit with only a minimum of joint allowed. When the hinge is in place, the door is inserted into the cabinet and the position of the hinges is marked on the frame. Recesses are made for the hinge leaf or alternatively the hinge is simply screwed to the frame.

Be careful to use the correct size of screw. If the heads are too big and do not fit into the countersunk holes in the hinge they will bind on each other when the door is closed. Should too little be cut out of the hinge recesses, the door will strike the cabinet and not close. If too much is cut out of the recesses, the door will bind on the hanging side. This will also occur if the door edge is not planed square but bevelled slightly to the front. It is best to err slightly on the side of taking off a shaving too much on the inner edge of the door as this will prevent the door binding when it is closed.

Four-legged constructions

Where constructions such as chairs and tables are being made, the mortises for the rails, which are at right angles to each other, meet inside the leg. This means that

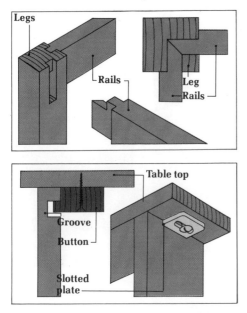

the tenons must be mitred at their ends to give the maximum length to each.

Tops of solid-wood tables must be fixed by means of slotted metal plates or by wooden buttons which engage in grooves in the inside face of the top rail. This is to enable the wide wooden top to move with changes in atmospheric conditions. Solid tops which are battened on the underside must also be allowed to move. This is done by not gluing the battens, and making slots for the screws instead of tightly fitting holes. Failure to provide for the movement of natural timber tops could cause serious splitting in a warm atmosphere.

Side panels fitted into grooves in the framework must also be allowed to move and therefore they are not made a tight fit and they are not glued or pinned. Chipboard and laminated boards do not suffer this and can be securely fixed.

The legs and rails of chairs and tables, for example, must be cramped up carefully to avoid the whole article becoming twisted. Sight across the construction, viewing one rail against the same one on the opposite side, and you will be able to see whether they are in line or whether they are sloping in opposite directions. If they are not all in line, the piece of furniture will rock or wobble on its feet.

To make a wobbly chair or table stand firmly, wedge it level on a flat, level surface. Take a strip of wood about 3mm thicker than the amount the leg is short and mark a cutting line against the top of it on each leg. Never cut one leg to suit the others.

Top *Mitred haunched tenon joining rails to top of table or chair leg.*

Above *Join wooden table-top to base with wooden button (left) or slotted metal plate to allow for movement of timber.*

Right *Trim all four legs to level a wobbly table.*

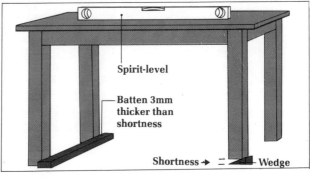

Working with man-made boards requires different techniques to conventional joinery and involves very few cut joints.

Chipboard

Much modern furniture is basically boxes made from veneered chipboard. Construction is often of the knock-down type so that the units can be taken apart and fitted into a cardboard box which will go in a car boot or on a roof-rack. Any permanently constructed units are generally joined by means of dowel joints. There are two main requirements for making furniture like this and they are the ability to cut a straight,

square line and to drill neat, perpendicular holes. This latter requirement is easily met with a dowelling jig or vertical drill-stand.

This type of furniture is ideal for the beginner to make, as the boards can be bought cut to length and plastic blocks can be used for the joints and for supporting shelves. The blocks are simply screwed into place using double-threaded chipboard screws, enabling you to produce the furniture quickly. Doors can be of the lay-on type so that there will be no need to plane them to fit into an opening. Hinges can be of the concealed lay-on type which need no cutouts and are just screwed into place.

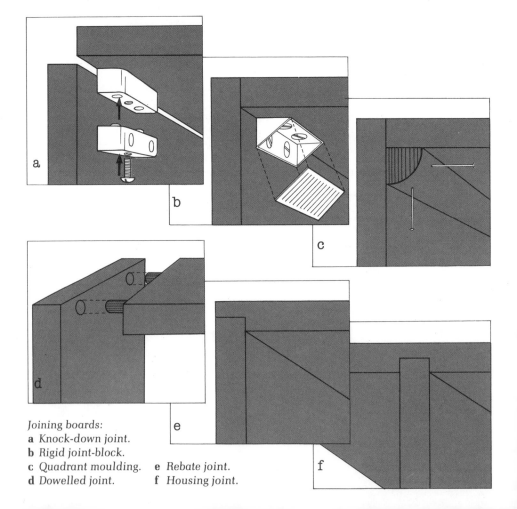

Joining boards:
a Knock-down joint.
b Rigid joint-block.
c Quadrant moulding.   **e** Rebate joint.
d Dowelled joint.   **f** Housing joint.

Laminated boards

Working in blockboard and pine-board follows a more traditional method, as some woodworking joints can be employed. This kind of board will accept a mortise and tenon joint as well as a notch or a rebate in the edge. The boards will also accept screws in the edge which is not a good practice when using chipboard. To some extent you can make housings into the board so that shelves can be fitted.

Hardboard

This can be used for making doors and for cladding other types of framing, but it must be conditioned first by damping the back of the board, using about 1 litre of water to a 2440 × 1220mm sheet. The wet sheets should be placed back to back for 48 hours before use. This process enables the board to stretch so that when it is fixed and dries to the moisture content dictated by the conditions in which it is being kept, it will tighten up and will not buckle. It would do so if it were perfectly dry when it was fixed to the framework and was then taken into a more moist atmosphere. The treatment is not necessary for free-moving panels.

Cutting boards

Sheet materials, especially thin boards like hardboard and plywood, are cut most easily if they are supported along the whole length of the cutting line on both sides of the cut. Lack of support allows the sheet to sag or bend and jam the saw.

Rigidity

Because there is no basic framework to hold the whole construction rigid, stability depends on the hardboard back of the unit being fixed securely to the sides and rails or shelves. In addition, any plinth or top rail will help to prevent the front of the unit swaying. This can prevent sliding doors from meeting the sides properly and it will make hinged doors swing open or closed.

Right *Maximum span between supports for various types and thicknesses of shelf.*

Finishing

The plywood facing of blockboard and the surface of pine-board can be stained, polished or varnished without preparation other than sanding. This also applies, of course, to veneered chipboard and plywood, but plain chipboard needs some degree of filling, or preferably veneering, before a suitable finish can be applied.

Cut edges of chipboard can be a problem, but they can be trimmed using iron-on veneer strips which are obtainable in finishes to suit the finish of the boards you are using. Careful planning will enable you to use standard sizes and therefore reduce the number of cut edges. You can also arrange for the cut edges to be at the back, where they will be covered by the hardboard back of the unit, or in a position where they will be covered by other boards.

When plain chipboard is being used and is to have a decorative laminate applied to it, it is important that a similar laminate, which be cheaper because it is not decorative, is applied to the back as well. Without this balancing veneer, the chipboard will tend to bend. However, the balancer is not essential when the board is being used for worktops or table tops because these can be screwed securely to the frame which will restrain it. Unlike natural timber, chipboard does not need to have the freedom to move with the changes in the atmosphere.

Type of board	Thickness (mm)	Maximum span (mm)
Chipboard	12	400
	19	600
	25	760
Blockboard & Plywood	12	450
	19	810
	25	1000
Pine-board	19	810
Timber	16	500
	22	914
	25	1000

Free-standing shelves must be well made and braced if they are to be secure when carrying heavy weights. It is always best to try to have one end fixed to a wall as this will do away with the need for bracing the structure.

The size of the uprights will depend on the weight likely to be carried; an average size suitable for general storage would be 40mm square. All the uprights must be cut off to the same length and their ends squared. One of the pieces is then set out with the positions of all the bearers. Then all the uprights are put together with their ends level so that the marks can be transferred by squaring them across. This will ensure that all the members are marked exactly the same and all the bearers will be in line.

Bearers can be either screwed directly to the face of the uprights or they can be partly let in for extra strength and stability. A housing about 10mm deep would be sufficient and would not weaken the upright too much. The housing is cut with a tenon saw; extra cuts in the central waste will make chiselling it out easier. Chisel from each side of the housing

1 When making free-standing shelves all four legs are set out together.
2 The legs should be held firmly while the notches for the bearers are cut.
3 If the bearers and notches are a good fit, they will make a square frame.
4 Notching the ends of the shelves helps to make the structure rigid.
5 A brace will be necessary and it can be let into the legs and shelves for greater strength.

towards the middle to make a neat joint. Drill the bearers and screw them to the uprights. If neat joints have been made the ladder sections which you have made will be fairly rigid.

The shelves can be fitted either between the uprights or they can be cut to fit round the uprights to finish flush with the front edges. The latter method helps to make a more rigid structure. In either case some bracing will be required if the shelves are to support any great weight. Even if only open slat shelves are used, it is best to notch the outer slats round the uprights to give the extra stability.

At least one brace will be needed at the back. Lay a piece of timber, usually 50 × 25mm, from the top shelf down to the rear upright. Mark where it crosses the shelves and, if there are any, intermediate uprights. It should cross at least two shelves. Notch out these joints to a depth of about 10mm and screw the brace into place ensuring at the same time that the framework is square. This is done by measuring both diagonals of the structure from corner to corner, and adjusting it until they are equal.

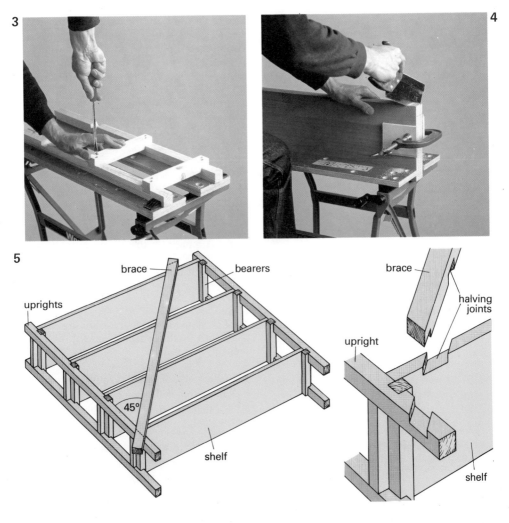

3

4

5

uprights
brace
bearers

45°

shelf

brace

halving joints

upright

shelf

The main difference between the fixings for a normal shelf and the fixings required for a folding or drop-down shelf is that the latter needs a horizontal board on which to hinge the shelf.

When fitting a simple flap support stay, the horizontal board need be wide enough to take only the wall section of the stay. This timber, which is as long as the shelf, must be securely plugged and screwed to the wall close to the point where the stay will be attached. One screw at the top of the board and one at the bottom will be sufficient for general purposes, but for heavy weights double the number.

The shelf is hinged to a narrow timber of the same thickness as the shelf, which is screwed firmly to the top edge of the horizontal board attached to the wall. The width of this board depends on the projection of the flap stay when in the closed or down position as obviously the shelf must fall freely in front of it.

You can hinge the shelf using ordinary butt hinges set into its edges and its bearer in the usual manner. To avoid having to make recesses, you can use piano hinges, available in lengths of up to about 2m, or mount butt hinges on the underside of the shelf and support. Alternatively, use hinged brackets.

Folding table tops and worktops can be supported on wooden brackets. Timber 50 × 25mm will make a strong bracket. The right-angle halving joint at the top is made first and is screwed together, then checked with a square to ensure its accuracy. The bracing piece is then laid across the two legs of the bracket at an angle of 45 degrees. Both timbers are then marked where they cross and the depth of the joint is marked on the edge of the timber. If possible, this is best done with a marking gauge, but if you have not got one you can make a gauge by driving a countersunk-head screw into a small piece of scrap wood until the head projects just the right

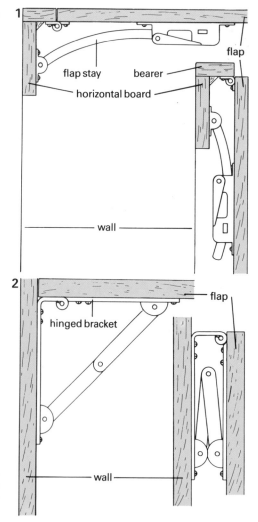

1 & 2 *Two methods of making folding shelves using flap stays or hinged brackets as supports.*

1 *Folding shelves or tables can be supported on gallows brackets.*
2 *The brackets can be made using halved and lapped joints which are glued and screwed together.*
3 *The butt hinges for the flap support brackets can be surface mounted.*
4 *Let the hinges for the flap into the bearer and the edge of the flap for a neater finish.*

amount for the depth required. Slide this gauge along the face of the wood so that the head of the screw cuts a line into the side. Then square the joint lines down to this depth line to guide you when cutting the joint.

Saw down to the depth line at each side of the joint and into the waste to make chiselling easier. Cut the waste from the face of one half of the joint and from the back of the other. Screw all the joints together and fix the bracket, with hinges, to an upright plugged and screwed to the wall.

1

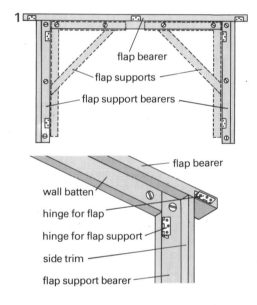

flap bearer

flap supports

flap support bearers

flap bearer

wall batten

hinge for flap

hinge for flap support

side trim

flap support bearer

2

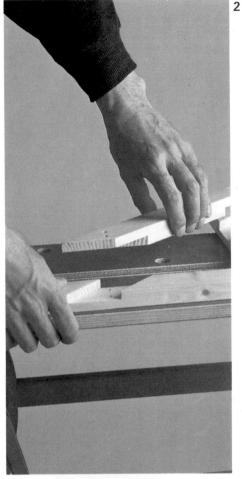

3

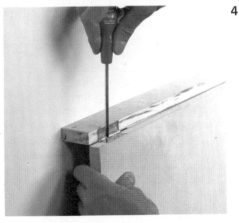

4

A display cabinet need be only a light wooden case with glass or wooden shelves and either with or without glass doors. As the cabinet is intended to be looked at, it is best to make it using some form of concealed joint rather than the plastic blocks which make storage cupboards easy to construct.

One of the simplest concealed jointing systems is the dowel joint. It does require some form of jig to get the holes in exactly the right places. If only a few dowels are to be used, twin-point locators are all that you need. These are metal discs with a centre point at each side. The board edge is pierced by the locator at the required position. A dowel or small tube can be used to press it home. The board to be mated is then positioned accurately and pressed on to the exposed point of the locator. Both board and locator are then separated and the pin marks are used to centre the drill. For accuracy, the holes should be bored using a purpose made dowel bit which is similar to a metal twist drill except that it has a centre point and side spurs for clean cutting and accurate centring.

When a lot of dowel joints are to be made, it is better to buy a dowelling jig. There are two or three different types but the basic principle is the same. A metal block contains holes of various sizes and set at right angles to each other. These holes are used to guide the drill for face and edge boring. Usually they take bits of 6, 8 and 10mm diameter.

Methods of adjustment for the positioning of the holes for the dowels and the sizes of timber that can be accommodated vary according to the make of the jig.

Glass shelves for ornamental displays can be supported by studs let into the side of the cabinet. Decide on the number of shelves and the adjustment needed, then drill a plywood strip with holes at the required spacings and use this as a templet when drilling the holes in the cabinet sides.

If possible, drill these holes before assembling the unit. A bush is then pressed into the hole and into this is pushed the stud on which the shelf rests. Always use a depth stop of some kind when drilling these holes, to prevent you boring too deep and damaging the face side of the boards.

A well made dowel joint will make a fairly rigid cabinet, but rigidity and appearance are improved if a back is fitted. This can be hardboard painted to match the woodwork or for better finishes use veneered plywood. If you have the facilities a rebate can be made to take the back, otherwise bevelling the edge of the board will make it less obtrusive when viewed from the side. Do make sure that the fit is very close.

1 *Two methods of fitting the back of a cabinet.*
2 *Using a dowelling jig when drilling dowel holes in the edge of a board. Note the depth stop on the drill bit.*
3 *Drilling holes for shelf support studs through a pre-drilled templet.*
4 *An exploded view of a simple display cabinet showing shelf supports and dowel joints with, inset, a detail of the pivot hinge for the glass door which needs no holes or cut-outs.*

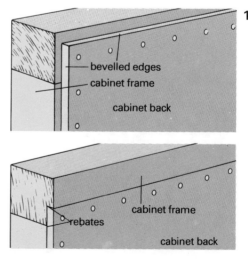

1

bevelled edges
cabinet frame
cabinet back

rebates
cabinet frame
cabinet back

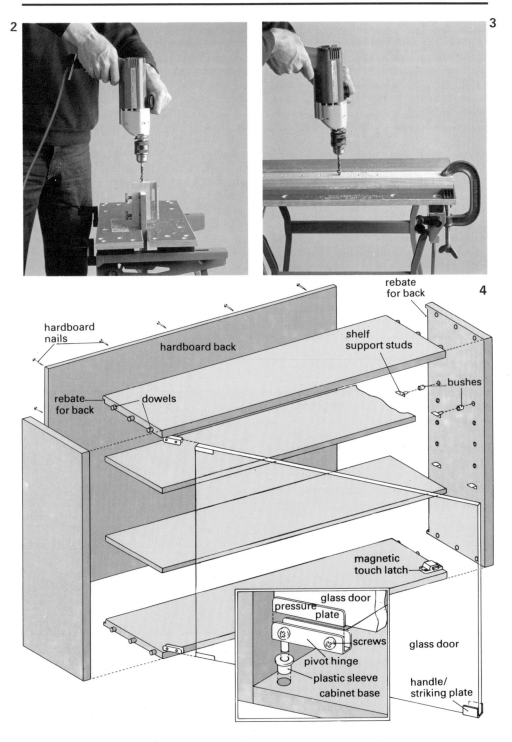

2

3

4

rebate
for back

hardboard
nails

hardboard back

shelf
support studs

bushes

rebate
for back

dowels

magnetic
touch latch

glass door

pressure
plate

screws

pivot hinge

plastic sleeve

cabinet base

glass door

handle/
striking plate

There are two main types of storage cabinet. One is of the quality suitable for use in living rooms and the other is the more sturdy store room type.

Cabinets for use as furniture are made using veneered boards and for these the dowel joints described in making display cabinets are most suitable. Plastic block connectors are quite suitable for general storage cabinets and for kitchen cabinets.

As these units have a fair weight of materials to support, it is more usual to house the shelves into the side of the cabinet, unless plastic blocks are being used. For the best appearance, the housing should be stopped and not cut right through to the front of the side pieces. Mark the position and thickness of the shelves, then square the lines across the boards. Mark the depth of the housing and bore two or three shallow holes at the stopped end of the housing. Clean out these holes to make a small recess and you will find this a help when sawing each side of the housing. The waste is best cut away with a chisel and finished off with a hand router. If a router is not available, you will have to take great care in getting the housing level and even.

The front edge of the shelf is cut back to clear the end of the stopped housing and the shelves are glued into place. These shelves are slid into the cabinet from the back after the top and bottom have been dowelled and fixed.

When the shelves are installed the back can be fitted. This is either set in a rebate, or if that cannot be made the cabinet must be squared by measuring the diagonals, which must be the same length, and the back nailed to the sides and bottom edges. Extra nails into the shelves will make an even more rigid job.

Rigidity is very important if a door is to be inset as any movement of the cabinet would cause the door to bind and jam. Face fitted doors hung on adjustable concealed hinges are the best for this type of unit as any slight discrepancies can be overcome by the adjustment of the hinge.

Wall-hung cabinets must be firmly fixed and this means making provision for fixing when making the cabinet as well as

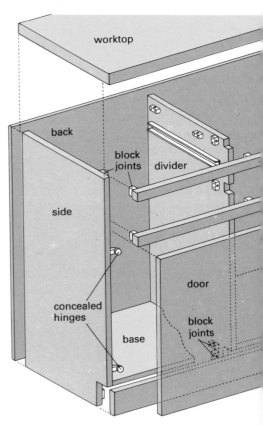

worktop

back

block joints divider

side

concealed hinges

door

base

block joints

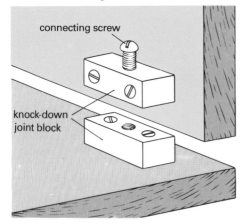

connecting screw

knock-down joint block

providing a secure fixing in the wall. One method for use where heavy weights are expected, is to fit a supporting batten underneath the top and the shelves. The shelves and the top can be screwed down into these battens and the battens then plugged and screwed to the wall.

Brass mirror plates, which are screwed to the edges of the top or sides and then fixed to the wall are really satisfactory only when solid timber is being used. Chipboard soon gives way at the edges.

Measurements have not been included in the illustrations as they are intended to show the methods used when constructing the complete unit.

A typical storage cabinet with details of the joints used. Although the entire unit can be constructed using plastic blocks, secret fixings such as dowel joints and housings look more professional for living room furniture. The cabinet top can either overhang the sides or be inset between them. Dowel joints can be used in either case. The back will hold the frame rigid so the shelves can be fixed in housings or they can be made adjustable by using one of the support systems suitable for bookcases.

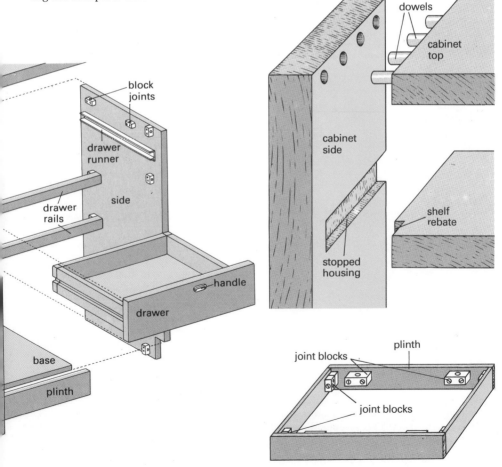

1 Making drawers can be a tedious and time-consuming job and it is unlikely that you would want to go to all the trouble of making dovetail joints for the fronts. Housed joints will do the job just as well and, if you prefer it, you can use plastic extrusions instead of wood.

There are one or two different plastic drawer systems, but most include a corner joint which enables the drawers to be assembled using only square cut materials. Using these drawer systems does limit the depth of the drawers to that of the extrusions. If you want to have a more varied choice you will have to use wood and chipboard.

The easiest type of drawer is the one with the front wider than the sides so that it fits over the face of the cabinet. The drawer itself is then made as a square box with the ends housed or rebated into the sides. These joints are glued and pinned.

2 Ideally, the bottom of the drawer is fitted into a groove in the sides and front, and the back of the drawer is made shallower than the sides, finishing level with the top edge of the groove so that the bottom can be slid into place and pinned to the bottom edge of the drawer back.

A rebate can be made for the drawer bottom, but it is not very good as it does not leave much for the drawer to run on. The drawer will not run freely if the bottom is simply fixed directly to the bottom edges of the sides.

Side runners are therefore the best solution. A strip of hardwood, glued and screwed to the outside of each side of the drawer, slides on a similar strip of hardwood fixed to the inside of the cabinet. This means that the drawer tray is made 20mm narrower than the opening to make a space for the two 10mm runners. The false front, which overlaps the sides of the cabinet, is screwed into place through the front of the drawer.

Using side runners means that there need be no cabinet rail showing between the drawers which will then present a flush finish. If rails are needed to

1 *The bottom of a drawer slides into grooves in the sides and then the back is fitted and fixed in place.*
2 *The bottom holds the drawer square so it must fit neatly into the back.*
Remember to allow for the depth of the grooves when measuring up for the size of the base.

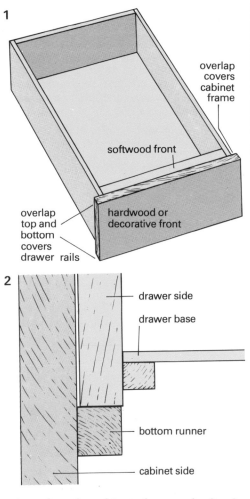

softwood front

overlap covers cabinet frame

overlap top and bottom covers drawer rails

hardwood or decorative front

drawer side

drawer base

bottom runner

cabinet side

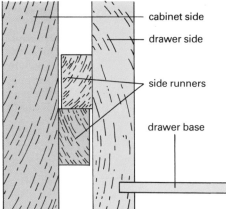

cabinet side

drawer side

side runners

drawer base

Methods of making drawers.

1 The drawer can have a decorative front screwed to a softwood backing.

2 The drawer slides on a hardwood runner screwed to the side of the unit.

3 Hardwood runners are screwed to both the sides of the unit and to the sides of the drawer.

The former method is often used where front rails form a feature of the unit. In the latter method the two hardwood runners wear better and the drawer fronts are not separated by the front rails of the cabinet.

4 This illustrates how drawers are made-up using one of the plastic drawer making systems which are generally obtainable as complete kits.

strengthen the cabinet, they can be fixed by letting them into the sides or screwing them through the sides, dependent on the quality of finish required. In this case the width of the drawer front will have to be adjusted to cover the rails.

Drawers can be run on bottom rails if the drawer bottom is fixed to battens glued and pinned to the inside of the drawer about 10mm above the bottom of the sides, but this reduces the storage depth of the drawer.

Always remember to make your drawers as strong as possible so that the weight they bear will be well supported.

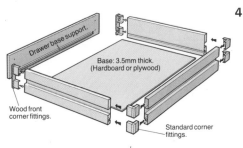

Drawer base support.

Base: 3.5mm thick. (Hardboard or plywood)

Wood front corner fittings.

Standard corner fittings.

Making a corner unit presents few problems as the sides can be screwed to each other at the back, as well as being screwed into the triangular top and bottom. When the unit is in position these screws will not show. The shelves can also be screwed into place through the sides; there is no need to house them if they will have little weight to carry. If preferred, they can be supported on studs so that they can be adjusted whenever necessary.

Corner display shelves are usually open at the front, but if a door is required a 50 × 25mm frame can be made and secured to the unit by plastic blocks behind the top and bottom rails. The doors can then be hung on butt hinges or piano hinges, or for glass doors pivots can be used.

As the sides of the cabinet will be of plywood or chipboard, they can be screwed directly to the wall. Drill a hole near the top at each side, then hold the unit in place and mark the wall. Drill the wall and fit plugs, then screw the unit into place.

Floor standing kitchen units are quite large as the units which they adjoin are about 600mm deep. This large corner area where two runs of floor cabinets meet, does present a problem of access. The easiest solution is to provide the corner unit with a lift up lid. The unit itself is made as a simple box joined at the corners by plastic blocks. The bottom, which can

A corner cabinet is constructed in the same way as an ordinary cabinet but the door can be a bit more awkward to hang. There are also more sawn edges to finish with veneer or plastic strip.

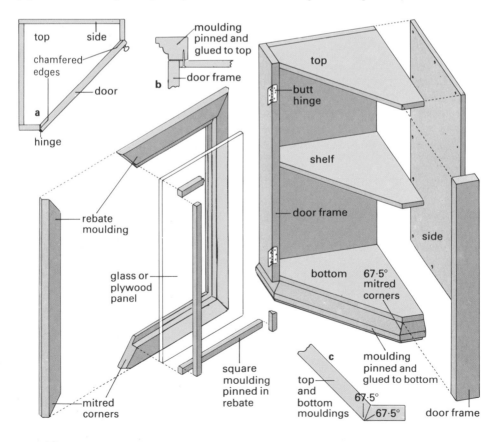

be made of chipboard, holds the unit square and can be supported on 25mm square bearers fixed to the sides, just above floor level.

A lift-up top is most easily provided by fixing a strip of worktop about 75mm wide to the top of the unit using plastic blocks. The flap can then be hinged to this strip by means of a piano hinge. The unit can then be fitted into place and screwed to the wall. It can be used for storing large items or as a linen box.

In order to get a front door access, the unit must be made a little bigger than the

Corner units in a run of kitchen units can be a bit of a problem. Here are two ideas for getting the most out of the space available. The lidded type fits the corner exactly. The door type is bigger.

depth of the kitchen units. The larger it is made the bigger the door that can be provided. A scale drawing, or a full-size drawing on the floor would help in ascertaining the size of opening needed to provide access for large items.

Construction is the same as that described for other cabinets, except that the top is fixed to the sides by small metal brackets. The doors can be hung one at each side so that they close to make an internal right-angle, or they can be hung one onto the other, like folding doors. In each case they are held closed by magnetic catches.

Shelves or a carousel can be fitted in the usual way. A carousel is a set of circular shelves on a central pivot which enables you to revolve them to get at the contents easily.

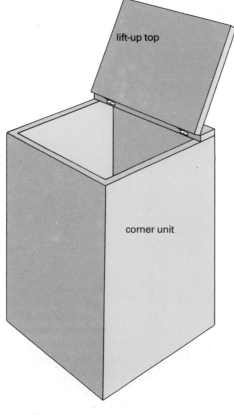

lift-up top

corner unit

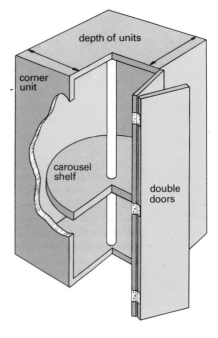

depth of units

corner unit

carousel shelf

double doors

All articles made of wood need treating with a preservative or finish, not only to preserve and protect the surface, but also to bring out the inherent beauty of the grain and the texture of the timber. The quality of finish is extremely important, as it is by this that the work is usually judged. Although painting will hide any slight surface defects, any blemish in wood becomes even more noticeable when a clear finish, or a stain and clear finish are applied. It is important also that all woodwork, except that which is being treated with a preservative such as creosote, is perfectly clean and smooth.

The main processes in finishing are filling, stopping, staining and applying the finish. When a clear finish is to be applied, it is essential when an orbital electric sanding machine has been used that the surface is still finished afterwards by sanding with the grain, by hand. If this is not done, small circular scratches resembling fish scales will be seen in the final coat.

Preservatives

Fences and sheds can be treated with creosote to BS 3051. If the brown colour is not acceptable, preservative of another colour can be used. Where the timber will be in contact with plants, such as on the inside of greenhouses and forcing frames, a green horticultural preservative should be used. Colourless preservatives are also available, for use on interior and exterior woodwork; these can be painted when dry.

Painting

Emulsion paint can be applied direct to sanded wood and no knotting, primer or undercoat is required. Before applying solvent-based paints, any knots in the wood should be sealed with pure shellac knotting and allowed to dry. Any cracks or dents should then be filled with wood-stopping, which should be applied slightly proud of the surface to allow for shrinkage and, when dry, papered smooth. Next, a pink or white primer, followed by an undercoat of a similar colour to the top coat should be applied. If a first-class finish is

required, lightly rub this smooth with fine glasspaper when it is dry, and apply a second coat. This too can be rubbed down before applying the finishing coat.

Because paint is pigmented it does not usually have as good a flow as varnish and, to make sure that no brush marks are left on the surface, it should be 'laid-off' to a greater extent than a varnish. The paint should be applied in one direction, then with a slightly lighter pressure at right angles, then with lighter pressure still

Left *Different finishes and veneers.*
Top to bottom: Gloss polyurethane on rosewood; Matt polyurethane on sen; Yacht varnish on padauk; Plastic coating on burr walnut; Teak oil on teak; Danish oil on Baltic pine; Satin polyurethane on coromandel.

Below *Selection of dyes on sycamore.*
Top to bottom: Light oak; Dark Burmese teak; Light Scandinavian teak; Dark oak; Walnut; Medium oak; Brown mahogany; Ebony; Red mahogany; Pine.

diagonally, finishing off with the minimum pressure, drawing the brush lightly across the surface in the original direction of application.

The best results are always obtained by using good quality brushes of the correct size. For example, it is no good using a 1″ brush for painting a door – a 2½″ brush would be more suitable. Immediately after use, brushes should be cleaned with white spirit or a proprietary solvent.

Exterior wood-stains can be used on timber instead of paint. These are not to be confused with the transparent wood-stains or dyes used for staining wood prior to the application of clear finishes. They contain a pigment and tend to obliterate the grain, but they are easier to apply and maintain than paint.

Non-pigmented finishes

All finishes alter the colour of wood to some extent and some woods, for example, mahogany and walnut, turn much darker even when a completely clear finish is applied. An approximate idea of the colour the wood will become when finished with a clear solution can be seen by damping a small area with water. If this colour is too light, then the wood can be stained before finishing. It is only possible to stain wood to a darker colour; for a lighter shade it must be bleached.

When staining wood, it is advisable to test the stain on a spare piece of wood, or on an area which would not normally be seen, as it is difficult to remove stain which has been recently applied. If the wood has an open grain, and a smooth finish is required, then a grain-filler should be used for filling the pores, or extra coats of the finish would have to be applied and then rubbed down with an abrasive paper. Any cracks or holes in the wood should be filled with wood-stopping before staining.

The final finish may be of a type which gives a surface film, such as French polish, varnish or polyurethane. The last two are available in gloss, satin and matt finishes. Varnish stains are also available which will

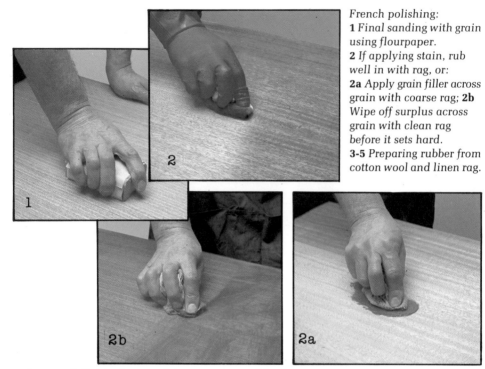

French polishing:
1 *Final sanding with grain using flourpaper.*
2 *If applying stain, rub well in with rag, or:*
2a *Apply grain filler across grain with coarse rag;* **2b** *Wipe off surplus across grain with clean rag before it sets hard.*
3-5 *Preparing rubber from cotton wool and linen rag.*

colour and finish the wood in one operation. It is important to note, however, that each extra coat of varnish stain will darken the colour and, unless brushed out very evenly, the colour will vary as the thickness of the film varies. When wood is stained with a penetrating dye, the colour will not vary however many coats of clear finish are then applied. When varnishing an external door, it is important that at least one coat is applied to the top, bottom and side edges to prevent water being absorbed at these points, which would eventually cause the varnish to fail.

Alternatively, oiled finishes may be used, such as teak oil and Danish oil. These finishes are far easier to apply than the previous types as they are merely wiped over the surface with a cloth. Teak oil leaves the wood with a soft, lustrous finish. When a high gloss finish is required on exterior woodwork, a yacht varnish should be used. These usually contain tung oil which has outstanding exterior durability.

Waxing

This type of finish is popular on wood such as pine and oak. Before applying wax the wood should be sealed with French polish if a golden colour is required, or with transparent French polish, which will not alter the colour of the wood. Two coats of French polish should be applied with a brush or rag and, when dry, lightly rubbed down with fine glasspaper. The surface can also be rubbed down with fine steel wool and wax polish. This treatment will give an acceptable satin finish. If, however, a higher gloss is required, then the wax polish should be applied with a soft cloth or a shoe polishing brush and allowed to harden. The surface should then be buffed with a soft yellow duster or soft shoe-brush.

French Polishing

For further information on this process send a stamped addressed envelope to the manufacturer of the product.

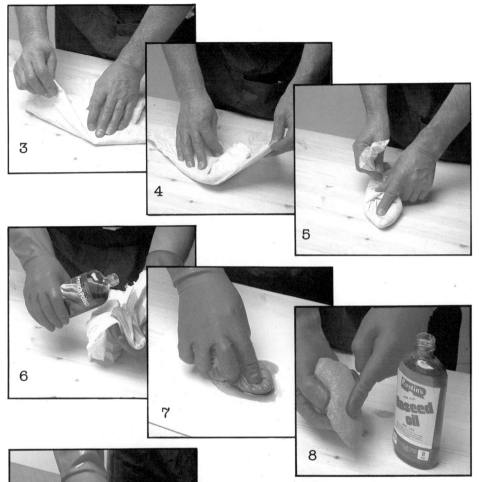

6 Saturate cotton wool with French polish.

7 Squeeze out excess polish on piece of card.

8 Dab a drop of linseed oil on to base of rubber.

9 Rub in overlapping circles, gliding rubber on and off surface. Finish by rubbing with grain in even backward and forward strokes with nearly dry rubber.

10 Put rubber in airtight jar between applications.

These bookshelves are a free-standing floor unit with some adjustable shelves. Construction of the shelves is in pine-board, which can support greater loads than the same thickness of chipboard.

The overall width of the unit is 900mm and its height is 1200mm. This means that two standard 1200mm boards will make the sides, while the shelves and top can be made from standard 900mm boards. The top is 36mm longer than the shelves as it goes over the top of the sides. The top and bottom are fixed by means of one-piece joint-blocks. One middle shelf is also permanently fixed in the same way, but the other shelves are adjustable. Alternatively, the unit could be assembled using dowels, with the fixed shelf set in housing joints in the sides. These techniques are described earlier in the book under Dowel & Halving Joints and Housing, Butt and Mitre Joints.

One-piece joint-blocks are neat, plastic, triangular blocks which are fixed by one screw into each panel. A plastic lid then covers the screws to provide a good finish to a sound and permanent joint.

The depth of the bookshelves depends on the type of books you intend to store on them. Paperbacks need shelves 150mm deep; the larger hardbacks require shelves about 250mm deep. If the sides, and top and bottom shelves, are made wider than the middle fixed and adjustable shelves, you can fit grooved sliding-door track to take glass or perspex doors.

The unit has a back made from hardboard and this strengthens the framework and makes it more rigid. This is necessary because it is free-standing. Having cut the sides to the required lengths, place them with their inside faces together and mark the position of the bottom and the fixed middle shelf on the edges. Then square the marks across the boards and screw the joint-blocks into place ready for the shelves.

Next, carefully cut the bottom and middle shelves to the same length and screw them to the joint-blocks. The top, which is long enough to cover the tops of the sides, is

Cutting list (millimetres)

Pine-board:

Top	900 × 225
Sides (2)	1200 × 225
Bottom shelf ⎱ Middle fixed shelf ⎰	864 × 225
Adjustable shelves (2)	854 × 225
Plinth	864 × 75

Hardboard:

Back	1122 × 894

Other materials:
16 Joint blocks (rigid) and screws
4 Bookcase strips, 914 long, and 8 supports
¾" Hardboard pins
Polyurethane (satin finish)

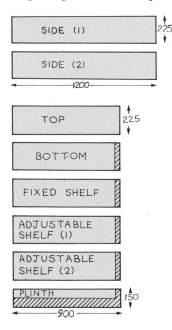

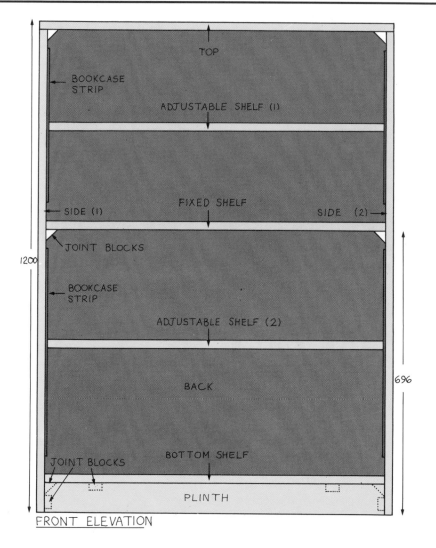

TOP

BOOKCASE STRIP

ADJUSTABLE SHELF (1)

SIDE (1)

SIDE (2)

FIXED SHELF

JOINT BLOCKS

BOOKCASE STRIP

ADJUSTABLE SHELF (2)

BACK

BOTTOM SHELF

JOINT BLOCKS

PLINTH

1200

696

FRONT ELEVATION

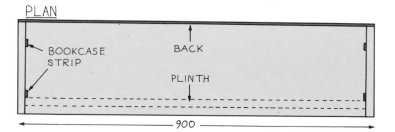

PLAN

BOOKCASE STRIP

BACK

PLINTH

900

SIDE SECTION

BOOKCASE STRIP

SIDE (1)

JOINT BLOCKS

BACK

PLINTH

225

SUPPORT STUD

BOOKCASE STRIP

fixed in the same way.

With the framework constructed, the metal bookcase-strips for the adjustable shelves can be screwed into place 50mm in from the front and back edges. They are designed to fit on the surface of the wood and do not need a rebate. When cutting the adjustable shelves to length you must allow clearance for these metal strips at each end of the shelves. The shelf-support clips engage in slots in the metal strip so it is important that these slots are in line at each side and at the back and front of the unit.

If you cut the hardboard squarely you can use it to square up the whole structure. It is held in place by 20mm hardboard pins. If you are using a clear finish such as polyurethane or Danish oil, then the inside of the hardboard back should be sealed and painted in a colour to suit the board finish before it is nailed into place. If the unit is to be painted then the hardboard can be sealed before it is fixed and then painted with the rest of the unit on completion.

At the bottom of the unit there is a plinth or kicking-board set back about 25mm to make it less vulnerable to scratching. This can be made from the same type of board as the rest of the unit, but as it is only 75mm wide you might find that stock sizes are a little wasteful, so it can be made from a length of matching timber.

To avoid damage to the plinth you can treat the timber with a plastic coating or face it with a laminate, either in a matching wood grain or a contrasting plain colour. Black makes a good plinth colour and it goes with most types of wood. The plinth is held in place by screwing one joint-block to each end and a couple under the bottom shelf, evenly spaced along its length.

Working with pine-board

Because pine-board is made from strips of timber glued together, it may swell and shrink with changes in atmospheric conditions. Where possible, therefore, it is advisable to apply one coat of the chosen finish to seal the timber before assembly.

However much storage space you already have, there always seems to be a need for more shelves. The construction of this small unit demonstrates a very simple technique for making modular shelving units. They can be of almost any length, width or height – the techniques for making larger units being identical. The unit shown is made with pine uprights and Contiplas shelves. Contiplas should have a maximum span of 700mm between supports for any loadbearing shelves. This 700mm can be increased if the shelves are strengthened by battens at the front or back.

All pieces of the same length and all holes must be marked out in a group for maximum accuracy. After marking out, saw the legs and cross-rails to length and bore all holes for the Scan fittings. The technique for using Scan fittings is explained in the instructions for making the coffee-table (see pages 64-67). Then clean up the legs and cross-rails and assemble using wood-working adhesive. Glasspaper well and finish with polyurethane.

Now cut the three shelves to length. The top shelf is fixed to the three frames using rigid joint blocks. The two lower shelves are screwed through into the frames and screw caps set into counter-bored holes are used to cover the heads.

Finally, cut the two backs to size and screw them into position between the frames using 1¼" No. 6 screws.

Cutting list (millimetres)
Contiplas:
Backs (2)   600 × 380
Shelves (3)   1200 × 230
Pine:
Legs (6)   755 × 47 × 22
Cross rails (9)   230 × 47 × 22

Other materials:
18 Scan bolts, nuts, and cover-heads
6 Joint blocks (rigid) and screws
1¼″ × No. 6 Chipboard screws
Plastic screw caps
Woodworking adhesive
Polyurethane

CUTTING PLANS

LEGS (1-3)   47×22

LEGS (4-6)

CROSS RAILS (1-9) 47×22

230 SHELF (1)   SHELF (2)

SHELF (3)
————2400————

380 BACK   BACK
————1800————

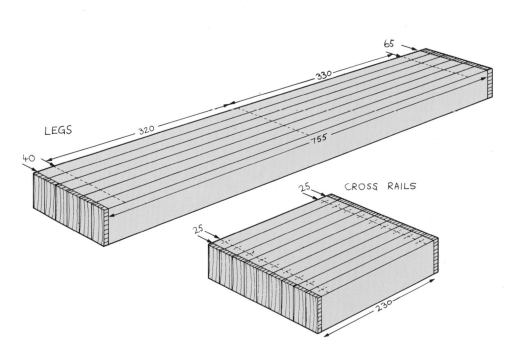

LEGS
65
330
320
755
40

CROSS RAILS
25
25
230

FRONT AND END ELEVATIONS

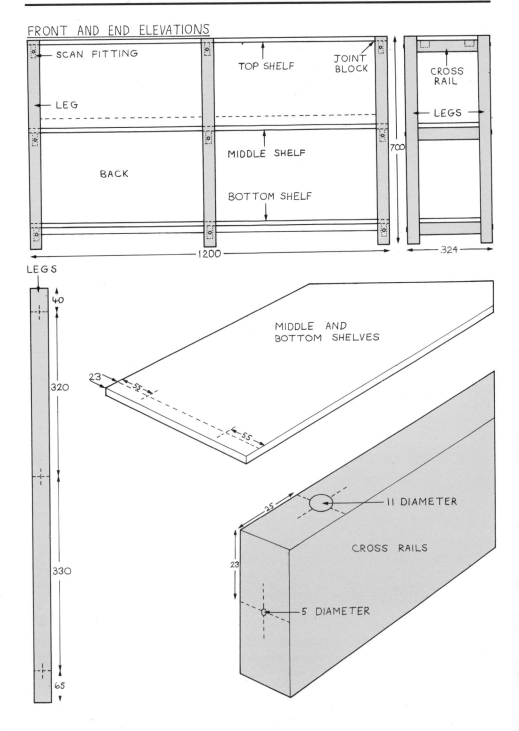

SCAN FITTING

LEG

BACK

TOP SHELF

MIDDLE SHELF

BOTTOM SHELF

JOINT BLOCK

CROSS RAIL

LEGS

700

1200

324

LEGS

40

320

330

65

MIDDLE AND BOTTOM SHELVES

23

55

55

23

25

11 DIAMETER

CROSS RAILS

23

5 DIAMETER

This bathroom cabinet is made from Contiplas which is suitable for the damp atmosphere of a bathroom and is easily wiped clean. There is room to store most of your bathroom requirements and it has a useful-size mirror attached to the outside of the door. There is also a hinged flap for putting items on while you are using them.

First, cut the Contiplas panel into the sizes shown in the cutting diagram, allowing an extra 20mm on the length of each. Then cut the 600 and 273mm long panels in half lengthways to form the shelves and sides

Place the two sides together in a vice or cramp, and mark them to length, with a marking knife. Square this cut line right round the panels, leaving approximately 10mm spare at each end. Repeat this operation to mark the top, bottom and two shelves to length, again leaving 10mm spare at each end.

Once the cut lines have been squared round the ends, all the panels can be cut to size. For this job use a panel saw with approximately 9 teeth to 25mm. Clean up each end using a sharp plane and then edge veneer the two side panels at both ends. There is no need to edge the shelves.

Next, mark the position of the screw holes in the sides of the cabinet. Bore these and then counter-bore to a depth of 4mm and 10mm diameter for the screw caps.

The cabinet can now be assembled. Cut the back to size and paint it to the colour required using emulsion paint, but do not fit it yet. Cut the door and flap to size and veneer the exposed edges. The door and the flap can now be hinged and the magnetic catches fitted, followed by the flap stays and the shelf studs.

Now fit the back using $\frac{3}{4}''$ countersunk screws, driving them well in. Attach the handles and mirror, and screw the cabinet to the wall using two mirror plates. These are screwed into the back top edge of the cabinet with countersunk chipboard screws. The third hole in the plate is used to attach the cabinet to the wall using screws at least $1\frac{1}{2}''$ long.

Cutting list (millimetres)

Contiplas:

Sides (2)	600 × 150
Top	
Bottom	
Shelf, fixed	273 × 150
Shelf, adjustable	
Door	393 × 303
Flap	205 × 303

Hardboard:

Back	600 × 303

Other materials:

2 Handles
4 Hinges, single-cranked, and screws
2 Flap stays, plastic
2 Magnetic catches
4 Shelf studs
1 Mirror, 350 × 255, and mirror screws
$1\frac{1}{2}''$ × No. 6 Chipboard screws
$\frac{3}{4}''$ × No. 4 Countersunk woodscrews
Plastic screw caps
Edging strip
Emulsion paint (for back)
Wall-fixing screws and plugs
1 Cupboard door lock (optional)

CUTTING PLAN

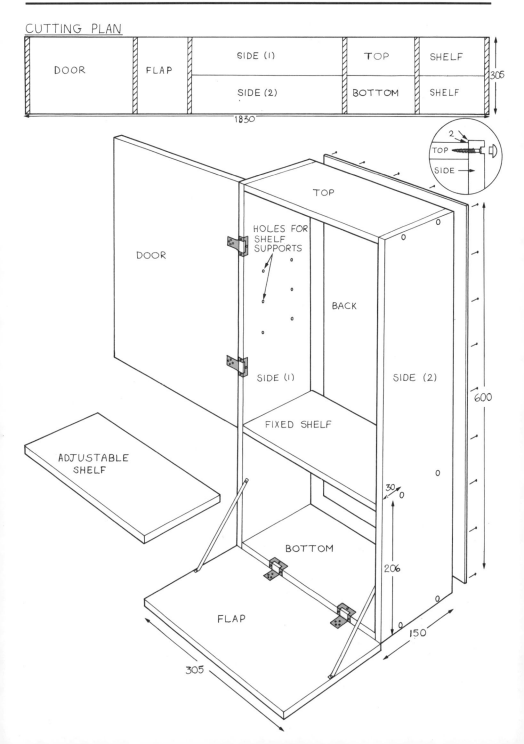

| DOOR | FLAP | SIDE (1) | TOP | SHELF |
| | | SIDE (2) | BOTTOM | SHELF |

305

1830

2
TOP
SIDE

TOP

HOLES FOR
SHELF
SUPPORTS

DOOR

BACK

SIDE (1)

SIDE (2)

600

FIXED SHELF

ADJUSTABLE
SHELF

30   0

BOTTOM

206

FLAP

150

305

This low table with a shelf for magazines is a useful piece of furniture for any living-room. The legs are made from timber and the top and shelf from veneered chipboard.

To ensure that each set of component parts matches, the marking out should always be done by the 'group' method as follows. Hold the four legs together as a group in a vice or cramp and mark these out as shown in diagram A. Cut lines, made with a sharp knife, are always used when a saw cut is to be made; all other lines are made with a pencil, sharpened to a chisel point. On the centre of each pencil line mark the position for boring the hole for the Scan bolt (5mm diameter), and bore these holes. Then saw off the waste.

Next, place the four long rails together and mark these as shown in diagram B. The four long rails are identical except for the position of the Scan bolt which goes through the thickness of the rails. On the

Cutting list (millimetres)

Contiboard:

Top	910 × 380
Shelf	700 × 286

Timber (to choice):

Legs (4)	360 × 32 × 32
Long rails (4)	700 × 45 × 20
Short rails (4)	286 × 45 × 20

Other materials:
16 Scan bolts, nuts, and cover-heads
4 Table plates and $\frac{1}{2}''$ screws
$1\frac{1}{4}''$ × No. 6 Chipboard screws
1" × No. 6 Countersunk woodscrews
Edging strip
Woodworking adhesive
Polyurethane

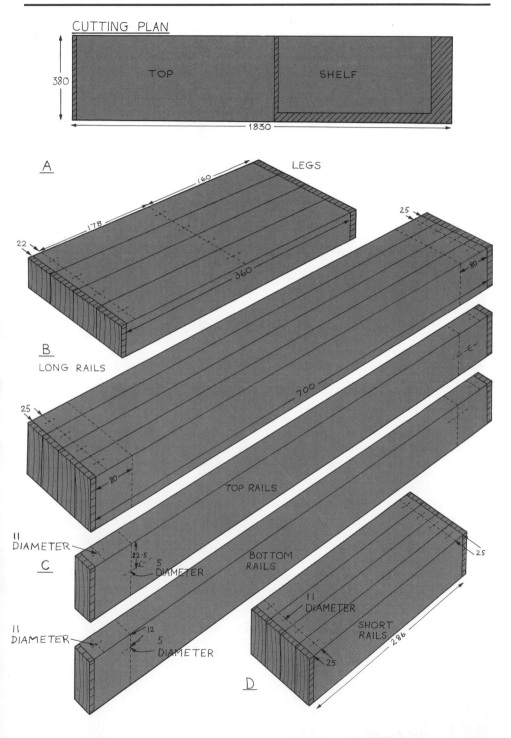

CUTTING PLAN

380

TOP

SHELF

1830

A

LEGS

160

178

360

22

25

80

B

LONG RAILS

25

80

700

C

TOP RAILS

11
DIAMETER

22.5

5
DIAMETER

BOTTOM
RAILS

25

C

11
DIAMETER

12

5
DIAMETER

11
DIAMETER

SHORT
RAILS

286

25

D

top rail the hole for the Scan fitting is dead centre, but on the bottom rail this hole is 33mm from the top edge as in diagram C. Saw off the waste from each end. Bore and counter-bore. The four short rails are marked out as in diagram D.

The ends of all the long rails and all the short rails are prepared for the Scan fittings in exactly the same way. Bore the 11mm diameter holes to the depth required using a vertical drill-stand. The holes in the ends of all the rails are best bored by making a small work aid as shown in diagram E. All marking out should be done using a marking gauge. The work aid is made using the vertical drill-stand and care should be taken to ensure that this is made with a good degree of accuracy. The work aid is cramped on to the end of each rail and guides the drill into the exact position. Once each rail has been bored, clean it up using a plane and/or glasspaper and then round the corners as shown in diagram F.

Next, counter-bore all positions for the Scan nut as shown in diagram G. Now insert a 1″ No. 6 screw into the 3mm hole at each end of each long rail. Screw these in so that 6mm of shank is left standing. Then cut off the screw with a small hacksaw leaving two steel 'pegs' protruding. These pegs prevent the rails from twisting round the Scan bolt once the framework is assembled (diagram H). Tighten each joint into position. The steel pegs will then mark their positions on to the mating surfaces. Take the joint apart, and bore holes 6mm deep to accept the steel pegs. Reassemble using a woodworking adhesive. Finally, cut the Contiboard top and shelf to size. Using a 550mm handsaw with approximately 9 teeth to 25mm, cut the board on the waste side of your cut line. Chipboard can be planed, but it is best to work from both sides to the middle to prevent damage to the board edge. Veneer the edges with edging strip. Attach the top to the top rails with table plates and screw through the bottom cross-rails into the underside of the shelf. Finish with polyurethane varnish for a stain-resistant surface.

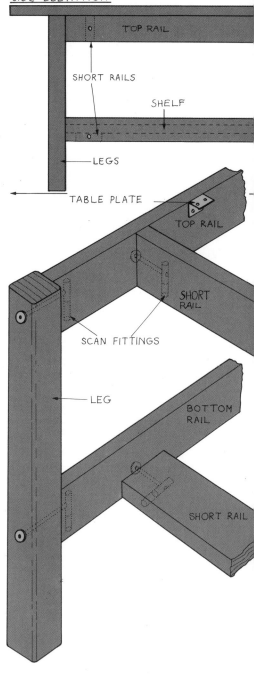

SIDE ELEVATION

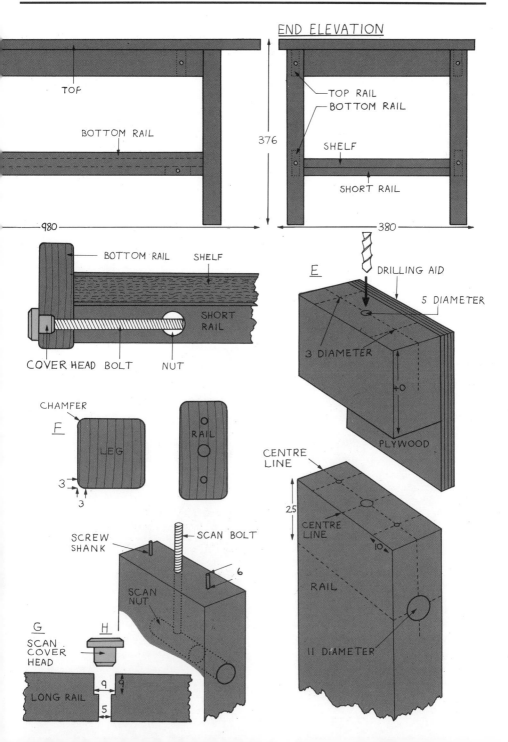

END ELEVATION

TOP

BOTTOM RAIL

376

980

TOP RAIL
BOTTOM RAIL
SHELF
SHORT RAIL

380

BOTTOM RAIL   SHELF

SHORT RAIL

COVER HEAD BOLT   NUT

E

DRILLING AID
5 DIAMETER
3 DIAMETER

PLYWOOD

CHAMFER

F

LEG
3
3

RAIL

CENTRE LINE

25

CENTRE LINE

10

RAIL

11 DIAMETER

SCREW SHANK
SCAN BOLT

6

SCAN NUT

G
SCAN COVER HEAD

H

LONG RAIL
9   9
5

Made in pine-board with white, plastic-laminate faced boards for the interior of the cosmetic-storage section, this dressing-table makes an attractive piece of furniture. Of straightforward box construction, without any fancy joints or legs to shape and fit, it can be made with the minimum of tools. If you should choose veneered chipboard you will have to finish any exposed edges with iron-on edging strip.

Standard-width boards are used throughout, but in order to provide an overhang so that the lid can be lifted without having to have a handle fitted, the ends and centre panel have to be reduced slightly. The top of the unit is 1066mm long and the lid, which is 616 × 375mm, is cut from it.

The top, end and centre panels are all

Cutting list (millimetres)

Pine-board:	
Top	1066 × 450
Lid	615 × 375
Ends (2) ⎫ Centre panel ⎭	647 × 447
Open shelf ⎫ Bottle-tray front ⎭	598 × 150
Top rail	1030 × 50
Back rail ⎫ Plinth ⎭	414 × 66
Upper drawer fronts (2)	412 × 150
Bottom drawer front	412 × 225
Contiplas:	
Shelf	598 × 182
Bottle tray	598 × 229
Hardboard:	
Back	1060 × 662
Drawer bases (3)	394 × 391

For timber drawers:
Plywood (9mm thick):
Bottom drawer back ⎫
Bottom drawer sides (2) ⎬ 400 × 203
Upper drawer backs (2) ⎫
Upper drawer sides (4) ⎬ 400 × 128
Timber:
Drawer base battens (6) 376 × 9 × 9
Drawer base battens (6) 391 × 9 × 9
Drawer runners (6) 400 × 12 × 12

Other materials:
4m Drawer profile, and corner connectors
1 Mirror, 450 × 300, and clips and screws
Adjustable braking stay or chain
Dowels 24 × 6 diameter
1 Piano hinge, 600 long, and screws
24 Joint blocks, and screws
$1\frac{1}{4}''$ × No. 6 Chipboard screws

Other materials (continued):
$\frac{5}{8}''$ × No. 6 Chipboard screws
$\frac{3}{4}''$ × Hardboard pins and Plastic screw-caps
Woodworking adhesive, Danish oil or other finish

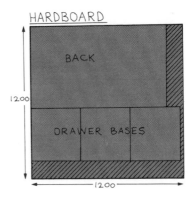

HARDBOARD

BACK

1200

DRAWER BASES

1200

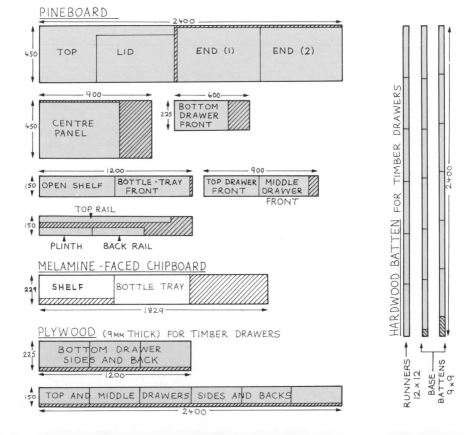

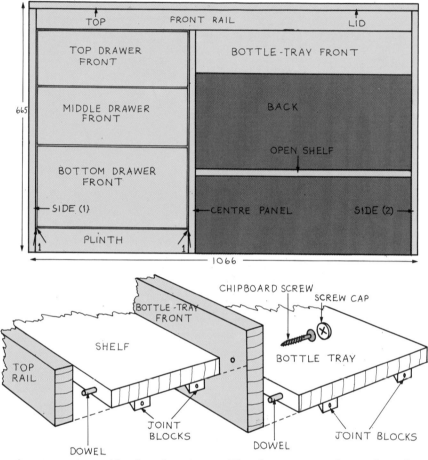

made from 450mm wide boards, the 647mm long end and centre panels being reduced in width by about 3mm so that the top will overhang them. The top of the centre panel has a notch 50mm wide and the same depth as the thickness of the board to take the 50mm wide top rail. Place the left-hand end and the centre panel together and mark on the edge the position of the top notch and the drawer fronts which are 150, 150 and 225mm wide. Allow 2mm clearance between the drawers and between the top drawer and the top rail, and 1mm at each side. Square these drawer marks accurately across the inside of the boards as they determine the positions of the drawer runners.

The drawers may be made either by using plastic drawer profile, following the manufacturer's instructions, or from timber as described below. In the latter case, the runners are made from 12mm square hardwood which is glued and screwed to the panels, with the bottom edge on the lines you have squared across them. The drawer runners also act as stops for the drawers so they must be positioned with the front end set back from the front edge of the board by the thickness of the drawer fronts.

Cut the 66mm wide plinth and the 50mm wide top rail from a 150mm wide board. The plinth is fixed by joint-blocks 18mm behind the edge of the end and centre panels, where it will butt up against the end

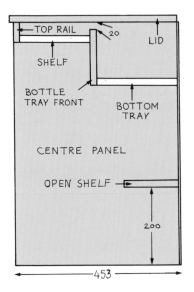

of the drawer runners. The top and the top rail are also fixed with plastic blocks, the top rail being flush with the panel edges.

A 150mm wide shelf is shown in the knee-hole of the dressing-table and this is positioned about 200mm up from the bottom of the panels. Its position is not critical and you can fit it where you think it will be most useful. Its main purpose is to hold the bottom of the end panel in place.

The shelf and bottle-tray inside the dressing-table are made from melamine-faced chipboard so that they can be cleaned easily and will not be damaged by spillage. As an extra precaution you should finish the sides of the inside of the dressing-table with hard gloss plastic-coating.

The shelf and bottle-tray can be assembled using screws with plastic caps, and dowels where the screws would show to the front. The whole assembly is fixed into place using plastic blocks underneath the shelf and tray where they will not be seen. A couple of short dowels into the front rail of the unit will provide extra support, and this joint should be glued as well. The top edge of this tray assembly must be about 20mm below the lid when it is closed, so that it will not foul the mirror when it is fixed in place.

At the back of the drawer section a rail of the same size as the plinth will be needed at the bottom to serve the same purpose as the small shelf under the dressing-table. This rail can be cut from the same board as the plinth and is fixed with two plastic blocks at each end.

At this stage the hardboard back can be fitted. It should be made about 6mm less than the width of the unit and 3mm less than the height so that when its edges are bevelled slightly, it will hardly be seen. Varnish or paint it and check that the unit is square by measuring the diagonals before fixing the back in place with glue and hardboard pins.

Plane smooth the cut edges of the lid and dressing-table top, and fix the piano hinge to the back edge of the lid so that it fits neatly back into the board from which it was cut and the grain pattern matches.

Support the lid by means of a chain, or a joint stay with a centre pivot. A standard mirror is fitted to the inside of the lid using the fixings provided with it.

The drawer fronts are made from the same type of board as the rest of the dressing-table, but the sides and backs are made from 9mm plywood. The drawer bottoms are made from hardboard or 3mm thick plywood.

The drawer fronts ought to be rebated to take the sides, but you can make simple butt-joints and fix the front to the sides using either joint-blocks or thin batten (9 × 9mm) glued and screwed to the sides and the front. Position the bottom of the sides 12mm up from the bottom of the front.

The back and the sides can be joined in the same way, but it is better to make a 3mm deep rebate in the sides.

Battens 9 × 9mm are also used to support the drawer bottoms. Glue and pin them round the inside of the drawer about 3mm above the bottom edge of the drawer sides so that they will not interfere with the sliding of the drawer on the runners. The bottom is then cut exactly square and rested on the battens where it is also glued and pinned. Fit handles as required.

This pine-board desk features a top which can be tilted up to form a drawing-board and also a wide drawer which can take large sheets of drawing paper. When in use as a desk or table, the top is quite firm and flat. A secondary top or dust board of thin plywood or hardboard covers the drawer when the desk top is raised so that the contents will not get dirty.

Only one shelf is shown under the desk, for stiffening the structure, but more can be fitted if required. If the drawer is not needed for large sheets of paper, it can be partitioned to take small articles without them becoming mixed up with each other.

Two brass hinges are used to fix the top, but a piano hinge could be used to avoid having to cut recesses. Butt hinges are used for the support legs of the top, or flush hinges which do not need recessing.

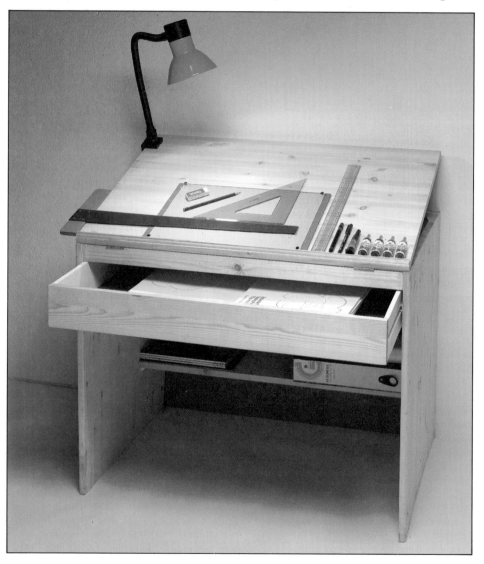

The side panels are 700 × 510mm and the top is 900 × 510mm. There is a narrow front-rail 40mm wide and a back rail 140mm wide; both of these and the shelf are 864mm long. The drawer front can also be cut off to this length, but the ends will require trimming to make it an easy fit when the cabinet has been constructed. When these parts have been cut square at the ends they can be assembled using joint-blocks. The small permanent type are most suitable for the wider back-rail and the shelf, where two will be required at each end. The front rail will have to be fixed with the two-part type

Cut a hardboard back to fit the unit so that it covers the back rail by about 25mm for nailing. If the side edges are bevelled slightly they will not show when the back is in place. Be careful to cut the hardboard exactly square as it will hold the desk unit square when it is glued and nailed into position. You can either paint the board before it is fixed or varnish it afterwards when the whole of the unit is given its finishing treatment.

Next, fix the battens for the dust board.

Cutting list (millimetres)

Pine-board:

Top	900 × 510
Sides (2)	700 × 510
Shelf	864 × 150
Drawer front	862 × 100
Front rail	864 × 40
Back rail	864 × 140
Support legs	175 × 50

Hardboard:

Back	896 × 575
Dust-cover	864 × 474
Drawer base	860 × 440

Timber:

Dust-cover supports (2)	864 × 9 × 9
Dust-cover supports (2)	456 × 9 × 9

Other materials:

900mm Scotia moulding, 18 × 18
2 38mm Butt or flush hinges, and screws
2 50mm Butt hinges, and screws
2m 100mm Drawer profile and corner posts
1m Drawer base support moulding
1m Drawer runner profile
8 Joint blocks (rigid) and screws
2 Joint blocks (knock-down) and screws
Polyurethane or Danish oil

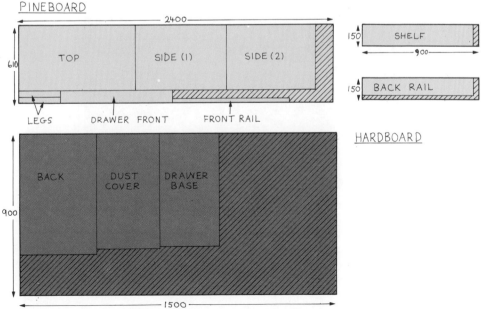

PINEBOARD

2400

610

TOP   SIDE (1)   SIDE (2)

LEGS   DRAWER FRONT   FRONT RAIL

150   SHELF   900

150   BACK RAIL

HARDBOARD

BACK   DUST COVER   DRAWER BASE

900

1500

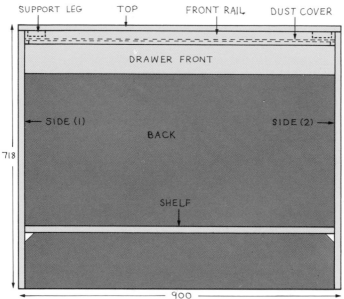

SUPPORT LEG   TOP   FRONT RAIL   DUST COVER

DRAWER FRONT

SIDE (1)   SIDE (2)

BACK

SHELF

718

900

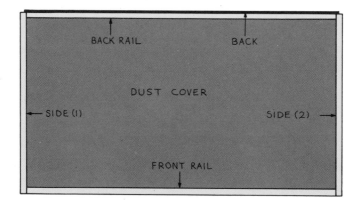

BACK RAIL   BACK

DUST COVER

SIDE (1)   SIDE (2)

FRONT RAIL

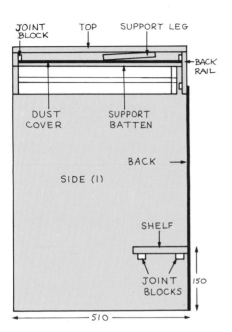

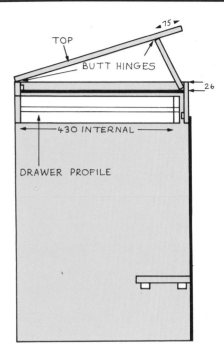

They are 9mm square and are pinned and glued with their undersides flush with the underside of the front rail. Then cut and fit the dust board, again remembering that it must be square because it will square up the whole unit when it is in place.

The supporting stays for the desk top are made from 50 × 18mm pineboard. Make them about 175mm long, and hinge them 75mm from the back edge of the top and 20mm in from the sides. They will then rest on the side supporting battens of the dust board and not just on the board which might bend and make the raised top unsteady.

These stays can be left in place, or taken off again to be refitted when the top has been hung on to the front edge of the desk. If butt hinges are used for the top, they should be let into the front rail with the knuckle projecting as little as possible. If a piano hinge is used, the front rail should be cut a little narrower to allow for the thickness of the closed hinge. A length of scotia moulding pinned and glued to the desk top,

flush with the front edge, prevents pencils and other drawing equipment from sliding off when the top is in the raised position.

With the framework complete, attention can be turned to the drawer. This is 100mm deep and should have an internal dimension from front to back of 430mm so that it will take A2 size paper. It is constructed (following manufacturer's instructions) from plastic drawer profile and corner posts using the three-sided method. The drawer front is attached using wood-front corner fittings, after cutting to size and fitting the hardboard base. The front edge of the base is supported on a drawer base support, screwed to the inside of the drawer front; this avoids having to cut a groove in the board. Mount the runner mouldings to give a clearance of 2mm between the drawer front and the top rail, and set them in from the front edge by 18mm plus the thickness of the front corner fittings. The desk, in its complete form can now be finished off with a protective paint or oil.

This versatile desk unit is made from pine-board using joint-blocks for most of the joints so that it can be easily constructed using only a basic tool-kit. Counter-flap hinges are used so that the work-top will fold back and the front portion will lie flat on the back portion when in the closed position. Butt hinges could be used as an alternative.

A foot rest or rail is fitted between the front legs to make them firm. The plastic blocks used to fix it are screwed to the front of the rail when it is in the down position so that they will be out of sight when raised.

No catches are needed to hold the legs when in the raised position as their own weight will be sufficient. However, if you would prefer them fixed, perhaps so that young children cannot pull them over, you can fit a bolt under the wall shelf-unit to shoot into the desk leg.

The wall shelf-unit is entirely separate from the folding base-unit and although it is shown with a single shelf, its storage space can be designed to suit your own requirements. Only the outer dimensions of the unit cannot be varied because the bottom shelf must be situated high enough up the wall to clear the work-top when it is folded, and the top shelf of the unit must fit underneath the foot rest when the legs are raised. If preferred, it can be fitted with doors, either solid wood or glass. This applies to the lower unit too, which is also shown as a simple shelf-unit. These shelves can be made adjustable and doors can be fitted. They would have to be sliding doors as hinged doors would not open because of the position of the foot rest when the desk is open. Both the top and the bottom unit are secured to the wall when complete.

Start by cutting the pine-board tops to size, followed by the two sides and the two legs. The length of these is 720mm less the thickness of the tops. Then set out one pair of sides for the shelves, if they are to be fixed, or if bookcase strips for adjustable shelves are to be used screw them into place, allowing for the top, plinth and bottom shelf.

At this stage the base unit could be assembled, but it would be better if the two halves of the top were hinged together first. This is done most easily on a bench or work table, even if the two halves are separated again afterwards for ease of assembly of the units.

Counter hinges are made of solid brass and have a double throw action which allows the flap to lie flat on the top of the fixed section. No special skill is needed to fit them – patience in marking out the recesses and chiselling them out is more important. Three hinges are used, one in the centre of the flap and the other two about 150mm from each end. Put each hinge in place and mark the position of the knuckle. Cut this recess so that the recess for the leaf can be marked using a sharp pencil or, better still, the pointed blade of a setting-out knife. Clamp the flap to your work-bench and, using a sharp chisel, cut out a little at a time so that the hinge leaf fits tightly into the recess. When properly hung the two flaps should have only the merest hint of a gap between their edges when they are opened up. Binding will occur when the flaps are folded if the hinges are let too far into the wood; one flap should lie on top of the other quite easily.

Having hinged the flaps successfully, the base unit can be constructed. It is simply joined together with joint-blocks using two to each joint at the top and bottom, and also for the shelves if they are to be fixed. The plinth is fixed in the same way, with a plastic block at each end and two evenly spaced under the bottom shelf.

The unit is held square by the hardboard back which must be cut accurately. It can be made about 4mm shorter than the width of the unit and the edges can be bevelled so that it does not show at the sides. The top edge is left square and fits flush with the top of the unit. The back will hold the unit 3mm or so clear of the wall so that when the legs are folded up they too will be just clear of the wall.

Cut a solid-timber foot-rest to the same length as the top, less twice the thickness of the legs. The leg unit can be assembled in the same way as the base by using joint-blocks, but as the underside of the flap becomes the top when the legs are folded up, a triangular wooden-fillet, glued and screwed to the legs and the flap, would look better. An alternative would be to use a piece of brass or aluminium angle-strip which can also be used instead of joint blocks to fix the foot-rest. When the two units have been completed the hinges are refitted.

As the wall unit has to fit neatly between the legs and has to clear both the arc of the flap and the foot-rest, it is best to check all measurements before starting to cut the boards to length.

A simple shelf-unit is shown here, but it can be divided up in whichever way will be most useful. Lay-on doors using concealed hinges can be fitted, either when the unit is made or later if they become necessary. Lay-on doors would not be suitable for the base unit as they would stand proud of the top when the legs were folded up.

Cut the top and bottom to the full length, but cut the sides to the thickness of the top and bottom less than the full length. Use two plastic blocks at each of the joints and under the shelf, which is cut twice the thickness of the boards less than the length of the top.

Cutting list (millimetres)
Pine-board.

Top Work-top	1000 × 225
Sides (2)	702 × 225
Desk legs (2)	702 × 150
Bottom	964 × 225
Adjustable shelves (2)	956 × 225
Wall-unit top Wall-unit bottom	900 × 150
Wall-unit sides (2)	300 × 150
Wall-unit shelf	864 × 150
Hardboard:	
Base-unit back	996 × 650
Wall-unit back	896 × 332
Timber:	
Foot-rest	964 × 75 × 50
Plinth	964 × 50 × 22

Other materials:
3 Counter hinges or butt hinges
4 Bookcase strips, 600 long, and 8 supports
28 Joint blocks, and screws
450mm Triangular fillet or metal angle
¾" Hardboard pins
Woodworking adhesive
Polyurethane or Danish oil

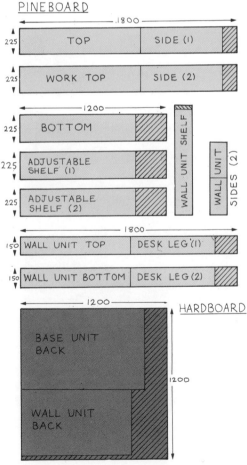

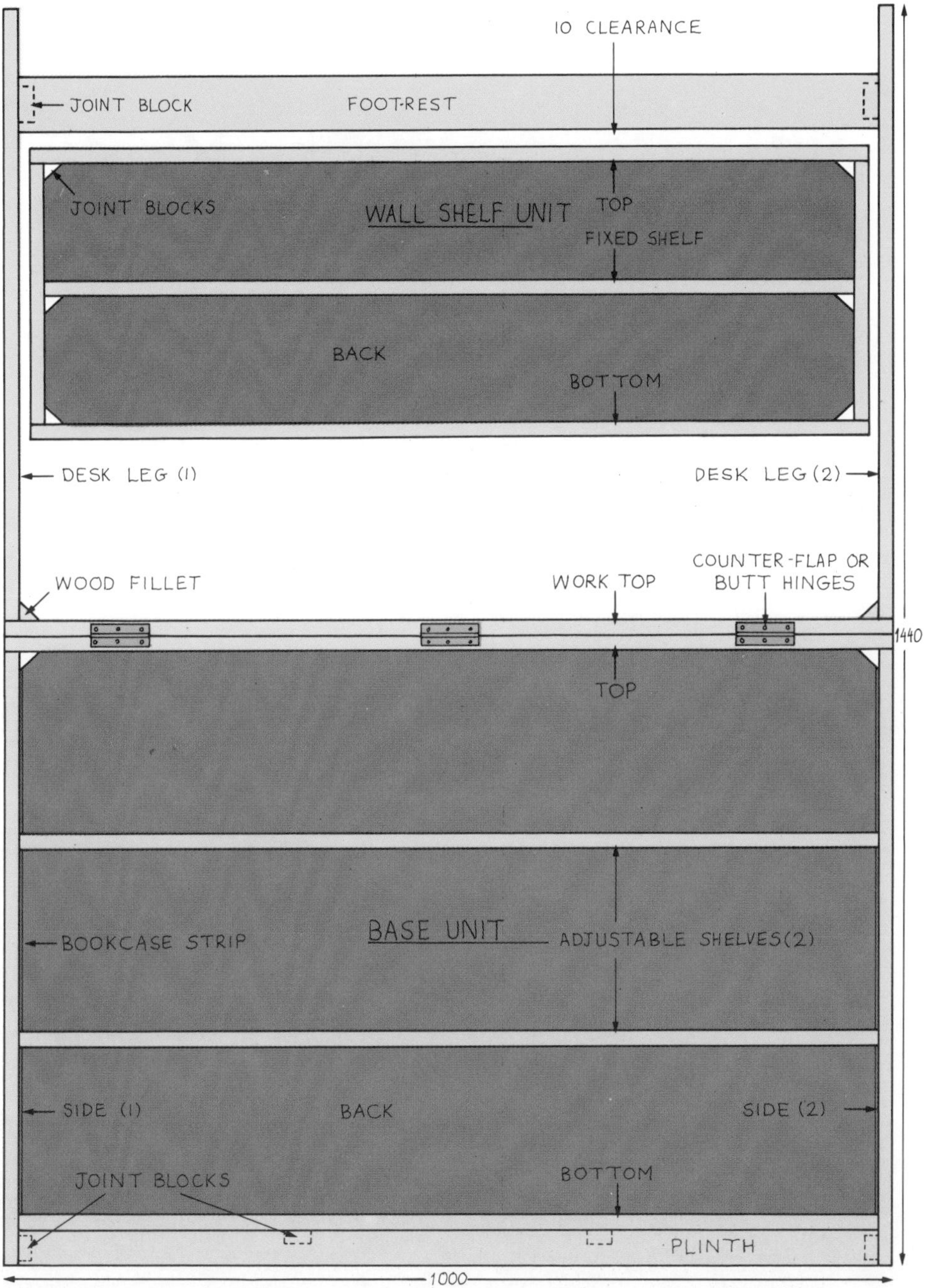

10 CLEARANCE

JOINT BLOCK   FOOT-REST

JOINT BLOCKS   WALL SHELF UNIT   TOP
FIXED SHELF

BACK

BOTTOM

DESK LEG (1)   DESK LEG (2)

WOOD FILLET   WORK TOP   COUNTER-FLAP OR BUTT HINGES

1440

TOP

BOOKCASE STRIP   BASE UNIT   ADJUSTABLE SHELVES (2)

SIDE (1)   BACK   SIDE (2)

JOINT BLOCKS

BOTTOM

PLINTH

1000

Electricity

Mike Lawrence

Consultant Editor Richard Wiles

82 THE ELECTRICAL NETWORK

We have all become so used to having electricity available in our homes at the flick of a switch that it is easy to forget how comparatively recent an innovation it is. Just over a hundred years ago, Swan and Edison invented the incandescent filament lamp — the first practical development of use in the home since Faraday's discoveries of half a century earlier — and in 1881 the first public supply of electricity in the country was established in Godalming, Surrey. In 1890 the country's first power station opened in Deptford, South London, with a 12-mile single-phase cable running to Bond Street and back.

With the introduction of three-phase transmission (still used today), it became possible to transmit electricity over greater distances, and sensible to begin (in 1911) the establishment of an interconnecting system of power stations. However, electricity generation was still a regionalised affair; in 1925 there were 572 separate electricity undertakings drawing their power supplies from 438 generating stations, and

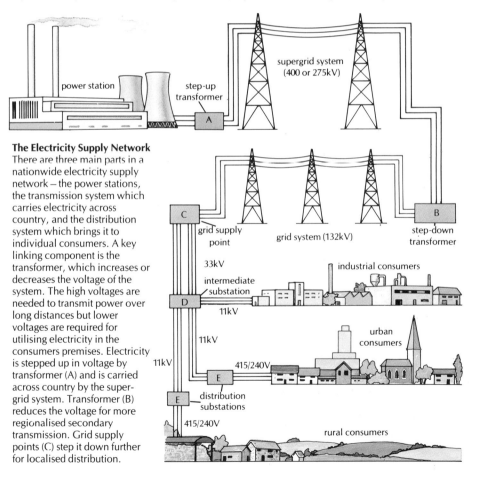

The Electricity Supply Network
There are three main parts in a nationwide electricity supply network – the power stations, the transmission system which carries electricity across country, and the distribution system which brings it to individual consumers. A key linking component is the transformer, which increases or decreases the voltage of the system. The high voltages are needed to transmit power over long distances but lower voltages are required for utilising electricity in the consumers premises. Electricity is stepped up in voltage by transformer (A) and is carried across country by the super-grid system. Transformer (B) reduces the voltage for more regionalised secondary transmission. Grid supply points (C) step it down further for localised distribution.

power station
step-up transformer
supergrid system (400 or 275kV)
A
C
grid supply point
grid system (132kV)
B
step-down transformer
33kV
industrial consumers
intermediate substation
D
11kV
11kV
urban consumers
11kV
415/240V
E
distribution substations
E
415/240V
rural consumers

THE ELECTRICAL NETWORK 83

it took the Electricity Supply Act of 1926 to set up the Central Electricity Board and to establish the National Grid system, which was brought into full commercial operation in 1938.

In 1947 the whole supply industry was nationalised, with a central authority and a number of area boards controlling the supply of electricity to commercial and domestic consumers. On March 31, 1990 the Electricity Act came into force. It made possible the privatisation of Britain's electricity generators and distributors and set up a Regulatory body to encourage competition in the electricity supply industry.

How electricity works

Before you embark on electrical work of any nature, it helps to have a basic idea of how electricity functions. The simplest analogy is with a flow of water through a pipe. Both water and electricity can do 'work' as they flow between two points; water, for example, can turn a water wheel or a turbine, while electricity can produce light if it flows through a lamp, or rotation (which can drive something) if it flows through an electric motor. What causes the flow in each case is a difference in pressure between the two points — the greater the pressure, the greater the flow.

Acting against this pressure is another factor called 'impedance'. Clearly, it's easier for water to flow through a wide pipe than through a narrow one; the latter has the greater impedance to flow, and so the same pressure difference between the ends of the pipe will result in a greater flow through the wider pipe. In electrical terms, impedance (or 'resistance', as it is usually — if incorrectly — called)

divides materials into two types, 'conductors' and 'insulators'. The former have low resistance to the passage of electricity, the latter have high resistance — to the point of not allowing it to pass at all.

Electricity will flow (and carry out work) if it has a circuit to flow round. The flow originates at the source of supply — the power station — and travels through one conductor (the 'live' wire) to wherever it is needed. Then, it returns via another conductor (the 'neutral' wire) to its source. The flow of current (measured in 'amperes' — amps or A for short) is driven through the circuit by the pressure difference (or potential difference, measured in 'volts' — V for short) acting against the resistance of the circuit (measured in 'ohms'). The three are related by the equation: $volts = amps \times ohms$. The amount of electricity consumed whenever work is done (driving a motor or illuminating a lamp, for example) is measured in 'watts' (W), and in practical terms the watts consumed are given by the product of the supply voltage and the current drawn — $watts = volts \times amps$.

In the home, cables deliver electricity to wherever it is needed and then return the flow to the system. Each cable contains a live (flow) conductor, a neutral (return) conductor and a third conductor called the 'protective' or 'earth conductor', or simply 'earth'.

Electricity can escape to earth on its rounds — for example, if you touch a live conductor the current passes through your body to earth, and will shock (or even kill) you. Therefore, everything metallic in your home's wiring system is connected to earth via the earth conductor in the circuit cables. If a fault occurs on an appliance, the voltage on any exposed metalwork cannot rise very high above earth voltage, so will not be dangerous.

84 SAFETY FIRST

The other protection built in to all wiring systems is the 'fuse'. This is a short length of conductor designed to heat up and melt if too high a current passes through it. Such a high current can occur if a circuit is overloaded with too many appliances, if a fault on an appliance occurs that lowers its resistance (such as a short circuit), or if, as already mentioned, electricity is leaking to earth. Fuses are provided in the live pole of all circuits in the house, and in addition are fitted within the rectangular-pin plugs used to link appliances to modern socket outlets. On the most modern systems, the circuit fuses (but not the ones in plugs) may be replaced by devices called 'miniature circuit breakers' (MCBs for short); these isolate a circuit by switching off the current in the event of a fault. In addition, where adequate earthing of the system is difficult to provide, an R.C.D. (Residual Current-Breaker Device) may also be installed.

Rules and regulations

Unlike most building, plumbing and drainage work (which by law must meet the requirements of the Building Regulations), there are no laws governing how electrical work is undertaken in the home . . . at least, not in England and Wales; in Scotland, electrical specifications are covered by the Scottish Building Regulations. However, there are regulations which professional electricians follow — the Regulations for Electrical Installations, published by the Institution of Electrical Engineers, and more commonly known as the IEE Wiring Regulations. It makes sense for the DIY electrician to follow these, too, since not only will the installation be safe but also it will satisfy any third party inspection.

It's impossible to summarise the Regulations in a few lines, but some of the most important points, so far as domestic work is concerned, are:

● ring circuits can serve a floor area of up to 100sq m (1076sq ft);

● radial circuits can serve a floor area of up to 50sq m (538sq ft) if wired in 4mm^2 cable AND protected by a 30A MCB or cartridge fuse, NOT a rewirable fuse; up to 20sq m (215sq ft) if wired in 2.5mm^2 cable and protected by any 20A fuse or MCB;

● you can connect as many spurs to a ring circuit as there are sockets or fused connection units on the ring itself;

● a spur from a ring circuit can supply only one accessory: a single or double socket, or a fused connection unit;

● in bathrooms, the only socket outlet allowed is a shaver supply unit containing a transformer. Wall heaters and towel rails should be connected to fused connection units but these must not be within reach of the bath or shower cubicle. Lampholders must be fitted with a protective skirt that prevents the metal parts being touched, unless the fitting itself is totally enclosed. Ordinary lampholders may be fitted if they are more than 2.5m (8ft 6in) from the bath or shower cubicle. Wall-mounted switches are allowed only if out of reach of bath or shower; otherwise use cord-operated switches;

● new sockets fitted to power outdoor appliances must have R.C.D. (Residual Current-Breaker Device) protection — either on the circuit itself, or at the fusebox. The R.C.D. is designed to detect any slight leakage of current in the circuit being protected, and it will cut off the power supply immediately to prevent accidental electric shock. You'll need expert advice on choosing the right type and model of R.C.D.

1

Never attempt any electrical work unless you know what you are doing, you understand how to do it and you are confident that you can carry out every stage of the job.

2

ALWAYS turn off the main isolating switch before beginning any electrical work. As an additional safeguard, hang a sign on the switch warning that the supply has been turned off so that no-one will turn it on again.

3

If working on one circuit only, remove the appropriate circuit fuse, or switch off the circuit MCB, before turning on the supply to the other circuits. Keep the fuse in your pocket until you've finished, so no-one can replace it in the fusebox without your knowledge.

4

Double-check all the connections, whether within accessories, plugs or appliances, to make sure that the cores go to the correct terminals, that terminal screws are tight and that no bare conductor is exposed.

5

Never touch any electrical appliance or fitting with wet hands, or use electrical equipment in wet conditions (in particular, out of doors). Never take a portable appliance into a bathroom on an extension lead.

6

Always unplug an appliance before attempting to inspect or repair it.

7

Don't use long trailing flexes or overload sockets with adaptors; fit extra sockets. If you have to extend a flex, use a proper flex extender; don't just twist the cores together and wrap them in insulating tape. If using an extension cable on a drum, always unwind it fully first or it may overheat; check the flex rating if the cable is supplying heaters.

8

Check plug connections and flex condition on all portable appliances at least once a year, remaking connections and replacing flex as necessary. Replace damaged plugs or wiring accessories immediately.

9

Never omit the earth connection. At accessories, take the earth core of the cable to the terminal on the mounting box or accessory as appropriate; on appliances with an earth terminal, use three-core flex and connect its earth core to the terminal.

10

Teach children about the dangers of electricity. The biggest danger areas are socket outlets (fit ones with shuttered sockets to stop them poking in metal objects) and trailing flexes (unplug unused appliances).

86 HOW OLD IS YOUR SYSTEM?

Before you can contemplate making any improvements or alterations to your home's electrical installation, you have got to find out exactly what sort of system exists already. This is particularly important if your house was wired up more than about 20 years ago, because older installations are more difficult to alter and there is also the risk that the system might already be in poor (and potentially dangerous) condition. This is because the materials used to insulate the cables deteriorate with age; once the insulation has failed, the whole system poses safety and fire risks.

Identifying cables
You can easily estimate the age of your system by looking for certain tell-tale signs. The most important, as already mentioned, is the cable itself. The earliest wiring systems used separate stranded copper wires; which were run round the house in surface-mounted steel conduit, lengths of which were screwed together and joined to cast-iron boxes containing light switches and, later, socket outlets for electrical appliances. Somewhat later, lead-sheathed cable containing two rubber-covered stranded copper wires was introduced, with the metal sheath providing earth continuity round the system. Steel boxes housed switches and socket outlets. Then, tough rubber-sheathed (TRS) cable, containing two insulated wires (called cores) and a bare earthing core, took over as the most common type, and plastic switches and sockets began to replace metal ones as plastic moulding techniques improved. Finally, PVC-sheathed cables, used on all modern wiring installations, came along in the late 1940s and early 1950s.

Since you are probably not the first person to want to extend your house installation, you may find there's a mixture of cable types in different parts of the house. The way to find out if this is the case is to turn off the power to the whole house at the main switch and to open up several light switches and socket outlets so that you can examine the cables running into them. Remember that conduit systems may have had new cables run inside them to replace the originals. It is also a good idea to check the condition of the cable insulation at the same time; if it is showing signs of deterioration, you should consider rewiring the whole system.

The second sign of your system's age will be found at the main fuseboard where the electricity supply enters the house — usually near the front door, but occasionally in a cupboard in a front room alcove. In an older installation, the cables from the electricity meter will pass to a main metal distribution box containing an on-off switch for the whole system and also several pairs of fuses in porcelain fuseholders. From this box, more cables feed similar but smaller sub-distribution boxes; two (or more) of these will supply the socket outlets in the main rooms, while at least one will feed the house lighting. A separate box, linked directly to the meter, may be fitted to supply the much heavier current needed for an electric cooker. You will notice that, throughout the system, a fuse is placed in both the live and neutral cables or 'poles' — so-called double-pole fusing.

Fuses and accessories
In a more modern installation, all these distribution boxes will have been replaced by a single box called a 'consumer unit'. This is a metal or plastic enclosure that contains the main system on-off switch and a number of single fuses. Each of these fuses protects one circuit, and is placed in the live pole only; all the neutral cores of the circuit cables are linked to the

unit's main neutral terminal, the earth cores to the main earth terminal.

The third (and least reliable) sign is the type of light switches and socket outlets fitted. The earliest switches you're likely to find will be round brass or brown Bakelite toggle types, probably mounted on small wooden blocks called 'pattresses'. Early socket outlets will probably be brown or cream plastic, again mounted on wooden blocks, and will have round holes. There were three sizes of socket outlet rated at 2, 5, and 15A; the smallest was for lamps and radios, the second for electrical appliances such as vacuum cleaners, and the biggest for heavy current-users such as electric fires.

Each type of socket was wired with cable of the appropriate size, a move intended to save running expensive heavy-duty cables to outlets feeding only light-duty equipment, and different-sized plugs were needed for each socket — they were not interchangeable. Since the 1950s, sockets rated at 13A with three rectangular holes have been used instead (although round-hole sockets are still available, and the smallest one is a useful way of providing power solely for table and standard lamps in a modern installation). There is only one size, designed to take the familiar flat-pin plug with its own internal fuse (round-pin plugs were not fused). If you have this type of socket, don't automatically assume that your whole system is modern; the old sockets may have been replaced by new ones, but the cables connected to them may still be original.

When inspecting an old wiring system, look out for tell-tale signs that indicate the need for a re-wire. These include double-pole fusing (above), switches on wooden pattresses and old roses and socket outlets (below).

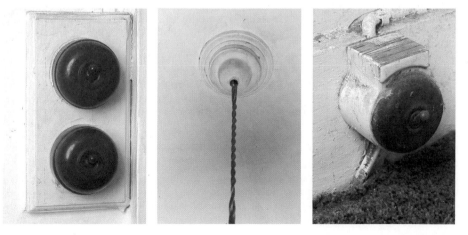

88 MODERN ELECTRICAL CIRCUITS

The basic electrical circuit, as we have already seen, consists of two wires. The current flows along one to wherever it is needed, and back along the other to its source. In house wiring circuits, the basic principle is the same, with electricity passing along the 'live' core of the cable and back down the 'neutral' core; the third core in modern cable is used to provide earthing continuity throughout the system.

Each circuit starts at the consumer unit or distribution box, where the live core of the cable is connected to the live terminal of one of the fuseways, and terminates at the neutral terminal. Most circuits are wired as 'branch' lines, with the cable feeding one or more outlets along the branch; whether this outlet is a light fitting, a socket outlet or a single major appliance, the live core loops in and out of one terminal of the outlet while the neutral core loops in and out of the neutral terminal, until the last branch outlet.

Ring circuits

The one exception to this is the 'ring' circuit, used on modern installations to provide power to socket outlets. This is a 'loop' line rather than a branch line, with a continuous cable running out from the consumer unit and returning to it. The two ends of the live core are both connected to the live terminal of the fuseway protecting the circuit; this means that electricity can flow to a socket outlet on the ring along two routes instead of one, and in practice allows the circuit to provide power to more sockets than a single branch line could. In effect, one modern ring circuit takes the place of a number of branch (or 'radial') circuits, with obvious savings on the cost of cable. However, radial power circuits are still used to take power to single major appliances such as cookers (page 132), instantaneous showers (page 134) and

immersion heaters (page 136), and also to outbuildings (page 138). Another use is to feed socket outlets in remote parts of the house where running a ring would mean a waste of cable.

Lighting circuits

Most houses have at least two lighting circuits, one for upstairs and one for downstairs. These are wired as radial circuits. What complicates them is the need to provide switching for each light at a convenient point in each room, and there are two ways of doing this so that the switch can 'break' the live core of the circuit cable and, in doing so, turn off the light.

One way is to fit a four-terminal 'junction box' (or joint box, as it is sometimes called) at an appropriate point on the circuit cable; this allows the supply to continue on to the next lighting point while providing connections for one cable to run down to the switch position and another to run to the light controlled by that switch. The light cable is then connected to the terminals of a 'ceiling rose', and the lampholder is connected to the rose by a piece of flexible cord (flex — see page 94). This is called the junction-box system; as you can see from the diagram, it could use up a lot of cable in certain situations.

The second and more recent way of wiring up lighting circuits uses ceiling roses containing extra terminals. The circuit cable simply runs from rose to rose instead of from junction box to junction box, and terminates at the furthest rose on the circuit. Only one

Right: Lighting circuits are wired up as branch lines or radial circuits, with a cable running from a 5A fuseway in the consumer unit to a number of connection points or outlets along the circuit. These may be junction boxes (A), from each of which run separate cables to a light fitting and to its associated switch, or loop-in ceiling roses (B) which act as junction boxes as well.

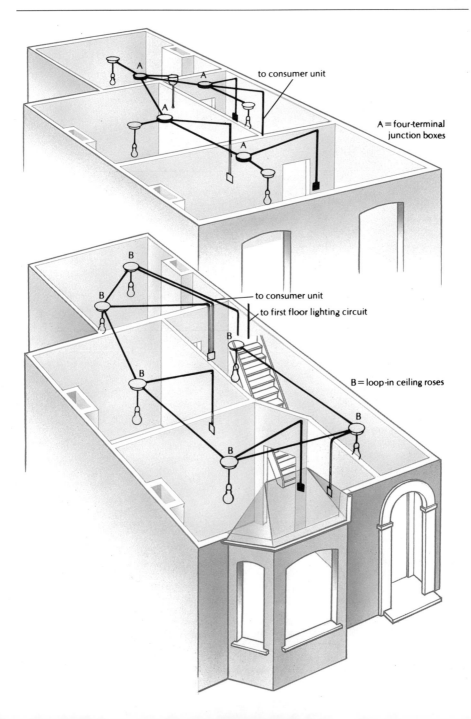

to consumer unit

A = four-terminal junction boxes

to consumer unit

to first floor lighting circuit

B = loop-in ceiling roses

90 MODERN ELECTRICAL CIRCUITS

extra cable is needed, to link the rose with the switch controlling it. This is the loop-in system, so-called because the cable loops in to one rose and out to the next.

Many houses are wired up with a mixture of both loop-in and junction box wiring, because maximum economy of cable can be achieved in this way. It all depends on the positions of the light and switch in each room as to which system is the best to choose.

In a modern installation, each lighting circuit is protected by a 5A fuse or more usually a Mini Circuit Breaker (MCB) in the consumer unit, and is wired up in 1 or 1.5mm^2 cable — see page 94. Therefore, each circuit can supply up to 1,200 watts — say, twelve 100W light bulbs. In practice, because you may want to fit some bulbs of higher wattage, each circuit is restricted to eight lighting points, so in a large house several lighting circuits may be needed.

Power circuits
As explained previously, modern power circuits to socket outlets are almost always wired up as ring circuits. The cable loops in and out of the back of each socket in turn, eventually returning to the consumer unit. One ring circuit can have as many socket outlets on it as you like; since it can carry current in two directions, and you are unlikely to want to use all your appliances at once, it's unlikely to be overloaded. However, kitchen outlets might warrant a separate circuit. The only restriction placed on the installation is that one ring circuit must not serve a floor area greater than 100sq m (1076sq ft). What's more, you are allowed to increase the number of socket outlets served by adding branch lines or spurs, each being a single cable connected to the ring at an existing ring socket outlet (or at a junction box cut into the ring cable) and taking power to

one single socket, one double socket or one fused connection unit. You are allowed as many spurs as there are sockets or connection units on the original ring. Before 1983, *two* singles or one double socket were permitted on each spur, but subsequent regulations have outlawed the second single socket.

Each ring circuit is protected by a 30A fuse or MCB, and is wired in 2.5mm^2 cable. Therefore, each can supply up to 7,200 watts. In addition to the protection provided by the circuit fuse, each plug or connection unit used to link appliances to the circuit contains a fuse which will 'blow' in the event of a fault on the appliance.

As mentioned earlier, you can also supply socket outlets via radial circuits in situations where a ring circuit would be uneconomical in use of cable. Again, there are no restrictions on the number of socket outlets on each circuit but there are restrictions on the floor area served. For a floor area not exceeding 20sq m (215sq ft), the circuit must be run in 2.5mm^2 cable and be protected by a 20A circuit fuse. For a floor area of up to 50sq m (538sq ft), a 30A MCB or cartridge fuse and 4mm^2 cable must be used.

Other power circuits to fixed appliances are quite straightforward — suitably-sized cable running from a fuseway in the consumer unit (where a fuse or MCB of the appropriate rating is fitted) to the appliance concerned. See pages 132 to 141 for more details.

Right: In modern installations, power circuits are wired up as a ring, starting and ending at a 30A fuseway in the consumer unit and looping into and out of socket outlets on the ring circuit. Branch lines or spurs can be connected to the ring circuit either at a ring circuit socket (A) or at a 30A junction box (B) — see text. Some power circuits — for example, to higher-rated appliances such as cookers, showers and immersion heaters — are wired up as radial circuits.

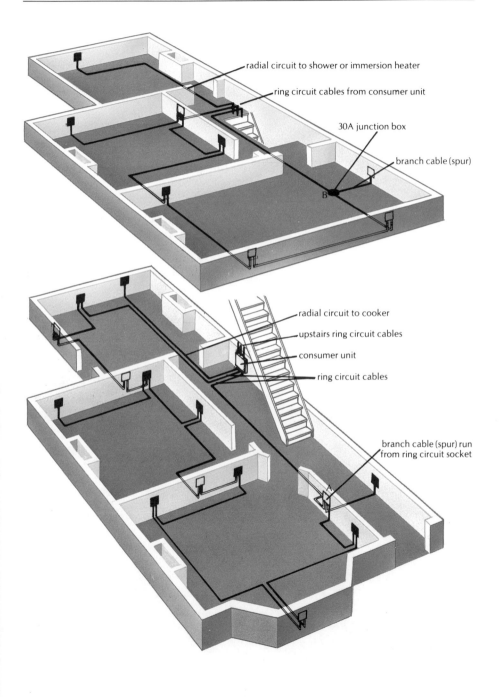

radial circuit to shower or immersion heater

ring circuit cables from consumer unit

30A junction box

branch cable (spur)

radial circuit to cooker

upstairs ring circuit cables

consumer unit

ring circuit cables

branch cable (spur) run
from ring circuit socket

92 **LIGHT AND POWER FITTINGS**

On lighting circuits, most lights take the form of pendant lampholders linked by flex to surface-mounted ceiling roses. In certain situations, the light bulb is fitted into a batten lampholder that is fixed directly to the ceiling or wall. Switches for turning these lights on and off come in a variety of types and sizes. The commonest type may have one, two, three, four or even six switches on a single faceplate. Each switch or 'gang' may have two or three terminals on the back; the former type is used for one-way switching, the latter for two-way switching (see pages 112 and 113). Slimmer versions of these

fittings, called architrave switches, are intended for fitting on door frames.

Specialist switches include dimmers (which vary the light level from fully on down to about 10 per cent) and time-delay switches (which turn a light off automatically at a preset time after it has been switched on). There are also cord-operated ceiling switches and weatherproof switches for use outside (see pages 138 to 141).

On power circuits, the most widely used accessory is the socket outlet, in single (one-gang), double (two-gang) and occasionally triple (three-gang) versions. The outlet may be switched

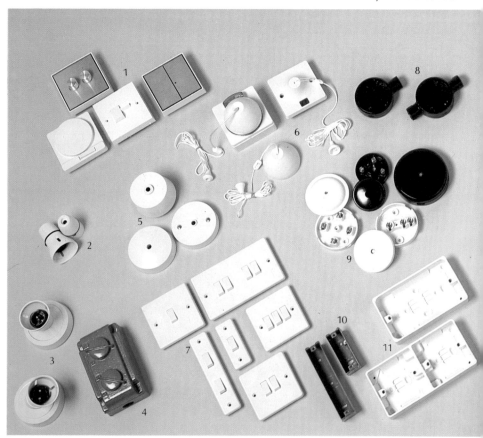

or unswitched, and may include a neon light to indicate when the socket is on. Most modern installations are fitted exclusively with sockets to take flat-pin plugs, but sockets for round-pin plugs are still available, and the smallest (2A) version can be useful on a fused spur circuit feeding table or standard lamps only. Fused connection units are used to connect up non-portable appliances such as freezers, electric towel rails and waste disposal units that are not unplugged regularly (and, indeed, should not be unplugged accidentally). Double-pole switches are used to isolate fixed appliances such as cookers, immersion heaters and instantaneous showers (an ordinary switch is single-pole, interrupting only the live pole). There are also special connection units for cookers, shavers, clocks and television aerials.

1: dimmers; 2: lampholders; 3: batten lampholders; 4: outdoor switch; 5: roses; 6: ceiling switches; 7: plateswitches; 8: BESA boxes; 9: junction boxes; 10: flush boxes for architrave switches; 11: surface-mounting boxes; 12: TV and phone outlets; 13: plug-in timer; 14: connection units; 15: cooker units; 16: blanking plate; 17: cable extender; 18: shaver adaptor and 3-pin plugs; 19; socket outlets; 20: shaver supply unit; 21: flush boxes.

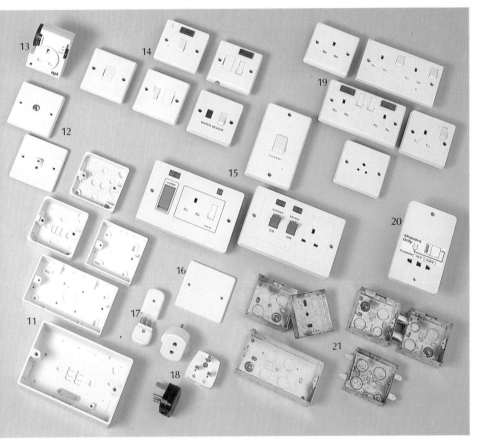

94 CABLE, FLEX AND LAMPS

It is important not to confuse cable and flex. Cable is used for all the fixed wiring on every circuit, running between the consumer unit and the various accessories fitted round the circuits. Flex is used to link appliances of all types to the fixed wiring — via plugs at socket outlets, between ceiling roses and lampholders at lighting points.

Cable for house wiring usually contains three cores. Two are insulated in colour-coded PVC — red for the live core, black for the neutral; the third core is a bare copper wire used to form the earth continuity conductor round the circuit. All the cores are covered with a thick PVC outer sheath; such cable is properly referred to as 'two-core and earth PVC-sheathed and insulated cable', and is usually grey or white. There is also special three-core and earth cable, used in two-way switching installations. Common cable sizes, measured by the cross-sectional area of the copper conductors, are 1, 1.5, 2.5, 4 and 6mm^2.

Flex usually contains three cores as well, all with colour-coded insulation — brown for live, blue for neutral and green-and-yellow for earth. You may find these cores coded red, black and green respectively in old flex. The outer sheathing of flex is normally white or coloured PVC, although a braided cover may be added. Two-core flex has no earth core, being used for lights and pendants with no metallic parts and double-insulated appliances such as power drills, garden tools, hair dryers, and food mixers. Special heat-resisting flex is used in powerful light fittings and to connect equipment such as immersion heaters.

Colour blindness may hinder the identification of the appropriate cable and flex cores when making connections. If you have difficulty in distinguishing colours, match the appearance of the wires with those shown in the wiring diagrams in this book.

Light bulbs and fluorescent tubes

Most light fittings take ordinary tungsten-filament light bulbs — properly called GLS (General Lighting Service) lamps. These have a two-pin 'bayonet'

From left: five sizes of two-core and earth PVC-sheathed and insulated cable (6, 4, 2.5, 1.5 and 1mm^2); three-core and earth cable; circular three-core flex; braided three-core flex; circular two-core flex; flat two-core flex; parallel twin flex. Note the uninsulated cable earth cores.

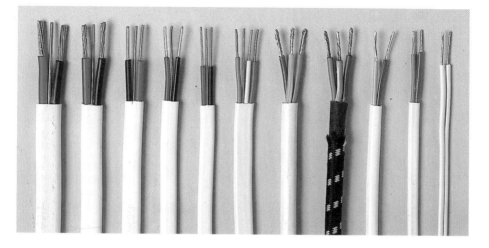

CABLE, FLEX AND LAMPS 95

cap, may be of clear or obscure (pearl) glass — this can also be coloured — and come in two common shapes; round and mushroom. There are also small candle, ball, pygmy and strip lamps for use in wall lights and other decorative fittings. For spot and flood lights, there are special internally-silvered (IS), crown-silvered (CS) and parabolic aluminised reflector (PAR) lamps, of plain and coloured glass. Many of these small and specialised lamps have a threaded Edison Screw (ES) cap instead of the more familiar bayonet fitting, and need special screwed fittings to hold them. A wide range of wattages is available.

Fluorescent tubes are usually 25 or 38mm (1 or 1½in) in diameter, and up to 2.4m (8ft) long, although narrower and shorter 'miniature' tubes are also available. You can even get circular fittings. Wattage depends on tube length — roughly 10 watts per 300mm (12in). The light emitted is described in terms such as 'daylight', 'white' or 'warm white'; coloured tubes are made as well. Most tubes have a bi-pin cap at each end, and are usually mounted in fittings that incorporate a starter (to initiate the discharge through the gas in the tube) and other components to control the discharge once the tube is lit. There may be a diffuser over the tube, or reflectors along both sides.

1: decor round lamps; 2: candle lamps; 3: pearl lamps with bayonet fittings; 4: internally-silvered (IS) lamps; 5: crown-silvered (CS) lamps; 6: double-cap filament and fluorescent miniature tubes; 7: fluorescent tubes; 8: circular fluorescent tubes; 9: coloured lamps; 10: PAR lamps; 11: SL lamp.

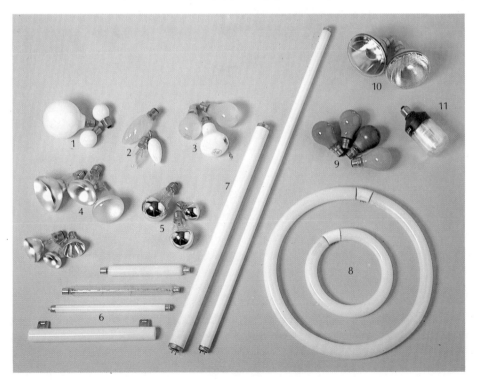

96 TOOLS FOR ELECTRICAL WORK

Even if you never intend to carry out any electrical installation work in your home, you should still have a small tool kit to enable you to cope with electrical emergencies and occasional jobs such as rewiring a plug or fitting a new length of flex to a light or other appliance.

This tool kit should be kept together in a box or bag, ideally next to your consumer unit so you can find it when you need it. You should include: a torch; fuse wire or cartridge circuit fuses to match the ratings of your light and power circuits; 3A and 13A fuses for flat-pin plugs; a roll of PVC insulating tape; a small electrical screwdriver with a sheathed blade; a sharp trim-ming knife; and a pair of wire strippers.

If you are likely to carry out some of your own wiring, you'll need: a pair of pliers (they will cut cable, too, if you pick a pair with cutting jaws; otherwise, add a pair of side cutters as well. Both should have insulated handles); a mains tester for checking that your connections are correct; brick bolster and cold chisel, plus a club hammer, for chopping out cable runs and recesses for flush-mounted accessories; power drill (with extension cable; the power may be off in the area where you are working) or brace and bits, for drilling through joists, and hand drill for drilling fixing holes in walls; a floorboard saw or circular saw for

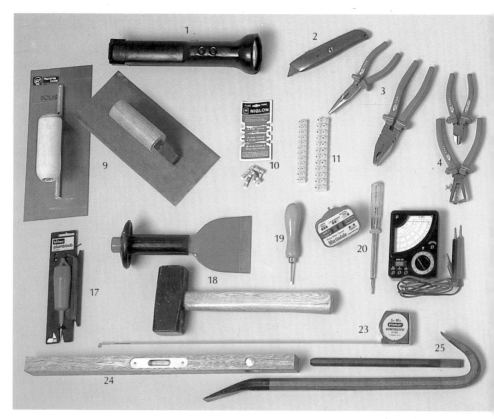

TOOLS FOR ELECTRICAL WORK 97

cutting through floorboards. In addition, you will need a number of everyday tools — for example, screwdrivers, chisels, hammers and saws, all of which you probably own already.

You will also need some cable clips (to hold cable in channels, or chases, cut in walls before you plaster over them, and to support cable runs along the sides of joists), and some green/yellow PVC sleeving (whenever you expose the cable's bare earth core at an accessory, you must cover the bare conductor with this sleeving). Some metal or plastic channelling to protect cables buried in plaster will be found useful, but it is not an essential part of the kit.

1: torch; 2: trimming knife; 3: two sizes of pliers with insulated handles; 4: side-cutters and wire strippers; 5: screwdrivers; 6: wood chisels; 7: assorted twist drills, flat bits and masonry drills; 8: electric drill; 9: plastering floats; 10: fuse wire and plug cartridge fuses; 11: strips of terminal connectors; 12: wood screws; 13: wall plugs; 14: green and yellow striped earth sleeving and red PVC insulating tape (needed for 'flagging' switch returns); 15: mini hacksaw; 16: tenon saw; 17: plumb bob and line; 18: brick bolster (with hand guard) and club hammer; 19: bradawl; 20: ring circuit tester, neon screwdriver and test meter; 21: claw hammer; 22: padsaw; 23: retractable steel tape measure; 24: spirit level; 25: cold chisel and crow-bar; 26: cable clips; 27: PVC grommets (for use with flush mounting sockets to prevent cables chafing where they enter the box); 28: extension cable on drum; 29: floorboard saw.

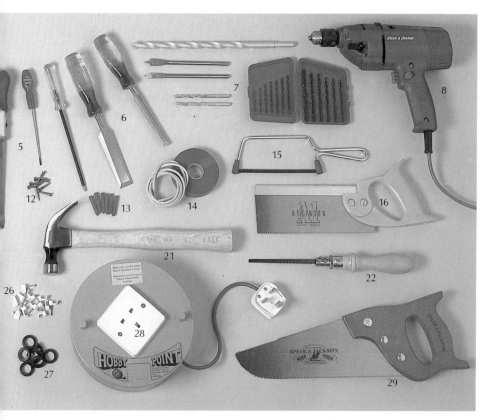

Before you begin to tackle any electrical work, it pays to stop and think about two points — design and ergonomics.

To most people, even a modern wiring accessory is just an uninspiring blob of white plastic that is functional rather than decorative. However, there are ranges of more attractive fittings around in coloured plastic, brushed aluminium, ornate brass and so on, all worth considering if you are prepared to pay more for your accessories. Lightswitches are particularly noticeable because they are less likely to be concealed, and money spent on updating these will certainly be well spent. You can cheer up portable appliances, too, by fitting them with coloured curly flex and matching coloured plugs.

Perhaps more important than the looks of your accessories is the question of ergonomics — making the system work in harmony with you. You must first decide what demands you're likely to place on your system, which appliances need a socket or other outlet full time and which ones can 'borrow' a socket when they're needed. You should also think about positioning light switches, pendant and wall lights and socket outlets for maximum convenience.

First, light switches. These are usually fitted beside the main door to each room, about 1.4m (4ft 6in) above the floor. Fine; but would it be worth having a second switch elsewhere, such as by the patio doors leading to the garden, or by the back door in the kitchen? What about wall lights; should they be switched by the door, by the light or at both points? What about two-way switching for the landing, stairs and hall, for the bedside lights, or even for the immersion heater (a remote switch in the kitchen could save unnecessary trips upstairs)?

Light positions need careful thought, too (although lighting design is a highly specialised field beyond the scope of this book). The central pendant fitted in most rooms is only any good for general lighting; it's hopeless for reading or sewing, or for illuminating dark corners. Would another position be more useful? Would a dimmer control help? What about a rise-and-fall fitting over a dining table?

So far as socket outlets are concerned, you can never (within reason) have too many, and it costs little to add more, either to an existing system or as part of a rewiring job. Remember that there are no restrictions on the number of sockets you can have on a ring circuit. As a guideline to numbers, ignore the Parker-Morris standards still followed by so many architects and specifiers; they were drafted 30 years ago and are pathetically out of date. Instead, aim to match the recommendations of the EIILC (Electrical Installation Industry Liaison Committee), which suggests the following numbers of *double* switched socket outlets:

Room	No. of socket outlets
Living room	6
Dining room	3
Kitchen	4
Hall	1
Landing/stairs	1
Double bedroom	4
Single bedroom	3
Bedsitting room	4
Garage	2

Remember, too, that they don't all have to be set at skirting board level. Some may be more useful at about 750mm (2ft 6in) above the floor — for appliances in alcoves or near fitted units in living rooms, and for freestanding appliances in kitchens — and sockets at this height are far more accessible. In kitchens, some sockets should be above worktop level.

DESIGN AND PLANNING 99

Supplying power to domestic appliances

Appliance	Needs	See pages
Kitchen		
Washing machine	Connection to ring main or spur; ideally, switched fused connection unit (13A fuse)	100, 106, 124, 126
Instantaneous water heater, chest freezer, dishwasher, waste disposal unit	Switched fused connection unit (13A fuse) on ring main or spur ·	100, 104, 106, 124, 126
Extractor fan	Switched fused connection unit (3A fuse) on ring main or spur; clock connector to link appliance flex to cable	100, 104, 106, 124, 126
Cooker	Separate 30A radial circuit from consumer unit to cooker control unit; cooker connection unit to link appliance trailing cable to supply cable	100, 104, 128, 132
Refrigerator, kettle, toaster, food mixer and other portable appliances	13A switched socket outlet	100, 104, 106, 122, 124
Bathroom		
Instantaneous shower	Separate 30A radial circuit from consumer unit; 30A double-pole pull-cord switch for appliance control (up to 7kW)	102, 104, 128, 134
Extractor fan	As kitchen above	
Immersion heater	Separate 15A or 20A radial circuit from consumer unit; control by 20A double-pole switch with flex outlet and neon indicator	100, 104, 106, 124, 126, 128, 136
Heated towel rail	Switched fused connection unit (13A fuse) on ring main or spur; flex outlet to link appliance to cable in small bathrooms	100, 104, 106, 124, 126
Wall heater	Switched fused connection unit on spur from 30A three-terminal junction box or socket outlet on ring main (also flex outlet in small bathrooms)	100, 104, 106, 124, 126
Living/dining rooms		
Wall lights	Junction box on lighting circuit or switched fused connection unit (5A fuse) on ring main or spur	104, 108, 116
Standard/table lamps	Socket outlets on ring main or spur; 2A round-pin versions suitable (spur must be fused)	100, 104, 106, 122, 124
TV aerial	Aerial socket sited near TV; coaxial cable link from socket to roof-mounted aerial	100, 104, 143,
TV, stereo and other portable appliances	13A switched socket outlets	100, 104, 106, 122, 124
Miscellaneous		
Loft light	Spur from four-terminal junction box on lighting circuit; one-gang, one-way switch on landing	102, 104, 108, 110
Central heating controls	Socket outlet or switched fused connection unit (5A fuse) on ring main or spur; ideally, separate 5A radial circuit from consumer unit	100, 104, 106, 124, 126, 128
Door bells	Via transformer fed by separate 5A radial circuit from consumer unit or spur from lighting circuit	104, 108, 128, 142
Outside lights	Spur from four-terminal junction box on lighting circuit	104, 108, 110
Garage	Separate radial circuit from consumer unit; separate switchfuse unit to control power and lighting circuits in outbuilding	100, 102, 104, 110, 124, 126, 128, 138, 140,
Garden	For temporary use: extension flex plugged into R.C.D.-protected socket outlet. For permanent use: separate radial circuit from consumer unit or switch fuse unit, or low-voltage supply via plug-in transformer for pond pumps etc	106,126,128, 140

100 FIXING WALL-MOUNTED ACCESSORIES

You can either mount your switches, socket outlets and other accessories on the wall surface, or recess them into the wall. The former is quicker and easier, but the latter looks much neater and is worth the extra effort (except, for example, in outbuildings where appearances matter less).

Boxes for surface-mounting are usually plastic or metal (to match heavy-duty 'metalclad' accessories) and are simply screwed to the wall where needed (below), using screws driven into wallplugs (solid walls) or cavity fixings (partition walls; alternatively, the box can be screwed to a vertical timber stud or horizontal noggin, if one is conveniently placed). Boxes for flush-mounting are of galvanised steel, and are screwed to the back of the recess in which they fit, as shown opposite. Any gaps between box and masonry are then made good with plaster or filler.

Most light switches are designed to fit a box only 16mm (⅝in) deep. The flush-mounted type is called a plaster-depth box, because in most houses only the plaster has to be cut out to fit them — far simpler than tackling solid brickwork.

Socket outlets, whether surface- or flush-mounted, usually need boxes 35mm (1⅜in) deep, but shallower boxes only 25mm (1in) deep coupled with accessories with thicker-than-usual faceplates are used in single-brick and cavity walls where chopping a deeper recess could result in a hole right through the wall. Certain special accessories such as cooker control units and shaver units need deeper mounting boxes — often 45mm (1¾in) in depth.

Boxes of both types have 'knockouts'; weak areas that are literally knocked out as necessary to allow cables to enter the box from any direction. With flush-mounted boxes, the cables usually enter through the

1 After feeding in the supply cable, remove one of the knockouts from the base of the mounting box. Then hold the box in place and mark the screw positions on the wall.
2 Drill and plug the wall, and then screw the box in place with two woodscrews. Check that it is level.
3 Sleeve the bare earth core with green/yellow PVC sleeving and then connect the live, neutral and earth cores to the terminals on the back of the accessory's faceplate. Make sure the insulation reaches right up to the terminals, and tighten the terminal screws fully.
4 If possible, push excess cable back into the wall or floor cavity, or fold it carefully into the mounting box. Push the faceplate into position and attach it to the box with the fixing screws provided.

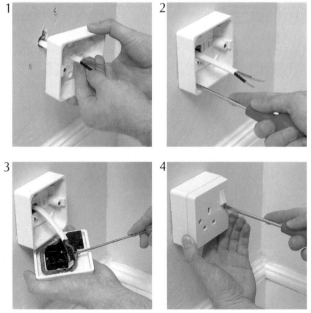

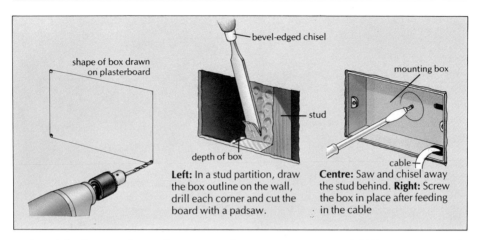

bevel-edged chisel

shape of box drawn on plasterboard

stud

depth of box

mounting box

cable

Left: In a stud partition, draw the box outline on the wall, drill each corner and cut the board with a padsaw.

Centre: Saw and chisel away the stud behind. **Right:** Screw the box in place after feeding in the cable

sides of the box (and must be protected from chafing on the metal edges by a rubber grommet fitted when the knock-out is removed).

With the surface-mounted boxes, the cable will enter through the back of the box if it is run below the wall surface, through its sides otherwise — see pages 104 and 105.

You need a one-gang (square) mounting box for single socket outlets, connection units, 20A switches, and one- two- or three-gang plateswitches; a two-gang (rectangular) box for double sockets and for four- or six-gang plateswitches.

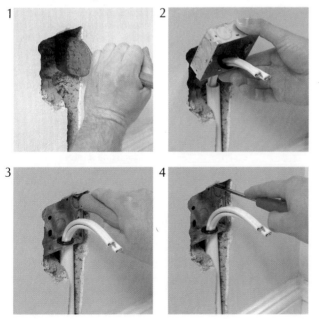

1

2

3

4

1 With a masonry wall, use a club hammer and brick bolster to cut out a neat chase for the cable, and to chop out a recess to match the size of the flush box being used. Drilling round the perimeter of the hole first with a masonry drill may ease the job on hard brickwork.
2 Lay in the cables, ideally in PVC conduit. Then remove a knockout from the side of the box, insert a grommet to stop the box chafing the cable and feed in the cable.
3 Check that the box fits snugly and squarely within the recess. Chop out more masonry if it's too shallow, fill with a dab of plaster if it's too deep. Then mark the wall for the mounting screws.
4 Remove the box, drill and plug the holes, replace the box and screw it firmly to the wall. Finally, make good the wall.

102 FIXING CEILING-MOUNTED ACCESSORIES

Fixing accessories to ceilings poses slightly different problems to mounting fittings to walls. For a start, such accessories are usually surface-mounted. Most ceilings are 'hollow' — like partition walls, with lath-and-plaster or plasterboard forming the ceiling surface — but the types of fixings used there can't be relied upon to support the weight of heavy light fittings. So any ceiling rose or fitting must be screwed to a proper support. This can be either a joist, or else a batten fixed between two joists. In the former case, the joist might not coincide with your required location. In the latter case, you will have to lift floorboards in the room above (or go up into the loft) so you can fix the batten.

Light fittings, other than simple pendants, have open-back ceiling plates, and the flex from the light is usually linked to the circuit cable via a multiway cable connector, which can cope with loop-in wiring. This connector has

to be housed within a non-combustible enclosure, consisting of a circular metal or plastic box (called a BESA box, or terminal conduit box) and the fitting's own ceiling plate, which is screwed to the ceiling or to the lugs of the BESA box itself (with M4 metric machine screws).

This BESA box is fitted flush with the ceiling surface, and is usually screwed to the underside of a batten fixed between the joists; in some cases, it may be possible to cut away the underside of the joist slightly and screw the box directly to it, but this is not recommended unless the joist is generously thick. In general, the side-entry type of BESA box is the most useful type to use.

Batten lampholders are either fitted on a backplate (called a pattress) which allows space for the connections, or else over a BESA box, as above. Modern loop-in batten lampholders have an enclosed backplate, so a BESA box is not needed.

1

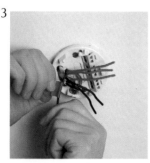

2

3

4

1 Draw the cable (or cables) down through a hole in the ceiling where the rose is to be fitted. Here, the rose will be wired as an intermediate rose on a loop-in system, so there are two circuit cables and one switch cable, identified with red PVC tape.
2 Remove a knockout from the base of the rose, feed the cables through and mark the positions of the fixing screws.
3 Wrap some red PVC tape round the switch cable neutral to show that it is live when connected up.
4 Connect the three live cores to the centre group of terminals, the sleeved earth cores to the earth terminal and the two neutral cores from the circuit cables to the neutral terminal bank. Link the switch cable neutral to the live load terminal at the end of the bank.

FIXING CEILING-MOUNTED ACCESSORIES 103

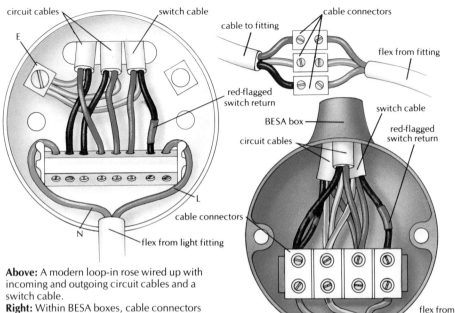

circuit cables

switch cable

cable connectors

cable to fitting

flex from fitting

E

red-flagged
switch return

switch cable

BESA box

red-flagged
switch return

circuit cables

L

cable connectors

N

flex from light fitting

cable connectors

flex from
fitting

Above: A modern loop-in rose wired up with incoming and outgoing circuit cables and a switch cable.

Right: Within BESA boxes, cable connectors link circuit cable cores to the fitting flex – on the loop-in system (bottom) or junction-box system (top).

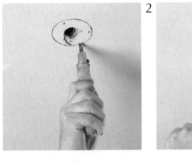

1

2

3

4

1 Mark the outline of the BESA box and use a padsaw to cut away the ceiling carefully.
2 If the box is to be screwed to the underside of a joist, use a large-diameter drill to remove just enough wood from the joist for the box to fit with its lower edge flush with the ceiling.
3 Offer up the box, checking that it fits reasonably accurately, and screw it in position.
4 Feed in the cables through the mouth of the box and use a terminal connector to link the cores as shown here and above. Note that the switch cable neutral is again flagged with red tape, and that a separate earth core links the earths in the connector with the BESA box earth terminal – necessary to provide earthing continuity with metal light fittings.

104 RUNNING CABLES

Modern electrical cable is a versatile material; you can run it almost anywhere round the house — under floors, in ceiling voids, buried in the plaster, fixed to the surface of walls and ceilings, or concealed in surface-mounted 'mini-trunking'.

Where cable is simply being fixed to wall or ceiling surfaces, it is usual to choose white-sheathed cable (and white cable clips) so that the installation looks less conspicuous against white walls or woodwork. The cable must be clipped at 250mm (10in) intervals on horizontal runs; 450mm (18in) intervals on vertical ones.

Mini-trunking makes for a neater installation when wiring is being run on the surface, and also protects the cables from accidental damage. It is often used with surface-mounted accessories, to which it is connected securely and neatly with special collars and adaptors. The trunking base is screwed, pinned or glued in position, the cable is laid in place and the cover strips are snapped on. Several sizes of trunking are available; alternatively, special skirting and architrave mouldings can be fixed in place of the existing timber ones, and used to conceal a number of cables.

Where cable is run in floor or ceiling voids, it can rest on underfloor screeds or ceiling surfaces without the need for any support. However, it should not be

1 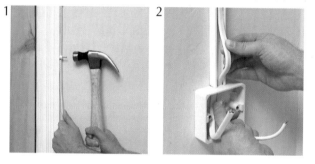 2

1 You can surface-mount cable on architraves and skirting boards using cable clips which have integral nails. Use white-sheathed cable to blend in with the clips and paint work.
2 Alternatively, run the cables in shallow surface-mounted PVC conduit. A snap-on cover hides the cables but allows ready access.

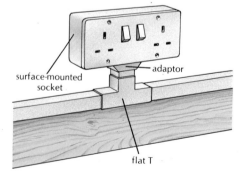

Mini-trunking is run along skirtings and beside architraves. Tees and adaptors link it to switches and socket outlets.

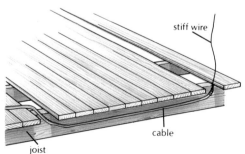

Running cables under floors is easy if you use stiff wire to draw the cable through the space underneath the floorboards.

left hanging in loops. Where the cable crosses a joist it should be threaded through a hole drilled at least 50mm (2in) below the top of the joist — *not* laid in notches cut in their tops, where floorboard nails could inadvertently damage it. In lofts, cables can cross joists, but should be routed away from loft hatches and walkways. Where polystyrene loft insulation has been laid, protect the cables with conduit or channelling; the insulation may attack and soften the cable sheathing.

Cable can be dropped down through the cavities of hollow partition walls (it's not considered good practice to run it inside exterior cavity walls, though). In stud walls (where a timber framework of vertical studs and horizontal noggins is screwed to the ceiling and floor and panelled with plasterboard), you may have to drill through the head and sole plates from the room above or below, and where there are noggins you will have to cut away a patch of plasterboard and noggin to feed the cable through. On solid walls, simply chop out a channel or chase 15 to 25mm (⅝ to 1in) deep, pin the cable in place (with conduit or channelling over it for additional protection) and plaster over it. Always run cables vertically or horizontally to and from electrical accessories, never diagonally. Then everyone knows where to expect cable if fixing things to their walls!

1 On solid walls, chop out a chase up to 25mm (1in) deep with a brick bolster and club hammer.

2 Measure the cable drop, cut a length of PVC conduit to match and feed the cable carefully down through it.

3 Feed the cable into the box via a grommet to protect it. The conduit should reach right to the edge of the box.

4 You can use small masonry pins to secure the conduit in place temporarily. Then fill the chase with plaster.

5 Where the cables have to pass across the line of floor joists, drill holes through the centres of the joists.

6 Feed the cable through the holes, leaving a little slack between joists. Never run cable in notches cut in the joists' tops.

106 **EXTENDING POWER CIRCUITS**

Don't be tempted to extend *any* of your power circuits if you have old rubber-sheathed cable, or you could dangerously overload an already suspect system. However, it's a comparatively easy matter to add a new socket outlet to a system with modern ring circuits. In principle, you simply add a spur (see pages 88 and 89) to one of the existing ring circuits, and you can install one spur for every socket on the original ring circuit.

You can do this in one of two ways. You can connect a branch cable into the back of an existing socket on the ring, or else cut the ring cable, insert a 30A three-terminal junction box and connect the branch cable to that. You can then run the branch cable to wherever you need the extra outlet,

and fit a single socket, a double socket or a fused connection unit. Under new wiring regulations you may have only one outlet on each spur (formerly two singles or one double).

The problem with all this is determining which cables form the ring circuit, since you aren't allowed to extend from a socket that is already on a spur, or fit a junction box on a spur cable. So far as sockets are concerned, you can eliminate two of three possibilities by unscrewing the faceplate of the socket where you want to add your spur. If you find only one cable, the socket is at the end of a spur, while if you find three cables, the socket is a ring socket with a spur already attached to it. You cannot connect a spur to either of these two sockets. If the socket

1 At a ring circuit socket (see text), connect in the new branch cable after sheathing the earth.

2 At the new socket position, fix a mounting box and draw in the new cable; note the grommet.

3 Prepare the cores and link them to the appropriate terminals. Then screw the socket faceplate into position.

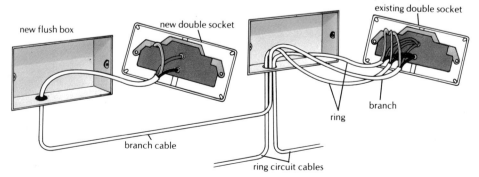

new flush box

new double socket

existing double socket

branch

ring

branch cable

ring circuit cables

EXTENDING POWER CIRCUITS 107

has two cables it could be a ring socket, the intermediate socket on an old two-outlet spur, or an intermediate socket on an old radial circuit (there used to be restrictions on how many sockets a radial circuit could supply, but these have now been superseded — see pages 90 and 91.

Unless you are prepared to trace cables all over the house, the only way you can check whether the socket is on a ring or not is with the simple continuity tester shown below. Turn off the current at the mains. At the socket in question, disconnect the two live (red) cores from their terminals. Touch one tester lead to one core, the second to the other; if the socket is on a ring, the bulb will light, but it will stay out if the socket is on a spur or a radial circuit.

You can use the same test to find out if a cable you want to cut into is a ring or spur cable, by turning off at the mains, cutting the cable and linking the red cores as before.

If your socket is a ring socket, you can add a spur to it. That leaves the spur/radial dilemma. If you can trace the cables leaving the socket in question *back* directly to a ring socket and *on* to a socket with only one cable feeding it, then you have a spur and you must not extend from the intermediate socket. If the cables can be traced back to the consumer unit and loop on to more than one socket it's a radial circuit and you *can* extend it, provided the radial circuit serves an area of less than 20sq m (215sq ft) and is wired in 2.5mm² cable.

1 Cut the circuit cable and screw a three-terminal junction box to a batten between the joists.

2 Link the cable cores to the box terminals as shown. Note the earth sleeving.

3 Run in the branch cable and link its cores to the appropriate terminals as shown below.

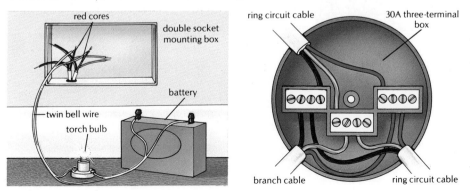

108 EXTENDING LIGHTING CIRCUITS

The concept of extending a lighting circuit is similar in principle to that of extending a power circuit. However, a similar caution must be given. Firstly, don't extend a circuit wired in rubber-sheathed cable. Secondly, don't overload existing circuits; you can have up to twelve 100W lighting points on each circuit, but in practice eight is a safe maximum, to allow for the use of more powerful lamps.

Start by removing the fuse (or switching off the MCB) on the circuit you want to extend and count up how many lights don't work (and how many

watts they consume). If it's less than eight lights or the total wattage is less than, say, 1,000W, then you can safely extend the circuit.

Assuming you've given the system the all-clear, you can extend it in one of two ways. Whatever system your house is wired with, you can cut the existing cable and install a four-terminal junction box, running new cables from it to the new light and switch. If you have loop-in roses with three terminal banks, you can add a spur from an existing rose without the need to use a junction box. The spur cable

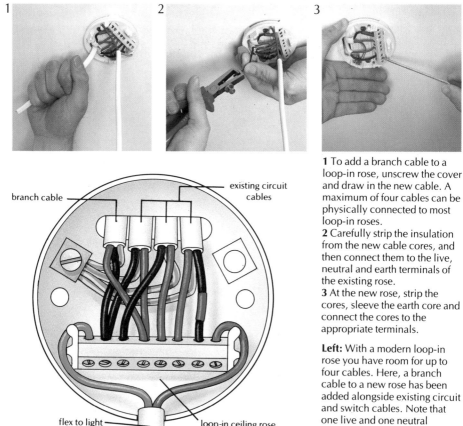

existing circuit cables

branch cable

flex to light

loop-in ceiling rose

1 To add a branch cable to a loop-in rose, unscrew the cover and draw in the new cable. A maximum of four cables can be physically connected to most loop-in roses.
2 Carefully strip the insulation from the new cable cores, and then connect them to the live, neutral and earth terminals of the existing rose.
3 At the new rose, strip the cores, sleeve the earth core and connect the cores to the appropriate terminals.

Left: With a modern loop-in rose you have room for up to four cables. Here, a branch cable to a new rose has been added alongside existing circuit and switch cables. Note that one live and one neutral terminal have to accept two cable cores each.

EXTENDING LIGHTING CIRCUITS 109

then runs on to the new rose and the new switch cable is connected to the new rose to control the new light.

Two points are worth bearing in mind when you are extending existing circuits. You may find that your circuits were wired in two-core PVC-sheathed cable . . . *without* an earth. Many types of light fitting — fluorescents and decorative pendants for instance — have metal parts which should be earthed for safety, and if they are to be installed you should run a single sheathed earth core back from the new light to the main earthing terminal at the consumer unit. It can be taken via any other ceiling roses where earthing is needed but is absent.

Secondly, you can provide power for wall lights in the same way (see pages 114 and 116). However, it may be more convenient to take a spur for your wall lights from a nearby ring main instead. This is permissible *so long as* you run the spur to a switched connection unit containing a 5A fuse (so that the lighting sub-circuit is protected by the same fusing level as an ordinary lighting circuit) before taking the cable on to the wall lights themselves.

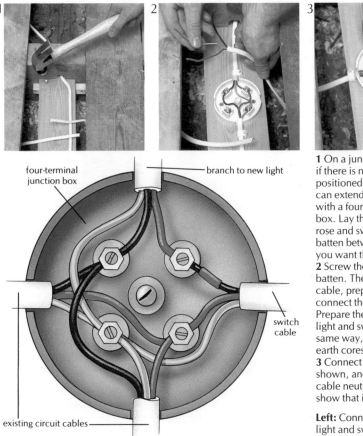

four-terminal junction box

branch to new light

switch cable

existing circuit cables

1 On a junction-box system, or if there is no conveniently-positioned loop-in rose, you can extend the lighting circuit with a four-terminal junction box. Lay the cables to the new rose and switch, and fix a batten between the joists where you want the box to be.
2 Screw the junction box to the batten. Then cut the circuit cable, prepare the cores and connect them up as shown. Prepare the ends of the new light and switch cables in the same way, sleeving the cable earth cores.
3 Connect the new cables as shown, and flag the switch cable neutral with red tape to show that it is, in fact, live.

Left: Connections for a new light and switch using a junction box.

110 FITTING A SWITCH OR DIMMER

Most lights are controlled by wall-mounted switches, usually sited by the entrance door and placed about 1.4m (4ft 6in) above floor level. They may be flush- or surface-mounted, and require a box 16mm (⅝in) or 25mm (1in) deep according to type. The commonest type is the plateswitch, which has one or more rocker switches in the centre of a large flat faceplate — about 85mm (3⅜in) square for one-, two- and three-gang units, and 146 × 85mm (5⅞ × 3⅜in) for four- and six-gang units. A 'one-way switch has two terminals marked L1 and L2 on the back, and provides on-off control from this switch position of all lights connected to it. Two-way switches have three terminals marked L1, L2 and C on the back, and are used in pairs to provide on-off control of one or more lights from two positions. Intermediate switches, with two pairs of terminals each marked L1 and L2, are used between pairs of two-way switches where control of a light or lights is needed from three (or more) positions.

Where there is no room to mount a plateswitch, you can use what is called an architrave switch instead. This is only about 32mm (1¼in) wide, and comes in one and two-gang versions (in the latter, the two rocker switches are placed one above the other).

Lights can also be controlled by ceiling switches with pull cords (and usually must be so controlled in bathrooms). These switches come in one-way and two-way versions, and can be fixed to a surface mounting box or fitted flush to a BESA box recessed into the ceiling.

Dimmer switches are light switches containing a variable control for raising

1

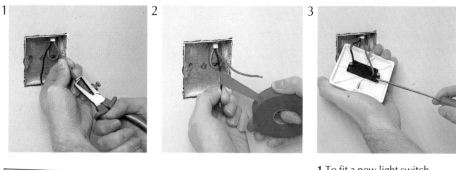

1 To fit a new light switch, install a plaster-depth box and feed in the switch cable. Strip the cores carefully.
2 Flag the neutral core with red PVC tape to show that it is live.
3 Connect the red core to terminal L1, the black core to L2. Then lay the cable neatly in the box and fit the faceplate. With plastic switches the earth core should go to the terminal on the mounting box (left); with metal switches it is usually linked to an earth terminal on the faceplate itself.

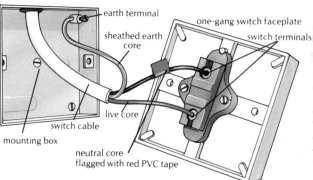

earth terminal
one-gang switch faceplate
sheathed earth core
switch terminals
live core
switch cable
mounting box
neutral core flagged with red PVC tape

FITTING A SWITCH OR DIMMER 111

or lowering the light level as well as an on-off switch. The control may be a knob, a roller or a touch-sensitive plate. Most are one-gang models, though up to four gangs are available in some ranges. When fitting one in place of an existing plateswitch, you may have to fit a deeper box (or even a two-gang box in the case of multi-gang dimmers) but the connections are usually the same as for ordinary switches.

A point to remember when fitting new plateswitches in place of existing ones for purely cosmetic reasons is to save the old fixing screws. The screws supplied with the new switch may not thread into the lugs on the old box if this pre-dates the introduction of metrication.

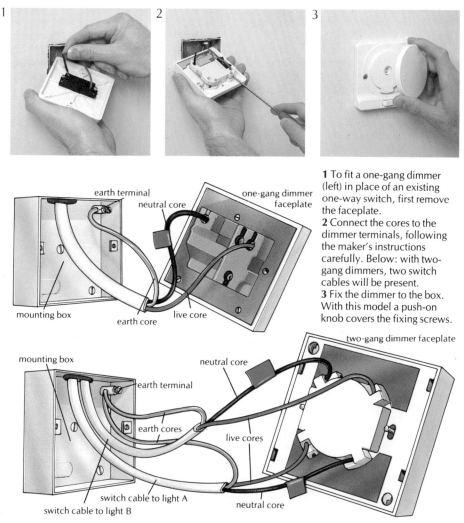

1 To fit a one-gang dimmer (left) in place of an existing one-way switch, first remove the faceplate.
2 Connect the cores to the dimmer terminals, following the maker's instructions carefully. Below: with two-gang dimmers, two switch cables will be present.
3 Fix the dimmer to the box. With this model a push-on knob covers the fixing screws.

112 TWO-WAY SWITCHING

It's often convenient to be able to switch a particular light on or off from more than one place in the house — for example, to control the hall light from hall or landing, or a bedroom light from near the door or bedside. So instead of having a single one-way switch breaking the live core of the mains supply, you use two two-way switches, one at each switch position. Each switch has three terminals, labelled L1, L2 and C; the live supply goes to the C terminal of one switch while the C terminal of the other switch is linked to the light being controlled. The pairs of L1 and L2 terminals are linked by strapping wires — L1 to L1 and L2 to L2 — so that, whatever the position of one switch,

the light can still be controlled from the other. That's the theory.

In practice, things are a little more complicated, since special $1.0mm^2$ three-core and earth cable is used. This has cores colour-coded in red, blue and yellow (plus the regular earth core); red should always be used for the C to C link, yellow for the L1 to L1 link and blue for the L2 to L2 link between the two switches. The switch 'drop' cable from the junction box or loop-in rose on the lighting circuit is run to the nearest two-way switch, its red core being connected to L1 and its black core to L2. The earth core of the three-core and earth cable links the earth terminals of the two switches, so

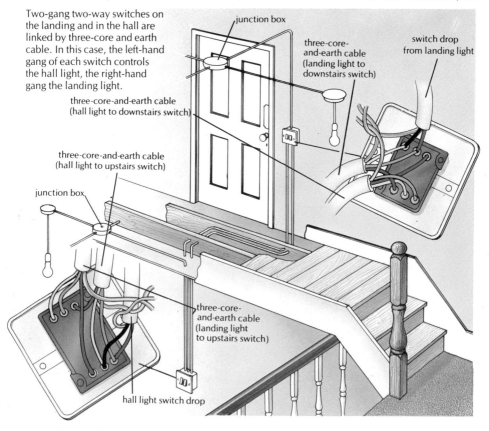

Two-gang two-way switches on the landing and in the hall are linked by three-core and earth cable. In this case, the left-hand gang of each switch controls the hall light, the right-hand gang the landing light.

junction box

three-core-and-earth cable (landing light to downstairs switch)

switch drop from landing light

three-core-and-earth cable (hall light to downstairs switch)

three-core-and-earth cable (hall light to upstairs switch)

junction box

three-core-and-earth cable (landing light to upstairs switch)

hall light switch drop

providing earth continuity throughout the switching circuit. The earth core must, of course, be sleeved with green and yellow PVC when exposed.

So to convert control of a light to two-way switching you simply replace the existing one-way switch with a two-way unit, and run three-core-and earth cable on to the new switch position. You can then provide further intermediate switches between the two-way switches at any point.

If you have partial two-way switching — say, you can switch the landing light on from hall or landing, but the hall light from the hall only — you follow a similar sequence. Replace the one-gang one-way switch on the land-

ing with a two-gang two-way switch and run a second three-core and earth cable alongside the one already linking the two switches. One gang of each switch is then linked by three-core cable, so enabling you to switch each light from upstairs or downstairs.

Lastly, you may want two-way switching of more than two lights — in a bedroom, say, with two independently-switched bedside lights. This could obviously involve a great deal of cable, but you can avoid a lot of the extra work by fitting a multi-terminal junction box in the ceiling void and making your cable connections through this. One typical wiring arrangement using this system is shown below.

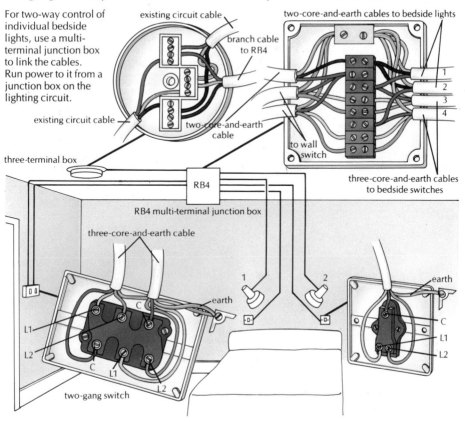

For two-way control of individual bedside lights, use a multi-terminal junction box to link the cables. Run power to it from a junction box on the lighting circuit.

existing circuit cable

branch cable to RB4

existing circuit cable

two-core-and-earth cable

three-terminal box

RB4

RB4 multi-terminal junction box

three-core-and-earth cable

two-core-and-earth cables to bedside lights

1
2
3
4

to wall switch

three-core-and-earth cables to bedside switches

earth

earth

C
L1
L2

1   2

C
L1
L2

C
L1
L2

two-gang switch

114 *MOVING OR ADDING A PENDANT LIGHT*

It's a relatively simple job to move an existing pendant light to a new position, especially if the switch is to be left where it was, or to add a new light to an existing circuit. In the first case, what you do depends on what you find under the cover of the old rose.

If you find only one cable present, it's wired on the junction box system and all you have to do is mount a suitable junction box to a joist above the old light position, connect the existing cable to its terminals and then run a new cable from the box to the new light position (shown below and top right).

If you find two (or more) cables at the old rose, it's wired on the loop-in system, and in this case you need a four-terminal junction box to which the existing cables, plus the spur to the new light, are connected (right). In either case, connect the new spur to the new rose and make good the ceiling where the old rose was removed.

In the case of loop-in wiring, you could choose instead to leave the existing rose where it is (but disconnect the pendant flex, leaving the option open of replacing it in the future should the lighting point be needed again) and to loop-in a spur cable from this rose on to the new rose position.

To install a completely new light, a little more work is involved. First of all, you have to check out how many lights are already on the circuit. You then have to lift floorboards or go into the

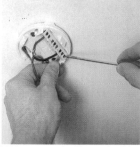

1 Disconnect the flex and cable from the old rose, and draw the cable into the ceiling void.

2 Connect the existing and new cables to a junction box mounted on a batten.

3 Fit the cover on the box. Then remove the old rose from the ceiling below and make good.

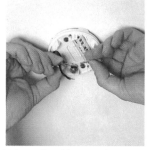

4 Mount the old rose in the new position, feed in the new cable and sleeve the earth core.

5 Connect the cores of the light flex to the rose terminals; hook them over their hangers.

6 Connect the other end of the flex to the lampholder after threading it through its cover.

MOVING OR ADDING A PENDANT LIGHT 115

attic to locate a circuit cable or loop-in rose near to your proposed light position. Make sure any cable *is* a circuit cable, *not* a switch cable: it must link two junction boxes or roses. If a circuit cable is nearby, isolate it at the consumer unit, cut it and insert a four-terminal junction box. Then run new cables from the box to the new rose and the new switch (remember that if you want the new switch at an existing switch position, you can run the new switch cable to that position and simply fit a new plateswitch there with one extra gang). If a loop-in rose is nearest, add a spur to the rose terminals, run it to a new rose at the new light position and then run a new switch cable from the new rose to the new switch.

Below: An alternative way of adding an extra light is to connect it to an existing light and switch which then controls both lights.

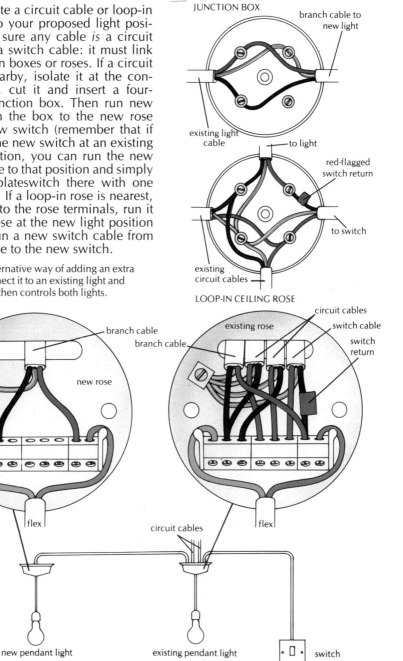

JUNCTION BOX

branch cable to new light

existing light cable

to light

red-flagged switch return

to switch

existing circuit cables

LOOP-IN CEILING ROSE

circuit cables

existing rose

switch cable

switch return

branch cable

branch cable

new rose

flex

flex

circuit cables

new pendant light

existing pendant light

switch

116 FITTING WALL LIGHTS

Wall lights help to add variety to a lighting scheme, providing localised illumination that can be decorative or functional, depending on what type of fitting you choose (and there is an enormous range available). Installing whatever light you finally decide on is a comparatively simple matter, but the job will make a mess of your decorations unless you are prepared to put up with surface-mounted cable, since cables have to be chased down walls to the light and any new switches required.

Mounting the light on the wall is the easy part. The fitting must be screwed over a flush-mounted enclosure that houses the connector block linking the fitting flex to the circuit cable; this can be a circular BESA box — ideal for fittings with circular base-plates, since the fitting can often be screwed direct to the box's fixing lugs — or an architrave box if the fitting has a very narrow baseplate (in this case, the fitting will probably be mounted via screws and wallplugs driven into the wall).

Next, you have to decide how to wire up the lights. You can either feed them from a convenient lighting circuit, as described on pages 114 and 115

1 To fit a wall light with its own separate switch, channel out the wall and fit a BESA box. Continue the chase on down to the switch position.

2 Feed the switch cable down to the BESA box, and then on down to the position of the switch. Pull it through so it lies neatly in the base of the box.

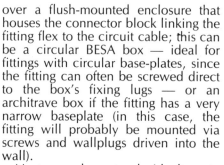

3 Next, feed in a second cable to supply the light fitting itself. The two are linked at a four-terminal junction box in the ceiling void above.

4 Strip the cable cores and then connect them to a three-terminal insulated connector block as shown.

5 Strip the cores of flex attached to the light fitting (three-core flex for a metal fitting) and connect them to the terminals.

6 Screw the fitting to the box with machine screws. If the fitting has a large baseplate, screw it to the wall instead.

FITTING WALL LIGHTS 117

(using three-terminal junction boxes to split the feed cables to two lights), or from a ring main. The latter method is particularly convenient in ground floor rooms, since it avoids having to lift first floor floorboards to make the circuit connections.

You should be able to pick up power from a ring main in two ways; the first involves cutting a nearby ring circuit cable, inserting a 30A three-terminal junction box and running a spur from there; in the second case, you simply run the spur cable from a conveniently-sited ring main socket (*not* a spur socket — see pages 106 and 107). In

either case, the spur must be in 2.5mm^2 cable, and must run directly to a switched fused connection unit containing a 5A fuse, so that the new lighting circuit is protected by a smaller fuse than the 30A ring circuit fuse, and can be isolated if necessary for maintenance or alterations.

You can then run a length of 1mm^2 cable on from the fused connection unit, either direct to the light (in which case, the fused connection unit acts as the light switch, too), or to a four-terminal junction box from where cables run on to the light and to a separate switch position.

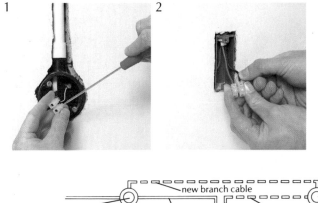

1 If the light fitting has an integral switch you can mount it over a BESA box or . . .
2 . . . an architrave box. Note that in each case the box is connected to the cable earth.
Below: You can supply wall lights from an existing loop-in rose (A) or from a three-terminal junction box (B). A new four-terminal junction box provides switch connections.

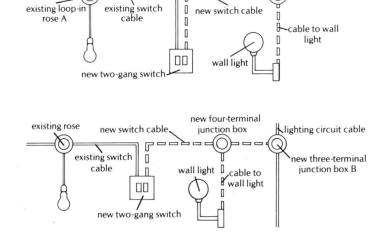

118 FITTING DECORATIVE LIGHTS

You don't have to restrict yourself to having pendant lights at all your ceiling fittings. The central light in many rooms is now usually supplemented by wall lights, table and standard lamps, and so on. However, it still has an important role to play, even if the tendency is towards fittings that are decorative rather than purely functional. You can, of course, simply change lampshades to transform an ordinary pendant fitting, but much more attractive effects can be obtained with other types of decorative fitting.

Such fittings usually either hang down from the ceiling on a rod, chains or cords, or else are close-mounted on the ceiling surface. What's involved in installing them varies from fitting to fitting, but one or two general guidelines can be given. With pendant-type fittings you will usually have to install a flush-mounted BESA box, screwed securely to a batten so it can carry the weight of the fitting screwed to it. The box then houses the connector blocks that link the fitting flex and the mains cable — you'll need four connectors instead of three if you're replacing an existing loop-in rose.

With surface-mounted fittings, you often have to mount a fixing bar on the

1 Most decorative light fittings are mounted over a BESA box. Connect the cable cores to a four-terminal connector block on a loop-in wiring system.

2 Follow the fitting manufacturer's wiring instructions. Then fit the block neatly into the box and fix the fitting baseplate to it.

3 With this downlighter, all that remains is to offer up the cowl, locking it on to the lugs on the baseplate by twisting it slightly, and fit the lamp.

1 If the fitting does not need to be earthed, link the block to the box with a short length of sleeved earth wire.

2 As before, offer up the new fitting and connect the flex cores to the terminals of the connector block.

3 Finally, position the fitting baseplate accurately over the BESA box, and tighten up the fixing screws fully.

FITTING DECORATIVE LIGHTS 119

ceiling, screw to it a base plate carrying the lampholder and terminal block, make the connections (if there are only three terminals, you can't handle loop-in connections) and fit the lamp cover. With rise-and-fall fittings, a base plate and hook (for the rise-and-fall unit) are usually screwed to a BESA box and concealed by a plastic cover.

Another versatile form of decorative lighting is the track fitting, which is surface-mounted on the ceiling and carries a number of sliding spotlights. Electrical conductors along the length of the track allow the spotlight position to be adjusted at will. There are no

facilities for loop-in wiring with track lighting, so if you have such a circuit you will have to break into it with a four-terminal junction box and run cables to the track and its switch.

Take care when installing decorative fittings to follow the manufacturer's instructions about the maximum bulb wattage to be used. In the case of enclosed fittings, it's also a good idea to slip lengths of heat-resistant sleeving over the flex and cable cores before connecting them to the terminal block; otherwise, the build-up of heat inside the enclosed fitting could make the insulation brittle and eventually fail.

1 With rise-and-fall fittings, link the cable cores to a connector block. Then attach the base plate and hook to the BESA box with machine screws.

2 Next, hook the rise-and-fall unit over the hook. You can adjust the up-and-down movement simply by tightening or loosening the control screw.

3 Connect the flex cores from the rise-and-fall unit to the correct terminals of the connector block.

4 Push the plastic cover up to the ceiling to conceal the rise-and-fall unit and secure it with a grub screw.

Track lighting

Above: Mark the track position on the ceiling and screw the track fixing brackets into place.

Above: Thread in the feed cable, attach the track to the brackets and connect the cores to the terminals.

120 INSTALLING A FLUORESCENT FITTING

Many people have mixed feelings about fluorescent lights because of the quality of the light they emit — harsh and bright. However, they need not look clinical; they are an ideal way of providing good all-round lighting in rooms such as kitchens, bathrooms and workshops, and can be used to provide all sorts of concealed lighting effects when fixed behind baffles and cornices, or above worktops.

Fluorescent lights cost more to install than ordinary pendant lights, but are more economical to run because they are more efficient. A 1500mm (5ft) tube rated at 65W gives out four times as much light as a 100W tungsten filament lamp.

A fluorescent fitting is installed in much the same way as any close-mounted ceiling fitting. It usually comes as an integral fitting in two parts; the base plate carries the two lampholders (one at each end of the tube), the control gear (to start the discharge through the tube and keep it running when the light is on) and the terminal block that links the circuit cable to the fitting. Over this is fitted a cover or 'diffuser'. You can also buy the lampholder and control gear separately — useful when you want to mount several

1 Remove the diffuser and tube from the fitting and take off the backplate cover by undoing the retaining screws and set it to one side.

2 Offer up the baseplate to the ceiling and mark the positions of the fixing screws through the holes in the backplate. Screw into a joist or a batten.

3 Feed in the supply cable, strip the cores and connect them to the appropriate terminal of the connector block on the baseplate of the fitting.

4 If using existing cables that aren't earthed, add an earth core between the fitting and the consumer unit (see page 109).

5 Offer up the baseplate cover, fitting it carefully between the ends of the unit, and do up the retaining screws.

6 Fit the tube and diffuser. In this case, the diffuser is held on to the tube by spring clips, so is actually fitted first.

INSTALLING A FLUORESCENT FITTING 121

tubes behind a pelmet to provide perimeter lighting, or below kitchen wall units to light a length of worktop, since one set of control gear can be linked to several tubes.

Incidentally, it is possible to dim fluorescent lighting; but you need to use a special model of dimmer switch made for the purpose.

When connecting up a fluorescent fitting in place of an existing rose, you should follow the same sequence of operations for wiring it as that given for pendant lights on pages 114 and 115 — what you do depends on the wiring at the existing rose.

Below: Connect the control units to a three-terminal junction box (A). With junction-box wiring, run new cable from the existing four-terminal box (B). With loop-in wiring, replace the flex to the existing fitting with new cable (C).

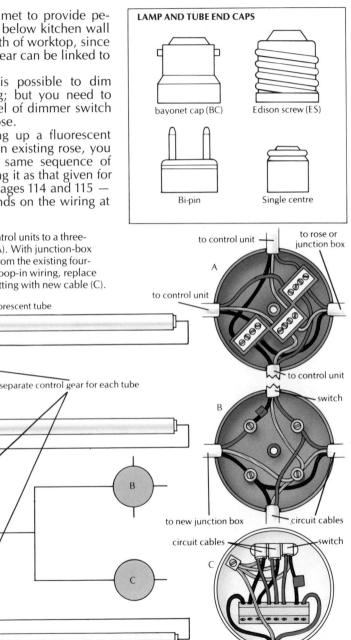

LAMP AND TUBE END CAPS

bayonet cap (BC)

Edison screw (ES)

Bi-pin

Single centre

fluorescent tube

separate control gear for each tube

new three-terminal junction box

to control unit

to rose or junction box

A

to control unit

to control unit

switch

B

to new junction box

circuit cables

circuit cables

switch

C

cable to new junction box

122 CHANGING SINGLE SOCKETS INTO DOUBLE

One of the simplest ways of getting extra power points around the house is to convert existing single sockets into double ones. Only do this if your house is wired in PVC-sheathed cable; you should not risk overloading any circuits wired in rubber-sheathed cable.

You can carry out the job in several ways, and which you choose depends on whether you have surface- or flush-mounted sockets already, and whether you want your new sockets to be flush- or surface-mounted.

The simplest option involves fitting surface-mounted sockets. First isolate the circuit, unscrew the existing socket faceplate and disconnect the cable from the terminals. If the existing socket is surface-mounted, unscrew the one-gang mounting box, fit a two-gang surface-mounted box in its place, connect the cable to the new double faceplate and screw it to the mounting box. If the existing socket is flush-mounted, leave the box where it is and screw the new two-gang surface-mounted box over it (holes in its rear face will line up with the lugs on the existing box) before adding the faceplate as before.

You may want your new double socket to be flush-mounted. In this case, disconnect the existing faceplate and remove the existing mounting box. If this was surface-mounted, cut a recess for a two-gang metal mounting box; if it was flush-mounted, simply enlarge the existing one-gang hole to take a two-gang box. Then secure the new box (having threaded the cable into it through a knockout fitted with a rubber grommet), connect the cable to the terminals and fit the new double faceplate to the box. Make good any gaps round the perimeter of the new box with plaster or filler.

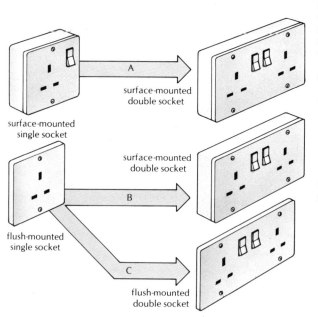

surface-mounted
single socket

A

surface-mounted
double socket

flush-mounted
single socket

surface-mounted
double socket

B

C

flush-mounted
double socket

Left: The simplest option is to change a surface-mounted single socket into a surface-mounted double one. Flush single sockets can be converted into surface-mounted or flush doubles quite easily, but in the latter case the wall recess has to be enlarged to accept the new, larger socket.

Below: The three options, shown in cross-section.

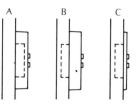

A   B   C

CHANGING SINGLE SOCKETS INTO DOUBLE 123

1 To change a surface-mounted single socket into a double, unscrew and disconnect the faceplate, then unscrew the mounting box from the wall. Lift it away carefully.

2 Remove a knockout from the base of the new double mounting box, thread in the cables and mark the fixing screw positions. After drilling and plugging, fit the box.

3 Finish off by connecting the cable cores to the appropriate terminals of the new double socket faceplate. Press the cables back neatly and fix the faceplate in position.

1 To change a flush single socket into a surface-mounted double, unscrew the faceplate of the single socket and disconnect the cable cores. Set the faceplate aside.

2 Remove a knockout from the base of the new double mounting box, and thread in the cables. Check which of the fixing screw holes coincide with the old box lugs.

3 Use the screws that secured the old faceplate to fix the new box in position over the existing one. This will ensure the threads match. Check the new box is level as you tighten the screws.

1 To convert a flush single socket to a flush double, remove the old faceplate and box. Chop out a larger recess.

2 Offer up the new box, thread in the cables and mark the positions of the fixing screws. Drill and plug the holes.

3 Fix the mounting box in place. Then connect the cable to the faceplate terminals and attach it to the box.

124 FITTING A NEW SOCKET

When you decide to fit a new socket outlet where none exists, you have two separate jobs to tackle. The first is to run a power supply to the new socket position (see pages 106 and 107), and the second is to fix a mounting box of whatever type you prefer to the wall, ready to receive the new cable and faceplate (see pages 100 and 101).

Most socket outlets need a mounting box 35mm (1⅜in) deep, but where you are fitting flush boxes in cavity and single brick internal walls, chopping such a deep hole can be difficult without cutting right through the wall, so shallow 25mm (1in) boxes are used

instead, coupled with accessories having thicker-than-usual faceplates.

Remember that you can also fit a special dual box instead of a two-gang box, and use two different one-gang faceplates — say, one single socket and one fused connection unit taking power to a freezer. You can combine any two accessories in this way, with one exception: you are *not* allowed to house a TV coaxial socket outlet in the same box as mains exceeding 50 volts; so you can't put one alongside the socket outlet powering the TV set; the Wiring Regulations forbid it.

With solid walls, making fixings is

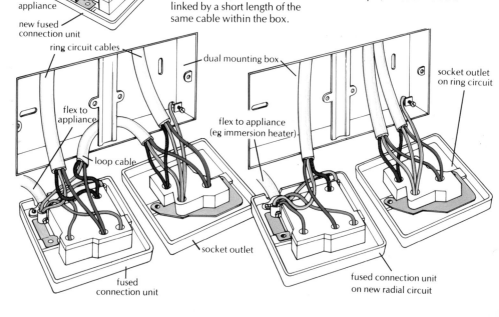

existing socket outlet
dual mounting box
branch cable
flex to appliance
new fused connection unit

Left: A dual box is designed to accept two one-gang accessories – such as a fused connection unit and a socket outlet.

Below left: The two accessories can be wired up on the same circuit. Here, the circuit cable runs into the back of the first accessory and out of the back of the second; the two are linked by a short length of the same cable within the box.

Below right: Where the two have to be on separate circuits, the cables are fed in independently. Here, a single socket is linked to a ring circuit, and a fused connection unit is wired up on its own radial circuit. You are not allowed to mix accessories operating at different voltages (socket outlets and TV aerial sockets, for example) in the same box.

ring circuit cables
dual mounting box
flex to appliance
loop cable
flex to appliance (eg immersion heater)
socket outlet on ring circuit
fused connection unit
socket outlet
fused connection unit on new radial circuit

FITTING A NEW SOCKET 125

obviously no problem: you simply drill holes where you need them, insert wallplugs and drive in the fixing screws, but with hollow stud partition walls life is not so simple. Obviously, if you are building the wall from scratch, you can fix the mounting boxes to noggins between the studs and cut holes in the plasterboard cladding ready for flush accessories to be fitted later. With existing walls, however, you have two choices. You can either use surface-mounted fittings (screwed to studs if they're conveniently placed, or secured with appropriate cavity fixings) or cut holes in the plasterboard and install a flush box. This can be done in two ways.

One rather fiddly method involves clipping metal lugs to each side of the metal box and offering it up to the inner face of the plasterboard; you need string to pull it tightly into place while you attach the socket faceplate, but once the fixing screws are tightened the whole assembly is quite secure. The other method involves the use of 'flange boxes', which are set into the hole and secured at each corner with screws and cavity fixings. The socket faceplate can then be mounted on the flange box.

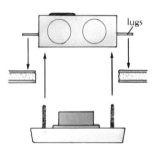

1 To mount accessories in hollow partition walls, clip small lugs to the mounting box. These are drawn against the inside of the partition as the faceplate is screwed on.

2 Cut away the plasterboard to match the size of the mounting box, drilling a hole in each corner and then cutting between the holes with a padsaw. Then fit the lugs to the box.

3 Draw the cable in through a knockout and feed a loop of string through the box base. Offer it up inside the recess and pull the string to hold it in place.

4 Holding the string taut, offer up the accessory faceplate and start to turn the fixing screws into the box lugs.

5 When you have almost fully tightened the screws, release the string loop and draw it out. Finish tightening the screws.

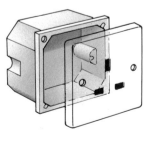

6 To mount accessories in holes cut in thin sheet materials, use a special flanged mounting box of the appropriate size.

126 FUSED CONNECTION UNITS

Fused connection units are mainly used instead of plugs and sockets to link certain electrical appliances — fridges and freezers, for instance — to the mains when you want to avoid the risk of the appliance being unplugged accidentally. They are more convenient, too, for items that are often in use — such as washing machines, extractor fans and waste disposal units — because they save you the bother of constantly plugging in and unplugging the flex.

A connection unit has a double-pole switch (one that breaks both the live and neutral cores of the circuit to the appliance) and a cartridge fuse that acts in the same way as a plug fuse to protect the flex or cable running on from the unit. Different types of unit are

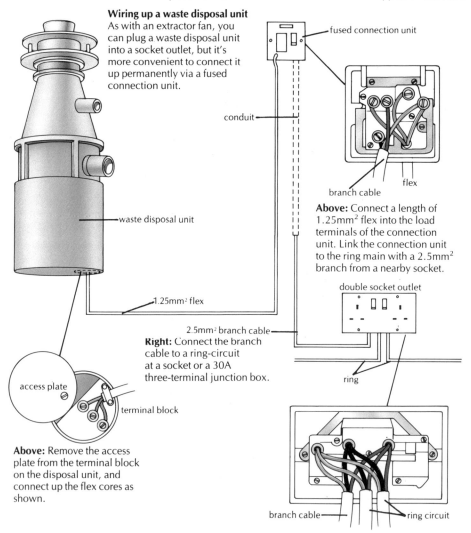

Wiring up a waste disposal unit
As with an extractor fan, you can plug a waste disposal unit into a socket outlet, but it's more convenient to connect it up permanently via a fused connection unit.

fused connection unit

conduit

waste disposal unit

flex

branch cable

Above: Connect a length of 1.25mm² flex into the load terminals of the connection unit. Link the connection unit to the ring main with a 2.5mm² branch from a nearby socket.

double socket outlet

1.25mm² flex

2.5mm² branch cable

Right: Connect the branch cable to a ring-circuit at a socket or a 30A three-terminal junction box.

ring

access plate

terminal block

Above: Remove the access plate from the terminal block on the disposal unit, and connect up the flex cores as shown.

branch cable

ring circuit

FUSED CONNECTION UNITS 127

available, with or without switches or neon indicators; some are designed for use in spur circuits, with cable entering and leaving the unit (as in the wall light installation described on pages 116 and 117), while others are designed to allow flex to run through an outlet in the face of the unit to the appliance.

Connection units are one-gang units and are fitted to 25mm (1in) or 35mm (1⅜in) deep mounting boxes. Slim and standard depth versions are available as for socket outlets. They can be mounted in pairs (or alongside a single socket outlet) in dual boxes.

A particular type of low-rated unit is the clock connector, containing a 2A fuse and intended to provide a permanent connection for mains clocks and other low-rated appliances.

Fitting an extractor fan

There's nothing to stop you simply plugging an extractor fan into a nearby socket outlet, but a far neater solution is to wire it in permanently.

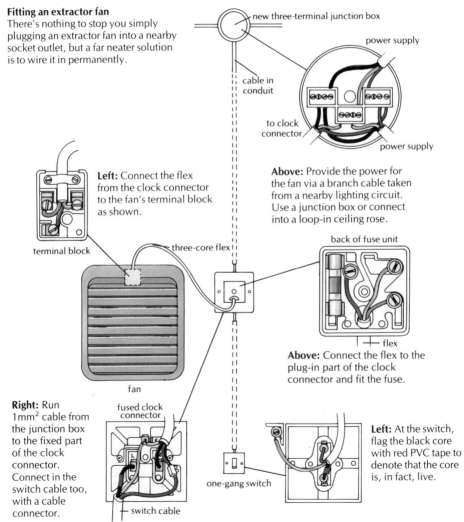

new three-terminal junction box

power supply

cable in conduit

to clock connector

power supply

Left: Connect the flex from the clock connector to the fan's terminal block as shown.

terminal block

three-core flex

Above: Provide the power for the fan via a branch cable taken from a nearby lighting circuit. Use a junction box or connect into a loop-in ceiling rose.

back of fuse unit

Above: Connect the flex to the plug-in part of the clock connector and fit the fuse.

flex

fan

Right: Run 1mm² cable from the junction box to the fixed part of the clock connector. Connect in the switch cable too, with a cable connector.

fused clock connector

switch cable

one-gang switch

Left: At the switch, flag the black core with red PVC tape to denote that the core is, in fact, live.

128 ADDING A NEW CIRCUIT

Unless your electrical system was extremely well-planned at the very beginning, it's quite likely that sooner or later you will want to add one or more new circuits. For example, you may have built an extension that requires its own ring main, or you may want to add circuits to such major appliances as an electric cooker, an instantaneous shower or an immersion heater, all of which must be fed from an individual radial circuit.

In a modern installation, you may be lucky enough to have a consumer unit with a number of unused fuseways that could be used to supply these circuits, but in most cases you will have to install extra circuit fuse capacity to power the new circuits. This involves installing either a second consumer unit alongside the first (worthwhile if you want several extra circuits; you could even consider removing the existing unit and fitting a much larger one to handle both existing and new circuits) or a smaller unit called a

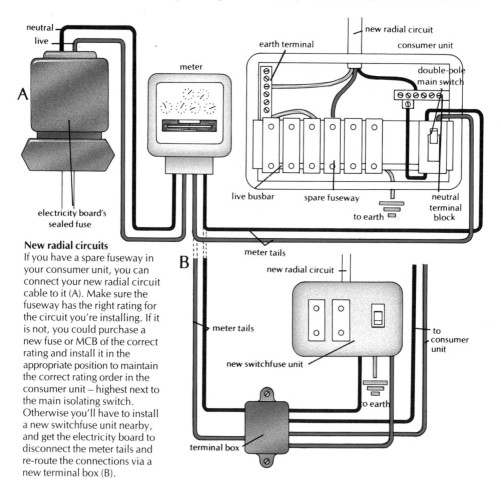

neutral
live

A

electricity board's
sealed fuse

meter

new radial circuit

earth terminal

consumer unit

double-pole
main switch

live busbar   spare fuseway

to earth

neutral
terminal
block

meter tails

B

new radial circuit

meter tails

new switchfuse unit

to earth

terminal box

to
consumer
unit

New radial circuits
If you have a spare fuseway in your consumer unit, you can connect your new radial circuit cable to it (A). Make sure the fuseway has the right rating for the circuit you're installing. If it is not, you could purchase a new fuse or MCB of the correct rating and install it in the appropriate position to maintain the correct rating order in the consumer unit – highest next to the main isolating switch. Otherwise you'll have to install a new switchfuse unit nearby, and get the electricity board to disconnect the meter tails and re-route the connections via a new terminal box (B).

1 When you want to add a new circuit, check at your consumer unit to see if you have any spare fuseways or room within the unit to insert another fuseway. If you have room to add one, switch off the main switch on the unit and undo the fixing screws holding the MCBs or fuseholders to the neutral busbar. This unit has room for two more circuits to be added.

2 Where the new MCB or fuseholder is fitted depends on the current rating of the circuit you want to add. In this case the new circuit is a 15A one, and so an MCB of the appropriate rating has to be inserted between the low-rated lighting circuit MCBs furthest from the main switch and the higher-rated MCBs nearer to it. This order of circuit rating must be followed.

3 With the new MCB or fuseholder clipped into place, the circuit cable can be fed into the consumer unit. Remove enough of the cable's outer sheathing to allow all the cores to reach the appropriate terminals within the unit. You can always cut the cores down if they are too long. Then connect up the cores; here, the neutral is being connected to the neutral block.

4 Next, the earth core, sleeved in green/yellow PVC, is connected to the unit's earth terminal (top right). Then, the live core is linked to the top terminal of the new MCB or fuseholder to complete the connection of the new circuit cable. All that remains is to fit the consumer unit's protective cover back in place and turn on the main switch and circuit MCBs.

130 ADDING A NEW CIRCUIT

mainswitch and fuse unit, which incorporates an isolating switch and usually one or two extra fuseways. This is mounted alongside the original consumer unit or fusebox. The meter tails are then disconnected from the existing unit and taken on to a terminal box; from there, two new sets of single-core double-insulated cables run to the existing unit and the new one. You can do all the installation work on the new unit, but you must leave the disconnection

1 If your consumer unit doesn't have any spare fuseways, put in a new switchfuse unit. Attach its baseplate to the board near the old box.

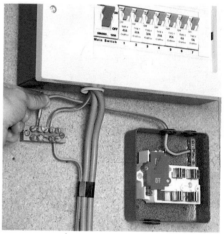

2 Link its earth terminal to the installation's main earthing point with a single-core earth lead of the appropriate size – usually 6mm^2.

3 Connect in live and neutral single-core tails to link the new switchfuse unit with a terminal box. This is necessary because only one pair of tails can be connected to the meter.

4 You can now feed in the cables that will take power to whatever new circuits you are installing. Here, the neutral cores are cut long enough to pass behind the fuseholders.

ADDING A NEW CIRCUIT 131

of the meter tails, and their reconnection to the new box, to the local electricity board.

A new switchfuse unit must also be properly earthed, which means that a length of single-core earth cable must be taken from the new unit's earth terminal to the installation's main earthing point. If you are not sure where this is, ask the electricity board to make the connection when they reconnect the meter tails.

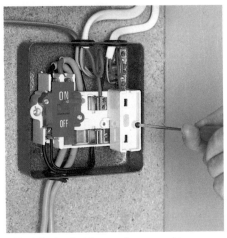

5 Now the fuseholders can be screwed into position over the terminals. Check that they sit squarely in place before tightening up the screw.

6 Fit the fuses or MCBs into the fuseholders, check that all connections are neat and secure, then replace the cover of the switchfuse unit.

7 Take the tails from the new unit to a terminal box mounted nearby. Then call in the electricity board to disconnect the consumer unit from the meter and connect up the new installation.

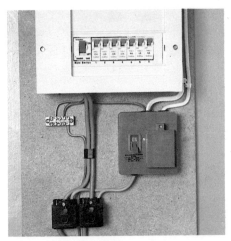

8 The completed installation looks like this. Note how the consumer unit and switchfuse unit are linked to the terminal box, from where one set of meter tails lead to the meter.

132 COOKER CONTROLS

Because cookers are heavy current users, they must be wired on a separate radial circuit run from the consumer unit. Its rating will depend on the wattage of the cooker — one rated at up to 11kW should be on a circuit wired in 6mm^2 cable and protected by a 30A fuse, while one with a higher rating should be wired with 10mm^2 cable on a 45A fuse. At the cooker end

of the circuit, what you do depends on the type of cooker you have.

With a freestanding type of cooker, the most common arrangement is to have a cooker control unit — an accessory combining a double-pole switch and a 13A socket outlet — or else just a double-pole switch (usually marked 'cooker'). The circuit cable runs to this switch unit (which must be

Wiring up a separate hob and oven
Right: If you want the control unit between the hob and oven, run separate 6mm^2 cables to each from the control unit. Each appliance must be no more than 2m (6ft 6in) from it.

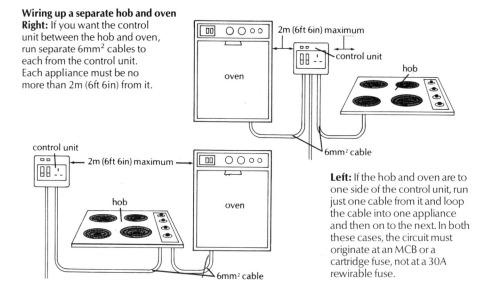

2m (6ft 6in) maximum
control unit
oven
hob
6mm^2 cable

control unit
— 2m (6ft 6in) maximum —
hob
oven
6mm^2 cable

Left: If the hob and oven are to one side of the control unit, run just one cable from it and loop the cable into one appliance and then on to the next. In both these cases, the circuit must originate at an MCB or a cartridge fuse, not at a 30A rewirable fuse.

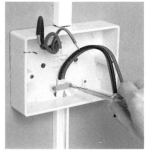

1 Feed the circuit cable and cooker cable into the mounting box. Secure the cooker cable in the clamp provided.

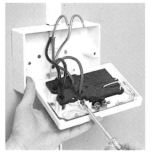

2 Prepare the cable ends, then connect the cores of each cable to the appropriate terminals on the control unit's faceplate.

3 Check the connections. Then snap on the conduit cover strips to conceal the cables, and fix the faceplate in position.

COOKER CONTROLS 133

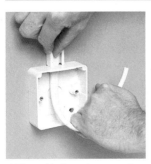

1 The cable from the control unit passes on to a cooker connection unit. Feed the cable into the box through a knockout. Cut off any excess cable with wire cutters.

2 Connect the cable that will run to the cooker into the lower set of terminals, and secure it in the cable clamp. Tighten the fixing screws fully to prevent the cable from being pulled out.

3 Now connect the cores of the supply cable from the control unit into the other set of terminals. Part the conductors if necessary to fit them under the terminal clamp.

4 Now snap on the conduit cover, and attach the connection unit's cover. Note that a cooker is the only appliance linked to the mains with cable instead of flex.

5 Feed the other end of the cable from the connection unit into the rear of the cooker. Make sure you use the cable clamp; follow the maker's instructions for connections.

6 Check that all of the connections are secure and that the cable earth core has been sleeved. Then tighten up the cable clamp and the cooker is ready to be switched on.

mounted within reach of the cooker) and then a further cable is run on to a connector unit which is fixed lower down the wall.

From here, cable (not flex; the Wiring Regulations allow this unusual exception) runs to the cooker's terminal block; this means that when repairs are necessary, the cooker circuit can be turned off at the double-pole switch and the cooker can be disconnected at the connector unit without having to disturb the fixed wiring.

With split-level oven and hob units, both can be linked directly to one cooker control unit or switch unit if they are both within 2m (6ft 6in) of it. Where the switch is between the oven and hob, two cables are run from the switch to the two units; where it is to one side, one cable is looped into the nearer appliance, and then runs on to the further one.

Cooker control units and double-pole switches can be flush- or surface-mounted; the former need a 55mm (2¼in) deep box, while the latter come complete with a special metal box. Cooker connector units are normally flush-mounted.

134 INSTANTANEOUS SHOWERS

Instantaneous electric showers take water direct from the mains supply, pass it over powerful electrical heating elements and supply it to a shower rose, which may be installed over a bath or shower tray.

Early models provided temperature control by varying the flow of water through the heater, but they were something of a disaster because their throughput of water was very low and the temperature was likely to be affected by any sudden draw-off from taps elsewhere in the system.

Recent models are more powerful (rating up to 8kW) and incorporate temperature stabilisers which iron out the problem of pressure fluctuations.

The power supply for these showers must be supplied from a separate radial circuit, wired in 6mm^2 cable, and the unit itself must be controlled by a 30A or 45A double-pole cord-operated switch. This can be surface-mounted on a plastic box fixed to the ceiling, or flush-mounted on a BESA box recessed into it and screwed to a batten fixed between the joists. This type of switch also incorporates a neon light to indicate when the unit is switched on. A wall-mounted double-pole switch can be used but must be outside the room.

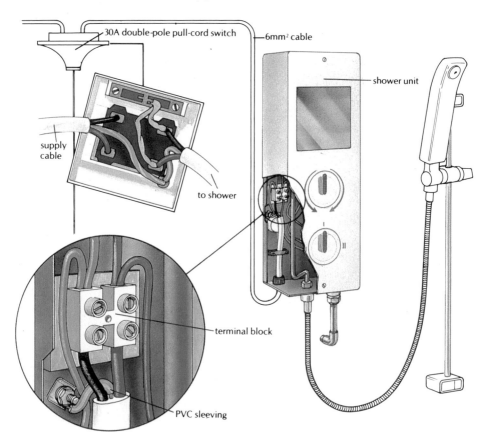

30A double-pole pull-cord switch

6mm^2 cable

shower unit

supply cable

to shower

terminal block

PVC sleeving

1
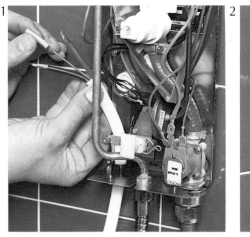

2
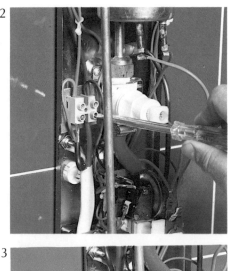

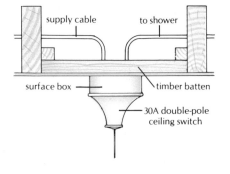

3
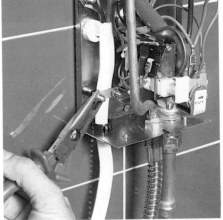

Above: Because of the pull exerted on a heavy-duty ceiling switch like this, firm mounting is important. Try to mount the switch on the underside of a joist. If you can't, fit a batten between the joists so that it sits against the upper surface of the ceiling. Then drill holes in the batten and the ceiling for the cables, remove a knockout from the base of the plastic mounting box and screw it in place. Finally, make up the connections as shown in the illustration.

Left: The new radial circuit cable is run above the ceiling to the 30A double-pole ceiling switch, and is connected as shown. Then a cable is run on to the shower unit, where it is fed in under a cable clamp before being connected to the terminal block. Note the sleeved earth connection to the terminal mounted on the shower unit's metal casing.

1 Feed the circuit cable into the shower unit through the grommet and cable clamp in the base of the case. Prepare the cable cores and sleeve the earth core.

2 Connect the live and neutral cores to the appropriate terminals within the unit and the earth core to its separate terminal. Make sure the terminal screws are tightened fully.

3 Tighten up the cable clamp – here, using long-nose pliers to grasp the nuts. Ideally, a small spanner should be used, but if you don't have one you can use pliers if you are careful. Check that the connections are correct, and replace the shower unit cover.

136 IMMERSION HEATERS

Immersion heaters provide an efficient way of heating water for domestic use when there is no central heating boiler, and they are also often used as an alternative heat source when there is full central heating, since it is more efficient to use the heater in summer than to run the boiler just to generate hot water.

Most immersion heaters — rather like large electric kettle elements — are designed to be fitted into a boss in the top of the hot water cylinder. There are two main types; one has a single element that extends almost to the bottom of the cylinder, while the other has two elements — one long as above, the other about 400mm (16in) long. Both types have to be supplied via a separate radial circuit protected by a

15A fuse and run in 2.5mm² cable (in theory, heaters rated at less than 3kW *could* be plugged into a socket outlet, but would hog that circuit's current-carrying capacity and present a grave risk of overloading it). The circuit cable is run to near the hot cylinder, where a 20A double-pole switch is fitted to control the heater.

In the case of a two-element heater, a 20A dual switch is installed instead; this has a double-pole on-off switch and a changeover switch (marked 'sink' and 'bath') for switching on the appropriate element.

Below: The circuit cable runs to a 20A double-pole switch (or a fused connection unit for heaters rated below 3kW). This is linked to the heater with 1.5mm² heat-resisting flex, connected up as shown.

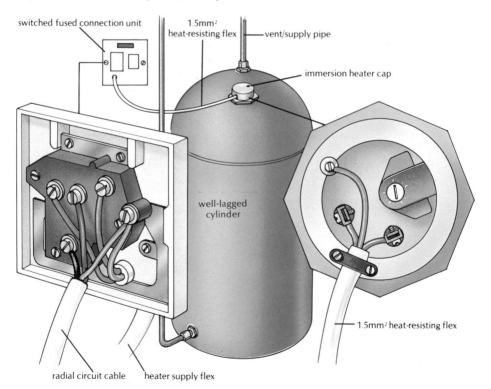

switched fused connection unit

1.5mm² heat-resisting flex

vent/supply pipe

immersion heater cap

well-lagged cylinder

1.5mm² heat-resisting flex

radial circuit cable

heater supply flex

You can, of course, plug an electric shaver into a special shaver adaptor that fits into a standard socket outlet, but you won't be able to use your shaver in the bathroom since you are not allowed socket outlets there because of the proximity of water.

It's more convenient to provide special shaver points in rooms where shavers are most commonly used — bathrooms, bedrooms and cloakrooms. These will accept most British, American, European and Australian two-pin shaver plugs.

There are two main types of shaver point: the shaver supply unit and the shaver socket outlet. The former is designed specially for use in bathrooms and washrooms where the proximity of water is so potentially dangerous. Power is provided to the outlet via a transformer, which means there is no direct connection between the shaver and the mains. A self-resetting overload device restricts the power supply to about 20W, so no other appliance could be connected to it without tripping the overload device. The unit usually supplies two voltages, 110V and 240V, selected either via a switch or by using only two of the three available socket holes.

The shaver socket outlet differs from the supply unit in not containing a transformer, so it cannot be installed in a bathroom or washroom. However, it's a much cheaper option for bedrooms. It contains a 1A fuse to protect the shaver, and may also be fitted with an overload device.

Some units are also available combined with a strip light (which is controlled by a pull-cord switch); these come in both shaver supply unit and shaver socket outlet versions. Make sure you get the right type for your chosen location.

You can provide power for a shaver supply unit in two ways: as a spur from a junction box or loop-in rose on a nearby lighting circuit, using 1mm^2 cable or as a spur from a junction box or socket outlet on a ring circuit, using 2.5mm^2 cable (see pages 106 to 109 for details of how to identify and extend lighting and power circuits).

A shaver socket outlet can be supplied as above from a lighting circuit, but if linked to a power circuit the spur must be run via a fused connection unit fitted with a 3A fuse. Then 1mm^2 cable is run on from the fused connection unit to the shaver socket (if you want to install several shaver sockets, simply loop this cable on from one unit to the next).

1 A shaver socket outlet fits a standard single box and can be wired from a lighting circuit. To fit it, connect the cable cores.

2 Tuck the cores neatly into the mounting box, then screw the faceplate into position. Check that it is level.

3 With a shaver supply unit you will need a special deep box if you want the unit to be flush-mounted on the bathroom wall.

138 POWER TO OUTBUILDINGS AND GARDENS

If you want light and power in a detached garage, garden shed or green-house, you must install a separate radial circuit to it — you are not allowed to extend your house circuits. There may be a spare fuseway in the consumer unit, which you can use (fit a 30A fuse or MCB), but it's better to install a terminal box and a separate circuit to a new switchfuse unit (see pages 128 to 131), complete with isolating switch and 30A fuse or MCB.

You can run the new sub-circuit in three ways: buried underground, carried overhead or fixed to a boundary or other wall (but *never* to a fence, which could be blown down in high winds). In the first case, you can use ordinary PVC-sheathed cable if the outdoor section is completely contained in steel or rigid plastic conduit; otherwise PVC-covered armoured cable must be used. Mineral-insulated copper-covered (MICC) cable could be used, but the cut ends of the cable have to be fitted with special glands to stop the insulation absorbing moisture, and this needs special tools — an unnecessarily complicated job for the do-it-yourselfer. Where armoured cable is used, a conversion box is fitted at each end of the underground run — one in the house,

Running overhead cables
Below: An overhead cable must be at least 3.5m (11ft) above ground, and 5.2m (17ft) if over a driveway. If the span is over 3.5m, a catenary wire must be fitted to support it. A strainer bolt keeps the wire taut.
Right: Within the outbuilding, the new sub-circuit must be controlled by a switchfuse unit, fed from a terminal box in the house. This then supplies the lighting and power circuits.

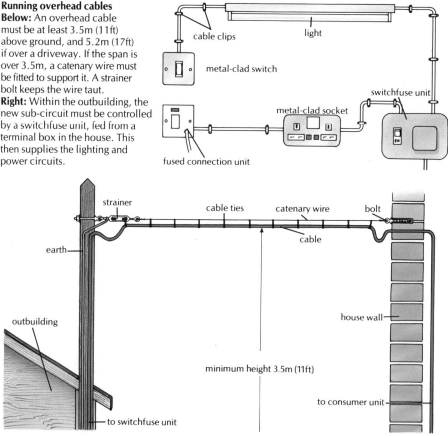

cable clips

light

metal-clad switch

switchfuse unit

metal-clad socket

fused connection unit

strainer   cable ties   catenary wire   bolt

earth

cable

outbuilding

house wall

minimum height 3.5m (11ft)

to consumer unit

to switchfuse unit

POWER TO OUTBUILDINGS AND GARDENS 139

one in the outbuilding — and the inside sections are run in cheaper ordinary PVC-sheathed cable.

With an overhead cable run, ordinary PVC-sheathed cable can be used unbroken, but certain rules have to be followed. It must be at least 3.5m (11ft) above the ground, 5.2m (17ft) if it crosses a driveway. If the span is over 3.5m (11ft), the cable must be supported on a 'catenary wire', and this catenary must have intermediate supports if more than 5m (16ft 6in) long.

The incoming cable from the terminal box is fed into a switchfuse unit containing one or more fuses or MCBs.

For a small installation, one 30A fuseway will be sufficient; any lighting circuit can be fed via a spur and a 5A fused connection unit. However, it's better to have separate 5A and 30A fuseways for lighting and power circuits. Under the Wiring Regulations, you must fit a 30mA R.C.D. in the new switchfuse unit to provide additional protection to users of outdoor power tools likely to be run from the new sockets. You can, of course, use any electrical accessories within the outbuilding, but surface-mounted metalclad accessories are the most durable in use.

1 To support an overhead cable run you need a catenary wire. First screw in a straining eye to a tall post fixed in the ground (or to the wall of the house).

2 Fix the catenary cable between post and outbuilding, and link it to the straining eye with an adjustable hook and eye. Take up the slack.

3 You can now run in the supply cable, leaving plenty of slack where it loops up to the catenary. Attach it with cable ties at regular intervals.

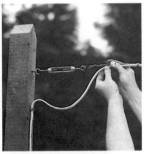

4 Within the outbuilding, install a small switchfuse unit with two fuseways: for socket outlets, and for lighting.

5 With metalclad accessories, run in the cable to each box, and add an earth core to link box and faceplate.

6 Sleeve this earth core and link it to the accessory's earth terminal. Connect the other cores and attach the faceplate.

140 POWER TO OUTBUILDINGS AND GARDENS

Unless you want your garden to look like an extension to the national grid, you'll find it much neater to bury long cable runs underground. This will mean digging a trench at least 500mm (20in) deep from where the cable leaves the house to wherever the run terminates. Try to avoid taking the cable across the flowerbeds or vegetable plots, where deep-digging could disturb or damage it; the best place is alongside a path or wall.

If you're laying armoured or MICC cable, put a layer of sand in the bottom of the trench first. Then lay the cable and cover it with a layer of sieved soil before refilling the trench. If you're using conduit lay out the run carefully, then thread the cable through and solvent-weld the couplers to link each length. Cut the last section to length,

add elbows and further short lengths to bring the cable up the house or outbuilding walls, and finish off the run with a further elbow and conduit length to take the cable through the wall.

Where the garden end of the cable is supplying a light or power point, make sure that you install weatherproof fittings; special sealed switches and threaded plug-and-socket outlets are available for outdoor use.

If you're powering pumps and lights for an outdoor pool, you may prefer to use low-voltage equipment and install a transformer in the house or garage. The low-voltage cable, usually at 12V, need not be buried since there is no risk of getting a dangerous shock if you were to accidentally cut the cable. Keep any socket outlets well away from the pool.

Running cables underground
Right: If you're laying cable underground, it must be buried at least 500mm (20in) deep. You can use ordinary PVC-sheathed cable if it's enclosed in conduit (A); armoured cable can be used unprotected, but has to be connected to a conversion box at each end of the run with a special coupler (B).
Below: Low-voltage cable fed from a transformer can be laid on or just below the surface. The transformer itself must be under cover.

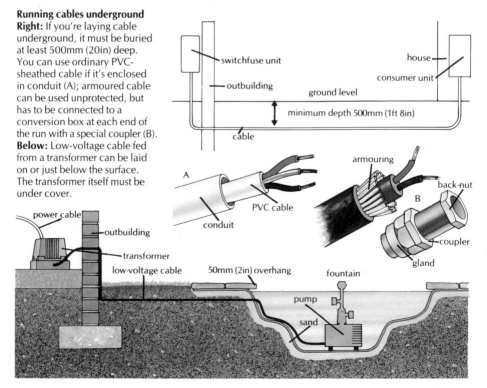

switchfuse unit

outbuilding

cable

house

consumer unit

ground level

minimum depth 500mm (1ft 8in)

A

PVC cable

conduit

armouring

back-nut

B

coupler

gland

power cable

outbuilding

transformer

low-voltage cable

50mm (2in) overhang

fountain

pump

sand

POWER TO OUTBUILDINGS AND GARDENS 141

1 You can run ordinary PVC-sheathed cable underground in rigid PVC conduit. Dig a trench and lay out the conduit sections, checking that they align neatly.

2 Thread the cable through the conduit, taking it through elbows where the run changes direction – passing through the house and outbuilding walls, for example.

3 When the cable is threaded through the whole run, work along it, solvent-welding the joins as you go. Brush on the solvent, assemble the joint and twist it to secure a good bond.

4 If you're using armoured cable you won't need conduit. To prepare the cable end for connection to the conversion box, slip on a PVC hood and gland nut.

5 Slip on the gland and coupler, and trim the armouring on the cable so that it ends at the bottom of the thread on the gland. Push up the gland nut and tighten it.

6 Feed the cable end into the conversion box and attach the back-nut to the coupler. Tighten it with a spanner. The coupler allows more room in the box for connections.

7 Attach an earth core to the box, and fit a block of three connectors to join the cores of the armoured and PVC cables.

8 Use PVC-sheathed cable to complete the circuit within the building. Link the box earth to the connector block.

9 Finally connect the other cores within the connector block and fit the lid. A similar box is used in the house.

142 FITTING A DOOR BELL

Most people choose battery-powered door bells because they are simple to install — all you have to do is to fix the bell housing to the wall, the bell push to the front door post, and link the two with a length of twin-core bell wire. But batteries do run down, and won't power an illuminated bell push for long. Instead, use a transformer and run your bell and bell push from the mains.

For this, you need a special bell transformer, usually having three different low-voltage outputs. Which you use depends on the model of bell or chime you have chosen; the manufacturer's instructions will tell you what

voltage is needed. From the transformer, run twin-core bell wire to the bell, on to the push and back to the transformer. The transformer is either linked to a spare 5A fuseway in the consumer unit with 1mm^2 cable, or is linked into a nearby lighting circuit via a three-terminal junction box.

You can add a second bell in series with the first; both will ring when the push is depressed. You can even wire in a change-over switch (an ordinary two-way light switch), as shown, so you can switch off the door bell and switch on a garden bell when you are out of doors.

Connecting up bells
Right: With battery bells the circuit is extremely simple – the bell push simply makes or breaks the circuit. In practice, the battery is within the bell housing, and a length of bell wire links it to the bell push.
Below: Mains bells are run from a 5A fuseway via a transformer. Here, two bells are wired up via a changeover switch, allowing one or the other to be switched off as required. One could be out of doors, or bells could be fitted at both front and back doors.

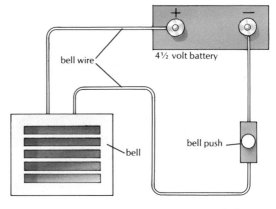

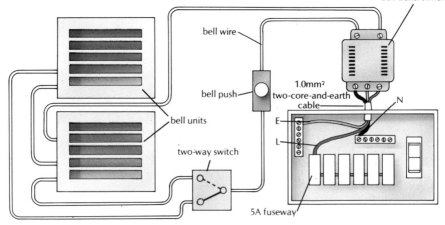

TV SOCKETS/HEATING CONTROLS 143

Television and FM radio sets are linked to their aerials with special coaxial cable. This is often run down the outside wall of the house from a chimney stack aerial, entering the house through a hole drilled in a wall or window frame. At that point a small junction box is usually fitted, and a second length of cable with a coaxial plug at each end is used to link the set to the junction box. This looks untidy, and it's much neater to run the coaxial cable inside the house. It can be fed into the roof under a tile near the aerial, and then taken in conduit to the room where the set is installed. The conduit terminates at a TV socket outlet (flush or surface-mounted), and the short TV lead is plugged into it.

When both TV and FM aerials are installed, two downleads will be needed — an added expense. The solution here is to fit a special isolated TV/FM twin socket outlet in the loft, a second one in the living room, and to link the two with just a single down-lead. Each appliance aerial lead is then plugged into its appropriate outlet on the socket faceplate.

Remember that you are not allowed to have a TV socket outlet and a mains socket outlet mounted in a dual box. They must be mounted in separate enclosures, even if for convenience and neatness they are set side by side on the wall.

Central heating controls

The way in which your central heating controls are wired up will depend to a large extent on what controls you have and on the manufacturer's own wiring instructions. However, power is usually provided via a switched fused connection unit containing a 5A fuse and linked as a spur to a ring main. The circuit can also be wired back directly to a spare 5A fuseway in the consumer unit; this means that a failure of the ring main fuse won't affect the heating.

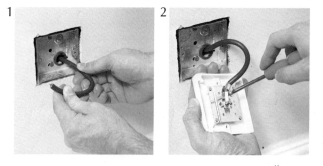

1   2

1 Run the coaxial cable from the aerial to the point where you want to install the socket. The cable can be run in conduit buried in the plaster, or can be dropped down wall cavities.
2 Strip back the sheathing and screening wires; clamp these in the special clip and then connect the central core to the aerial terminal. Finally, attach the faceplate to the box.

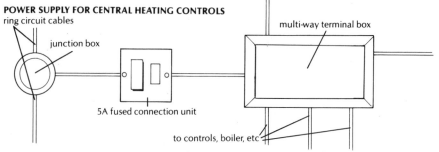

POWER SUPPLY FOR CENTRAL HEATING CONTROLS
ring circuit cables

junction box

multi-way terminal box

5A fused connection unit

to controls, boiler, etc

144 REWIRING YOUR HOUSE

Some of the tell-tale signs that your house needs rewiring have already been mentioned, and if you have been contemplating any electrical work you may already be aware of the short-comings of your wiring system. Here's a checklist of the danger signs:

Under the stairs . . .
● a multitude of separate old-fashioned switchfuse units
● double-pole fusing — a fusebox with fuses in both the live and neutral poles.

Around the house . . .
● round tumbler switches mounted on wooden pattresses
● round-pin socket outlets on pattresses or skirting boards
● old-fashioned ceiling roses, and pendant lights hanging from twisted twin flex
● adaptors being used to make up for a shortage of sockets
● overheating at sockets.

Behind the scenes . . .
● single-core cables run in light-gauge metal conduit, often rusty
● rubber or lead alloy sheathed cables
● crumbling core insulation behind switches and sockets
● missing earth continuity conductors on circuits.

You may find that parts of your system *have* been rewired — for example, a new cooker circuit or a ring main may have been installed. If these extensions were done properly, with PVC-sheathed cable run back to new switch-fuse units, they can probably be left as part of the new system. However, it's best to have them checked by your local electricity board or a qualified electrician first. Don't be deceived by the presence of new cable (which may just be a spur added to an existing — and dangerous — circuit) or new accessories (a popular and purely cosmetic dodge often perpetrated by house sellers); such recent additions

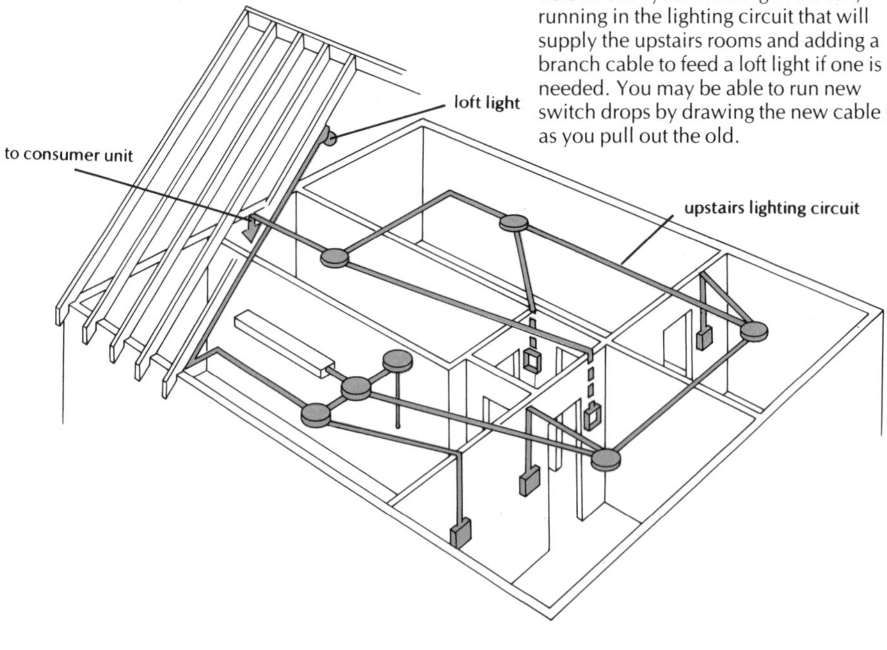

Below: Start your rewiring in the loft, running in the lighting circuit that will supply the upstairs rooms and adding a branch cable to feed a loft light if one is needed. You may be able to run new switch drops by drawing the new cable in as you pull out the old.

to consumer unit

loft light

upstairs lighting circuit

may be reusable, but only after proper rewiring has been carried out.

The actual task of rewiring a house is not especially difficult; it's really the sum of all the techniques and projects already described. However, it's a time-consuming and disruptive job best carried out in an empty house, or in planned stages in an occupied one. It needs some careful estimating for materials, too.

The first stage is to work out exactly where you are going to need lighting points, socket outlets and special provision for accessories such as cookers and immersion heaters, central heating electrics, showers and circuits to outbuildings. Start with a sketch plan of your house, and mark in everything you can think of. Then start to break the system up into circuits; remember, a lighting circuit should feed a maximum of twelve (and an optimum of eight) lighting points, and a ring main a maximum floor area of 100sq m (1076sq ft). In a typical home, your circuit requirements on a well-planned system could be:

Requirement	Rating
Upstairs lighting circuit	5A
Downstairs lighting circuit	5A
Radial circuit to immersion heater	15A
Radial circuit to instantaneous shower	30A
Radial circuit to outbuilding	30A
Ring circuit to first floor	30A
Ring circuit to ground floor (except kitchen)	30A
Ring circuit to kitchen only	30A
Radial circuit to cooker	45A

That's nine circuits already, not including 'luxury' circuits for freezers, mains bells or central heating electrics. This total will decree what size of consumer unit you need; remember to allow for

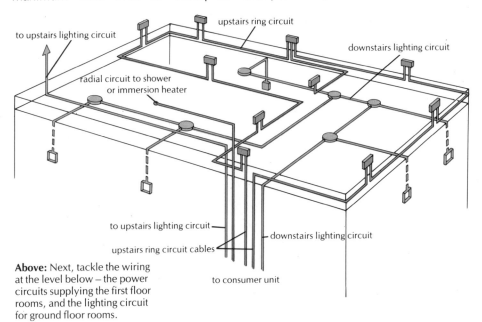

Above: Next, tackle the wiring at the level below – the power circuits supplying the first floor rooms, and the lighting circuit for ground floor rooms.

146 REWIRING YOUR HOUSE

further room in it if you want an integral R.C.D. instead of a mainswitch as an isolator unit. Choose a unit fitted with MCBs, or possibly cartridge fuses, not rewirable fuses.

The next job is to plan the room-by-room requirements in more detail so you can total the number of electrical accessories of each type you will need. Do not forget to include mounting boxes as required.

Thirdly, you need a rough estimate of the amount of cable to buy. There's little point in measuring cable runs accurately except on heavy-duty circuits such as those to cookers and showers, where the cable is very expensive; simply buy 50m drums of $2.5mm^2$ and $1mm^2$ two-core and earth cable for power and lighting circuits respectively, plus shorter lengths of other cable types required ($4mm^2$, $1mm^2$ three-core and earth for two-way switching, etc.). You can always buy another drum, or cable by the metre, later, should you run out. Add a quantity of $1mm^2$ round three-core flex for pendant lights, heat-resisting flex for immersion heaters, and other equipment and sundries such as PVC channelling or conduit, BESA boxes and cable clips. Then take your full shopping list to at least two wholesalers and ask for a quotation. Make sure that all accessories are made to the appropriate British Standards (BS 1363 for socket outlets, 5733 for connection units, 3676 for switches, 4177 for cooker control units, 3052 for shaver supply units, 67 for ceiling

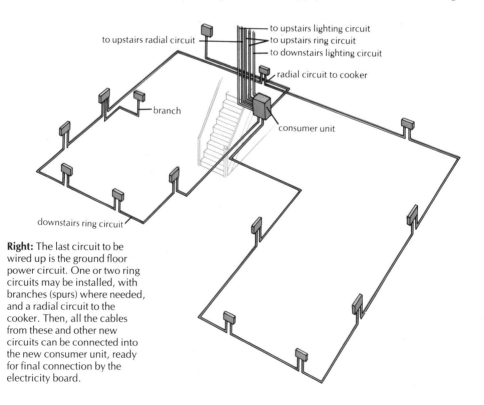

to upstairs radial circuit
to upstairs lighting circuit
to upstairs ring circuit
to downstairs lighting circuit
radial circuit to cooker
branch
consumer unit
downstairs ring circuit

Right: The last circuit to be wired up is the ground floor power circuit. One or two ring circuits may be installed, with branches (spurs) where needed, and a radial circuit to the cooker. Then, all the cables from these and other new circuits can be connected into the new consumer unit, ready for final connection by the electricity board.

roses, 6004 for cables and 6500 for flexes).

The actual job is best split up into stages to minimise disruption. Start in the loft, wiring up the bedroom lighting circuits and adding extras such as loft lights and TV aerial sockets. Then move to the next level down — the void between first and ground floors — and tackle the ground floor lighting circuit and the first floor power circuits. Finally, tackle the ground floor power circuits (unless you have solid ground floors, in which case these will also be run at ceiling level, with vertical chases in the walls carrying cable down to the socket outlets).

Throughout, chop out and fix mounting boxes first, so you can measure and cut cable runs precisely. On an exten-sive rewire, you're likely to be choosing new positions for most accessories anyway, so you can leave existing items working as you run in the new circuits. Then run all your circuit cables neatly back to the new consumer unit position, which doesn't *have* to be next to the meter. It may be more convenient on a hall or kitchen wall, and is simply linked via a sub-main cable to a new main isolator switch next to the meter.

At this point, you will have to notify your local electricity board to come and disconnect the old switchgear, connect up your new consumer unit and test the installation. This is the moment of truth, where good workmanship and careful planning will have resulted in a sound and safe job.

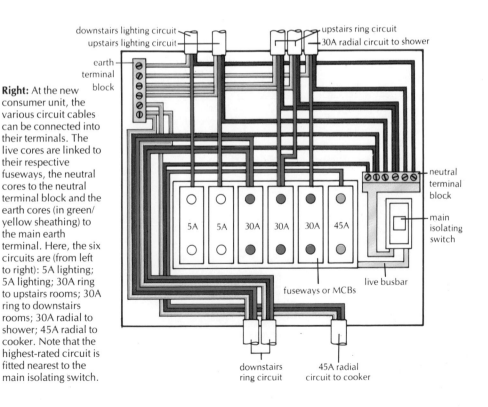

Right: At the new consumer unit, the various circuit cables can be connected into their terminals. The live cores are linked to their respective fuseways, the neutral cores to the neutral terminal block and the earth cores (in green/ yellow sheathing) to the main earth terminal. Here, the six circuits are (from left to right): 5A lighting; 5A lighting; 30A ring to upstairs rooms; 30A ring to downstairs rooms; 30A radial to shower; 45A radial to cooker. Note that the highest-rated circuit is fitted nearest to the main isolating switch.

downstairs lighting circuit
upstairs lighting circuit
upstairs ring circuit
30A radial circuit to shower
earth terminal block
neutral terminal block
main isolating switch
5A 5A 30A 30A 30A 45A
fuseways or MCBs
live busbar
downstairs ring circuit
45A radial circuit to cooker

148 PLUGS AND FUSES

Because many homes still have round-pin sockets, electrical appliance manufacturers usually sell their equipment without a plug (and most shops expect you to pay extra for one when you buy an appliance, even though you can't use it without one). So you will often need to fit a plug to any new appliance you buy, and you may also have to replace an existing plug that has been damaged. Because the plug is such a vital link between the appliance and the mains, it is vital that you do this properly. There are several rules to remember, whatever type of plug you are fitting:

1 colour coding of flex cores In appliances (and flex) made since about 1970, the live core is sheathed in brown PVC, the neutral core in blue PVC and the earth in green/yellow striped PVC. Earlier equipment and older flex had the same colour codes as mains cable — red for live, black for neutral and green for earth; make sure you know which is which. On continental appliances, check with the manufacturer or his agent if the colour coding is different from this.

2 terminals With the plug open and the inside facing you, the top terminal linked to the larger pin is the earth

1 To connect new flex to a plug, first split and cut away about 38mm (1½in) of the flex sheathing. Take care not to cut through the insulation on the inner cores.

2 Lay the cable in the plug and cut each core long enough to reach its appropriate terminal when the flex sheathing is positioned over the cable grip. Strip each core.

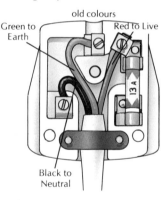

old colours

Green to Earth

Red to Live

13 A

Black to Neutral

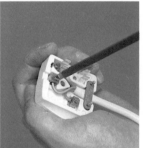

3 Clamp the flex sheathing in the cable clamp, and then link each core to the appropriate terminal as shown. Check that the terminal screws are tight.

4 Clip in a cartridge fuse of the correct rating for the appliance. Then check all connections again before fitting the top and tightening the screw.

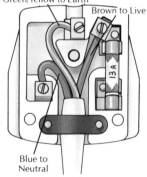

new colours

Green/Yellow to Earth

Brown to Live

13 A

Blue to Neutral

Old flex cores are a different colour to new flex cores, as shown above.

(usually marked E or ⏚). The bottom right terminal (marked L) is live and the bottom left (marked N) is neutral. Remember that the BRown core goes to the Bottom Right terminal, the BLue core to the Bottom Left terminal.

3 insulation There should be no bare strands visible inside the plug; the core insulation should reach right up to the terminal. The outer sheathing should be clamped securely in the cord grip.

4 two-core flex This is used only on double-insulated appliances (marked ▣) and certain table lamp fittings with plastic lampholders. In this case, there is no earth core; the other cores are connected as above.

5 fuses In fused plugs, fit a brown 13A fuse for appliances rated at over 700W (and for colour televisions), a red 3A fuse otherwise. You will find the appliance rating stamped on or attached to its body. Test whether fuses have blown with a continuity tester, or by holding them across the open end of a metal-cased torch with one end of the fuse on the casing and the other on the end of the battery. If the fuse is intact, the torch will work when switched on.

Mending a circuit fuse

When a circuit fuse blows, there is no point in mending it until you have tracked down and cured the fault that caused it to blow in the first place (see page 151). It may be obvious which circuit fuse has blown, but if not, switch off the main isolator switch and remove each fuse from its holder in turn. If you have rewirable fuses, you will be able to see at a glance which one is at fault, but with cartridge fuses you will probably have to test each fuse with a continuity tester (or by using the torch trick explained previously). Mend the fuse, then replace the other fuses and restore the power.

If you have MCBs, all you have to do to restore the power is to press the reset button or move the switch to ON.

1 To replace blown fuse wire in a rewirable fuse, loosen the terminal screws and remove the remains of the old wire. Then thread in new wire of the correct rating.
2 Cut off the excess, and connect each end to the terminals, winding it round once. Don't pull the wire taut. Tighten each terminal screw and then replace the fuse.
3 With cartridge fuses, simply open the fuse carrier, take out the old fuse and insert a new one of the same rating.
4 You can easily test whether cartridge fuses are intact by holding them across the open end of a metal-cased torch, one end touching the battery and the other resting on the torch body. With the torch switched on, the bulb will light if the fuse is intact.

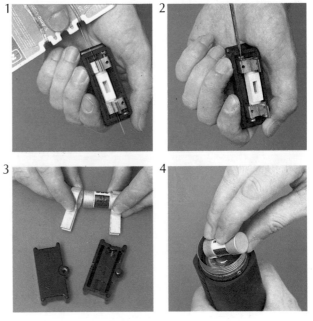

150 **FLEX**

Fit new flex to an appliance as soon as it shows any signs of damage or wear. You are more likely to get a shock or cause a short circuit from faulty flex than from almost any other fault in the electrical system, since live cores can so easily be exposed.

It's important to choose flex of the correct type and current rating for the job it has to do. Choose two-core flex for double-insulated appliances (marked with a double-square symbol ▣), and for pendant and table lamps with non-metallic fittings; go for three-core flex in all other cases. Use ordinary PVC-sheathed flex for most jobs, braided flex for electric heaters and

fires, unkinkable flex for portable kitchen appliances such as irons and kettles, and heat-resisting flex in light pendants with bulbs over 100W and also for wiring up immersion heaters. Choose the size of flex according to the appliance rating:

Flex size (mm^2)	0.5	0.75	1.00	1.5
Appliance rating (W)	700	1400	2400	3000

NEVER extend flex except with a proper one-piece flex connector. If you are using an extension plug-and-socket, connect the male part (with the pins) to the appliance, the female part to the mains — NEVER the other way round.

1 To replace a flex, unplug the appliance, and open the casing to reveal the terminals. Disconnect the flex, saving any protective sleeving.

2 If the flex is held by a cable clamp, undo this and then draw the old flex out through the grommet attached to the appliance casing.

3 Feed the new flex in through the grommet. It's easier to do this before you strip and prepare the cable ends.

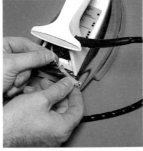

4 Finally, connect the new flex cores to the terminals within the appliance, reusing any protective sleeving.

Extending flex safely
Below: If you're extending flex with a two-part plug and socket, ALWAYS link the plug part to the appliance flex and the socket part to the mains. Otherwise, the pins will be live if the parts are separated.

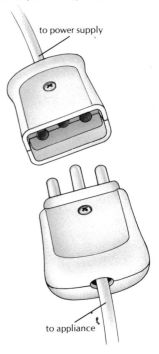

to power supply

to appliance

When something electrical fails to work around the house, the fault is usually fairly simple to locate and cure. With a knowledge of your electrical system and how it works, all you have to do is check things in a logical order until you pin-point the problem.

Turn off the power at the fusebox or consumer unit before investigating any faults on fixed appliances or circuit wiring; unplug any portable appliance before starting work on it.

A Pendant light doesn't work

1 turn off light switch, replace bulb.
2 turn off main switch, check lighting circuit fuse/MCB, replace/reset if necessary, restore power; if fuse blows again or light won't work, go to 3.
3 with power off, open rose and lampholder at offending light, look for loose connections or broken cores, and strip and remake connections as necessary; check that flex cores are hooked over anchorages, replace covers and restore power; if fuse blows again or light won't work, go to 4.
4 with power off, disconnect pendant flex and use continuity tester to check each core in turn; replace the flex if any core fails, replace rose/lampholder covers and restore power; if fuse blows again, go to FAULT C.

B Electrical appliance doesn't work

1 plug in appliance at another socket; if it works, suspect fault at original socket (FAULT C); if it doesn't, go to 2.
2 fit new plug fuse of correct rating.
3 check flex connections at plug terminals and remake if necessary.
4 with appliance unplugged, open casing and check connections at terminal block; remake if necessary.
5 check appliance flex continuity as in A4, and replace flex if necessary with new flex of correct current rating.
6 if checks 2 to 5 fail, suspect circuit fault (FAULT C) or appliance failure.

C Whole circuit is dead

1 switch off all lights/disconnect all appliances linked to affected circuit.
2 replace circuit fuse (using fuse/wire of the correct rating) or reset MCB.
3 switch on lights/plug in appliances one by one; note which one causes the fuse to blow/MCB to trip, then:
4 isolate the offending light/appliance (and check as in FAULTS A and B), then replace fuse/reset MCB again.
5 if circuit is still dead, check switches and socket outlets on circuit for physical damage or faulty connections at terminals, and replace or reconnect.
6 replace damaged circuit cable if pierced by drill or nail.
7 if the circuit fault persists, call in a qualified electrician.

D Whole house system is dead

1 check with neighbours to see if there is a local power cut.
2 if an R.C.D. is fitted to the system, check whether it has tripped off, and reset it if necessary; if it cannot be reset, there is a fault somewhere on the system. Run through FAULTS A, B and C, or call an electrician.
3 call electricity board to check main service fuse (you must not tamper with this yourself).

E Electric shock received

1 if the shock was minor, isolate the offending appliance for checking or replace the accessory concerned.
2 if someone receives a major shock, try to turn off the power, grab their clothes (NOT bare flesh, or you will get a shock if the power is still on) and drag them away from the power source; administer artificial ventilation or external chest compression — see page 152 for more details — and call a doctor or ambulance.
3 have the fault tracked down immediately and put right by an electrician; a repeat could kill.

152 FIRST AID FOR ELECTRIC SHOCK

If you or a member of your family receive a slight shock from an appliance, STOP USING IT. Unplug it immediately; check the connections at the plug (page 148) and terminal block (page 150), remaking them if necessary; check and replace the flex, too, if this is suspect (page 150). As an extra safety precaution, have it checked over by a qualified electrician. If the shock is received from a switch, socket outlet or other accessory, call a qualified electrician to check the circuit and look for any other faults that may be present.

If someone receives a severe electric shock, they may involuntarily grip the source of the current. IMMEDIATELY turn off the current if a switch is nearby, or drag them away by their clothing. DON'T TOUCH their flesh or you will receive a shock, too.

If conscious, but visibly shocked (deathly pallor, sweating, rapid and shallow breathing), lay the casualty flat on the back on a blanket with legs raised slightly on a pillow, unless you suspect leg fractures. Turn the head to one side to keep the airway clear, and cover the patient with a blanket. DON'T apply a hot water bottle. DON'T move the patient unnecessarily, nor give them anything by mouth (if thirsty, moisten the lips with water), nor allow them to smoke.

Cool any burns by flooding them gently with cold water. Then cover with a sterile dressing (a clean pad of non-fluffy material will do), securing it with a bandage. DON'T apply ointments, lotions or fats to the burn, and DON'T break any blisters or remove loose skin. CALL AN AMBULANCE.

If unconscious, lay the casualty in the recovery position shown below, placing the limbs so that they support the body in this position. Keep the airway clear by tilting the head back and bringing the jaw forwards. Cover with a blanket and CALL AN AMBULANCE IMMEDIATELY. Watch for signs of cessation of breathing and heartbeat, giving artificial ventilation and external chest compression respectively, as necessary (see opposite).

When correctly placed in the recovery position (right), the casualty's limbs provide safe and comfortable support for the entire body, ensuring that the airway remains open. For the latter, the head should be tilted back and the jaw brought forward. Rest the casualty's body on one side with the lower arm parallel to the back and the upper arm bent to support the upper body. Bend the upper leg as shown, bringing the thigh forwards to support the lower body. It is important that the head remains tilted back so that the casualty's airway is kept open. This position also ensures that any fluid or vomit is free to drain away.

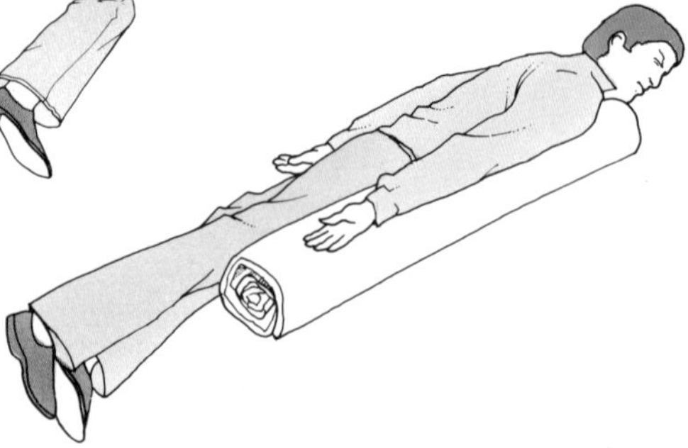

If you suspect fractures of the arms or legs, or if the casualty is lying in a confined space, use a rolled blanket or similar item to provide support as shown below.

FIRST AID FOR ELECTRIC SHOCK 153

1 Before commencing mouth-to-mouth ventilation, turn the casualty's head to one side and remove any obstructions from the mouth with your index finger. Don't delay doing this as you must begin ventilation immediately. Then open the casualty's airway by tilting the head backwards and pushing the chin upwards.
2 Making sure the casualty's head is tilted back to keep the airway open, take a deep breath and pinch the casualty's nostrils closed with your finger and thumb.
3 Seal your lips around the casualty's mouth and blow into it. Watch for the casualty's chest to rise, remove your mouth, exhale any excess air, and watch the chest fall. Repeat the process, making the first four breaths as rapid as possible. Check for a pulse at the casualty's neck by placing the tips of your fingers in the hollow of the neck between the voice box and adjacent muscle – just to one side of the throat. Continue at normal breathing rate until the casualty is breathing normally. Then place the casualty in the recovery position (opposite). If mouth-to-mouth ventilation is unsuccessful on its own (casualty has no pulse, is deathly pale and has developed a blueness around the mouth and ear lobes), it should be used with external chest compression (below) at once.

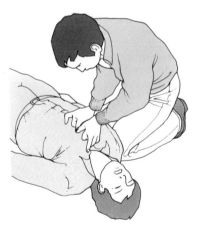

First, locate the centre of the lower half of the breast bone by placing your thumbs midway between the sternal notch at the top of the chest and the intersection of the rib margins at the bottom (above, left). Place your hands as shown at this mid point (above, right), locking the fingers together and keeping them clear of the patient's ribs.

With your arms straight, position yourself above the casualty until they are vertical and then press down 40-50mm (1½-2in). Release the pressure and repeat the procedure 15 times at a rate of 80 per minute. Give two full breaths of mouth-to-mouth ventilation (above) and then continue the compression procedure for one minute.

Check for heartbeat (as described above) and then continue the compression/ventilation cycle described, checking the heartbeat every three minutes. When the heartbeat returns, continue mouth-to-mouth ventilation until the casualty is breathing normally.

amp short for ampere (A), used to measure the flow of electricity through a circuit or appliance.

cable conductors (or 'cores') covered with a protective semi-rigid insulating sheath, used to wire up the individual circuits on a wiring system.

circuit any complete path for an electric current, allowing it to pass along a 'live' conductor to where it's needed, and then to return to its source along a 'neutral' conductor.

conductor the metallic current-carrying 'cores' within cable or flex.

consumer unit unit governing the supply of electricity to all circuits, and containing a main on-off switch and fuses or circuit breakers protecting the circuits emanating from it.

earthing the provision of a continuous conductor on circuits to protect the user from certain electrical faults. Earth conductors are sheathed in green/yellow striped PVC; earth terminals are marked E or ⊕ .

residual current-breaker device (R.C.D.) device fitted to circuits to detect current leakage that could start a fire or cause an electric shock.

flex short for 'flexible cord' — cores wrapped in a flexible outer sheath, used to link appliances and lights to the house's fixed wiring circuits.

fuse protective device designed to cut off the flow of current in a circuit in the event of a fault.

gang used to describe the number of units — switches or socket outlets — contained in one electrical accessory. A two-gang switch has two switches mounted on one faceplate.

insulation the PVC sheathing on and around the cores of cable and flex.

lamp correct 'trade' term for a light bulb or tube.

live used to describe the cable or flex core taking current to where it is needed, or any terminal or part to which the core is connected. Live cable cores are colour-coded in red, live flex cores in brown. Live terminals are marked L.

miniature circuit breaker (MCB) a device used instead of fuses to isolate a circuit.

neutral used to describe cores carrying current back to its source, or any terminal to which the core is connected. Neutral cable cores are colour-coded black, neutral flex cores are blue. Neutral terminals are marked N.

one-way used to describe a switch with on-off control of the circuit to which it is fitted from that one point only. Two-way switches, used in pairs, offer control of the same circuit from two positions.

radial circuit a power or lighting circuit originating at the consumer unit and feeding one or more electrical accessories, terminating at the remotest one.

ring circuit a power circuit wired as a continuous loop, both ends of which are connected to the same terminals of the consumer unit.

single pole used to describe a switch that 'breaks' only the live side of the circuit it controls. A double-pole switch breaks both the live and neutral sides of the circuit.

spur a sub-circuit run as a branch line from an existing circuit to extend the number of accessories supplied.

unit a measure of the amount of electricity consumed by an appliance or system, the product of the power consumed (in watts) and the time during which it was supplied. One unit is 1 kilowatt-hour (kWh) — used by, for example, a 100W light bulb burning for 10 hours.

volt unit of electrical pressure (potential) difference. In most British homes, the mains voltage is 240V.

watt unit of power consumed by an appliance or circuit, the product of the mains voltage and the current drawn (in amps). 1000W = 1 kilowatt (kW).

Plumbing

Alan Wakeford

Consultant Editor Richard Wiles

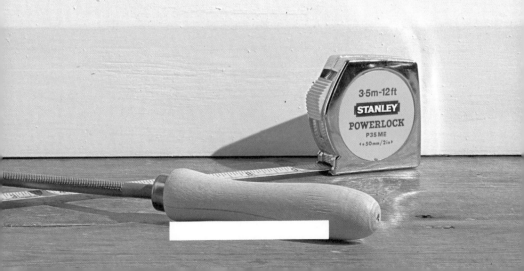

158 DOMESTIC PLUMBING EXPLAINED

How often do you think about the plumbing system in your house? Every day you use water for drinking and cooking, bathing and showering, and to flush WC cisterns, but for the most part because the system is out of sight it's usually out of mind as well. Indeed, a properly installed system will operate trouble-free for years, so why shouldn't you take it for granted that when you turn on a tap, water will come out of it?

This is not to say that you can ignore the plumbing totally, however. To work well, it does require some maintenance; leaking taps occasionally have to be dealt with, for instance, as do blocked drains. Emergencies, too, can arise unexpectedly, and sooner or later you may well want to make some modifications to the system.

There's something of a mystique about a plumbing system, but although the labyrinth of pipes may seem complicated, in reality it isn't. If something needs to be done, your first reaction may be to call in the plumber; however, with a basic knowledge of what's going on and a few practised skills, you'll be able to deal with most problems as they occur and to carry out a

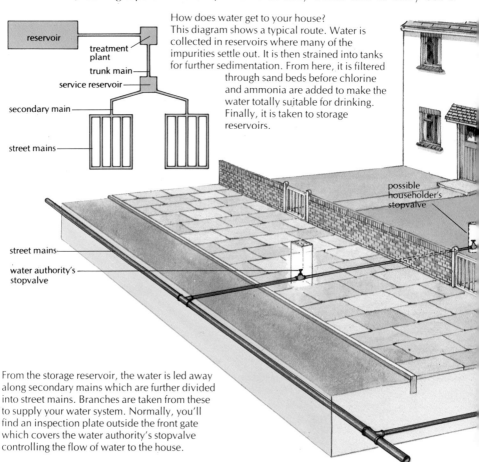

reservoir

treatment plant

trunk main

service reservoir

secondary main

street mains

How does water get to your house? This diagram shows a typical route. Water is collected in reservoirs where many of the impurities settle out. It is then strained into tanks for further sedimentation. From here, it is filtered through sand beds before chlorine and ammonia are added to make the water totally suitable for drinking. Finally, it is taken to storage reservoirs.

possible householder's stopvalve

street mains

water authority's stopvalve

From the storage reservoir, the water is led away along secondary mains which are further divided into street mains. Branches are taken from these to supply your water system. Normally, you'll find an inspection plate outside the front gate which covers the water authority's stopvalve controlling the flow of water to the house.

range of plumbing projects. You might eventually want to plumb in a new washing machine or bathroom suite, or replace a cold water cistern — each is well within your scope and nowadays made easier because modern fittings and copper or plastic pipe are light and easy to use. If you're prepared to take the time with plumbing projects, you can save a considerable amount of money in labour costs.

Normally, if you're replacing appliances and parts of the plumbing but you're not changing their positions, you won't need to obtain the relevant Building Regulations approval. But if you want to install a completely new handbasin, for example, there are regulations that you should take into account. These are pointed out later, but it is still worth contacting your local building inspector and local water authority to seek their guidance regarding your particular system.

Usually, there's little problem in supplying water to an appliance; what you have to be careful of is how you get rid of the waste, and the regulations are there to make sure this is done hygienically and efficiently. Don't ignore them.

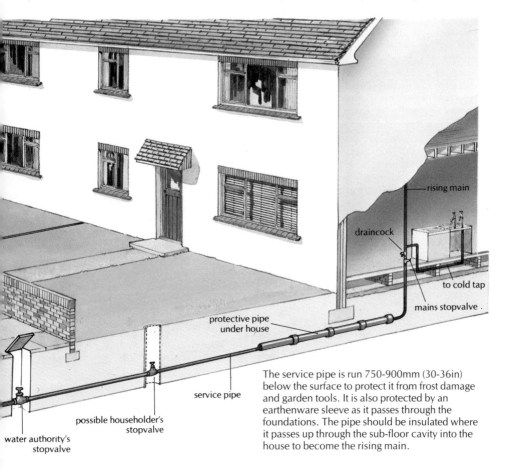

rising main

draincock

to cold tap

mains stopvalve

protective pipe under house

service pipe

possible householder's stopvalve

water authority's stopvalve

The service pipe is run 750-900mm (30-36in) below the surface to protect it from frost damage and garden tools. It is also protected by an earthenware sleeve as it passes through the foundations. The pipe should be insulated where it passes up through the sub-floor cavity into the house to become the rising main.

160 HOW WATER REACHES YOUR HOUSE

The local water authority is responsible for supplying your house with water and for the disposal of the waste and sewage. What happens on your property is your responsibility, although your plumbing system must still conform to regulations and byelaws.

The local water supply is distributed in a series of trunk mains, mains and submains — pipes that run underneath the street — and branches are taken from these to supply individual houses. Naturally, the water authority has ultimate control over the flow to your system by means of an isolating stopvalve situated at the foot of a guard pipe just outside your house. You'll recognise it by its metal cover, usually set in the pavement. Only the water authority should operate the valve.

From this valve onwards, the plumbing becomes your responsibility. Water reaches the house along what is now called the service pipe. Near to where it enters the house, there should be another stopvalve. You may find it under the kitchen sink or even under the stairs. It is vital to know where this valve is situated because it will enable you to turn off the domestic supply in an emergency.

Such a stopvalve has a habit of jamming open because it is operated so infrequently; it is sensible, therefore, to turn it off and on a couple of times a year. If you turn it back half a turn from fully open, it will be less prone to jamming, and won't affect the supply.

The stopvalve is where the plumbing really begins. Most houses have what is termed an 'indirect' cold supply, and at the hub of this system is a cold water storage cistern. Usually, it is sited in the loft and is supplied by the rising main, the pipe which continues from the service pipe. From here, water is fed under gravity pressure to the taps and WC cistern in the bathroom, and to the hot water cylinder. Water that has passed through the cistern is not considered to be suitable for drinking; the tap over the kitchen sink, then, is supplied direct from the rising main.

This type of system has a number of advantages, the most important being that there's a reservoir of water available — the cistern — for use if the mains supply is temporarily cut off. It also means that domestic water is supplied under an even but lower pressure than the mains, so reducing wear and tear on the system.

The alternative, largely outmoded set-up is known as a 'direct feed' system, whereby all the taps and WC cisterns are fed direct from the rising main, so they are all under mains pressure. However, this system still needs a cold water storage cistern to supply the hot water cylinder, and therefore the hot water pipes will be under gravity pressure.

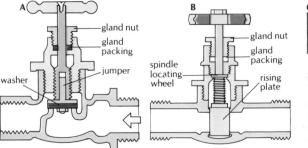

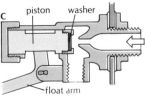

Stopvalves (A) are sited on the rising main, gate valves (B) on supply runs, and ballvalves (C) control the flow of water into cisterns.

HOW WATER REACHES YOUR HOUSE 161

The cold water system

Most of the cold taps and appliances in your home take their cold water from the main storage cistern. As the water flows under gravity pressure, the cistern must be higher than any of the outlets it supplies. Usually, it is situated in the loft, although it can be incorporated with a hot cylinder in what is termed a 'packaged' unit. The cistern itself is fed by the rising main which passes up through the house.

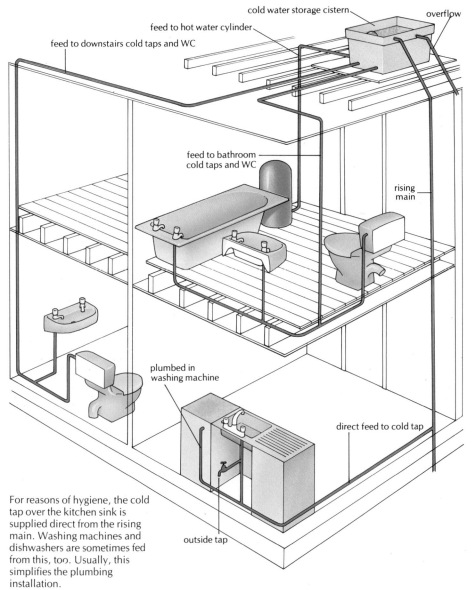

cold water storage cistern

overflow

feed to hot water cylinder

feed to downstairs cold taps and WC

feed to bathroom cold taps and WC

rising main

plumbed in washing machine

direct feed to cold tap

outside tap

For reasons of hygiene, the cold tap over the kitchen sink is supplied direct from the rising main. Washing machines and dishwashers are sometimes fed from this, too. Usually, this simplifies the plumbing installation.

162 HOT WATER SYSTEMS

Hot water at the turn of a tap whenever you want it is no longer considered a luxury — it's a necessity. There are now several ways in which this can be achieved, the simplest being an electric or gas instantaneous water heater (see page 219).

However, as with cold water systems, the commonest means of providing hot water is known as an indirect system. It revolves round a central heat source — a boiler or an immersion heater — and a storage cylinder which is fed from the cold water cistern. In the basic system, one where there's no combined central heating, a direct cylinder is used; water is drawn off from the bottom of the cylinder, fed to a boiler and then returned to the cylinder, where it's drawn off at the top

to supply the hot taps round the house. Or, there can be an immersion heater — rather like an electric kettle element — situated in the cylinder.

However, it is now more common to use an indirect cylinder, which is essential with a hot water central heating system. The cylinder incorporates a heat exchanger — a sort of 'radiator' made from a coil of tube or an enclosed jacket — which contains hot water heated by the boiler. As this water passes through the exchanger it heats the water in the cylinder, but, most importantly, it doesn't mix with it. The advantage of this is that it cuts down boiler scale as only a relatively small amount of water recycles round this 'primary circuit'. At the same time it cuts down boiler wear.

An indirect hot water supply

An indirect hot water system is really two hot water systems rolled into one. It incorporates a primary circuit which runs from the boiler to a heat exchanger in the cylinder. This heats the water that is drawn off for use in the bathroom, kitchen and possibly a cloakroom – the secondary circuit.

Because it is a separate circuit, the primary system needs its own feed and expansion cistern to ensure it never runs short of water. If it did, the boiler could overheat dangerously. Fortunately, it only requires a relatively small amount of water which is being continually recycled. This reduces the effects of hard water scale and allows corrosion inhibitors to be added to prolong the life of the boiler.

Providing the boiler has the capacity, a 'wet' central heating system can be run from the primary circuit as well.

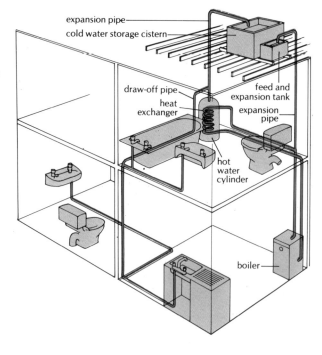

expansion pipe
cold water storage cistern
draw-off pipe
heat exchanger
feed and expansion tank
expansion pipe
hot water cylinder
boiler

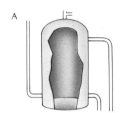

Depending on the type of hot water system being installed, different types of cylinder have to be fitted. A direct hot water supply requires cylinder (A), while cylinder (B) is used on an indirect system. (It can also be used as a direct cylinder if the primary tappings are blanked off.) The third cylinder (C) is part of an indirect hot and cold packaged system.

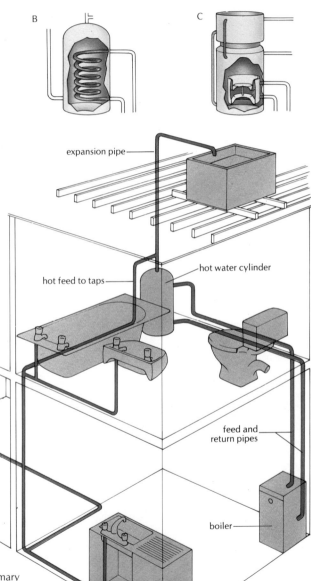

expansion pipe

hot water cylinder

hot feed to taps

feed and return pipes

boiler

A direct hot water supply
With this system there is no primary circuit. The water is fed into the cylinder from the cold water cistern. It passes through the boiler where it is heated and is returned to the top of the cylinder from where it is drawn off.

164 DRAINAGE SYSTEMS

When you pull the plug in a bath or basin, or flush a WC, it is obvious that the water has to go somewhere. It is the job of the waste water and soil system to carry this unwanted water away efficiently and hygienically through special seals called 'traps' and branch waste pipes, which feed into a large pipe known as the 'soil stack'. This is linked by an underground pipe to the main drainage system. Alternatively, in rural areas, the waste can be taken to a cess pit or septic tank. Sometimes, the system also has to deal with rainwater.

The regulations regarding the construction and adaptation of waste systems are quite stringent and are an important factor to take into account when modifying or extending the plumbing in your house. In fact, you are responsible for the waste system up to the point where it enters the main sewer; that means you have to clear any blockages. If your house was built before 1937 and has a shared drainage system where several houses discharge into the same branch of the main sewer, then the local authority is responsible for keeping the branch clean. You and your neighbours, however, have to deal with blockages and maintenance. So if you are in doubt about who is responsible for what, check with the local authority.

Single stack drainage

Now the preferred method of dealing with domestic waste, the 'single stack' system consists of a single soil stack, set inside on new buildings to give added

Single stack drainage
On a single stack drainage system, as shown on the right, there is only one soil pipe and this is sited in the house unless the system is a conversion from a two-pipe layout. Usually, all the waste pipes are fed into this pipe, except where it is more convenient for ground floor appliances to discharge over yard gullies, or for a WC to be connected directly to the branch drain via an inspection chamber.

Two-pipe drainage
The older two-pipe drainage system is illustrated on the facing page. Here, upstairs WCs discharge into a soil pipe while waste from other appliances is fed to hopper heads or trapped yard gullies.

In both types of system the soil pipe is continued above eaves level and vented to the atmosphere. It is topped by a wire mesh or plastic grille to prevent birds nesting in its end. Rainwater downpipes discharge into trapped gullies.

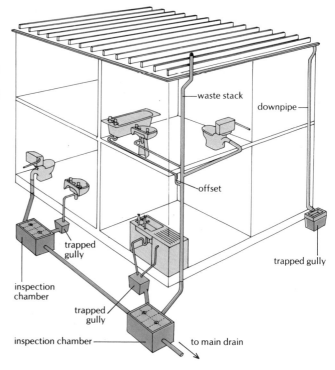

waste stack

downpipe

offset

trapped gully

trapped gully

inspection chamber

trapped gully

inspection chamber

to main drain

protection against frost. All the branch waste pipes from the bathroom, and sometimes the kitchen, discharge into this main stack. Kitchen waste water, however, can still be discharged over a yard gully, and a downstairs WC can be linked directly to the underground drainage system.

Two-pipe system

Before the single stack arrangement, the 'two-pipe' system was used. It differentiates between 'soil waste' from a WC and waste from a bath, basin or sink. Soil waste is fed into a soil pipe, which is connected directly to the underground drain, while the waste water is taken to a second pipe, which discharges over a gully incorporating a 'trap': this is an airtight seal of water in a U-shaped pipe. You'll recognise such a system by the open 'hopper head' at the top of this second pipe.

Where does rainwater go?

Rainwater falling on the roof of your home drains into the gutters and from here it is taken by a downpipe to discharge into an open gully, incorporating a trap. Then there are a number of options. Rarely is it fed into the main sewer because in periods of high rainfall it is doubtful whether that could cope with the excess water. Instead, there may be a storm drain which runs along with the main foul sewer, but if there isn't one the water is taken to a 'soakaway' (basically, a pit filled with rubble and covered with topsoil) where it can percolate back to the earth.

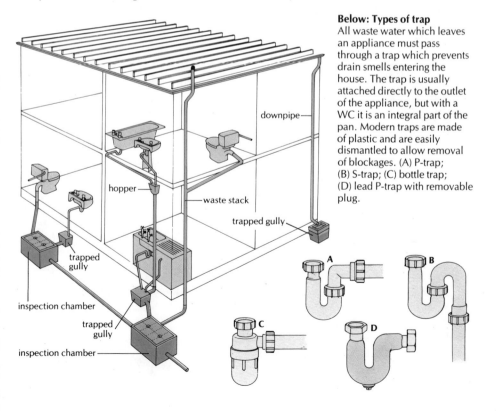

Below: Types of trap
All waste water which leaves an appliance must pass through a trap which prevents drain smells entering the house. The trap is usually attached directly to the outlet of the appliance, but with a WC it is an integral part of the pan. Modern traps are made of plastic and are easily dismantled to allow removal of blockages. (A) P-trap; (B) S-trap; (C) bottle trap; (D) lead P-trap with removable plug.

downpipe

hopper

waste stack

trapped gully

trapped gully

inspection chamber

trapped gully

inspection chamber

166 TOOLS AND FITTINGS FOR PLUMBING WORK

One of the beauties of modern plumbing is that you only have to learn a few techniques before you can tackle a wide range of plumbing jobs around the home, and you may already have many of the tools you will need. Of the few specialised tools required, most can be hired, but if you intend to carry out a considerable amount of plumbing it's worth buying at least some of them.

At the simplest level of plumbing, all the work may entail is disconnecting a couple of swivel tap connectors, unscrewing a trap, fixing a new basin where the old one used to be and then connecting all the fittings to it. Providing you can use a spanner, the job should not pose too many problems.

Invariably, however, the work is going to be more complicated than this, and you may end up having to modify or reroute the pipe runs themselves. More ambitiously, if you want to install, say, a completely new pipe run leading to a new basin, you'll have to fit a branch to the existing system and connect up a new waste run. It is in connection with this that most of the skills — measuring, cutting, joining, bending and connecting pipework to appliances — have to be used.

Although the use of hot and cold plastic supply pipes is becoming increasingly popular and adaptors are

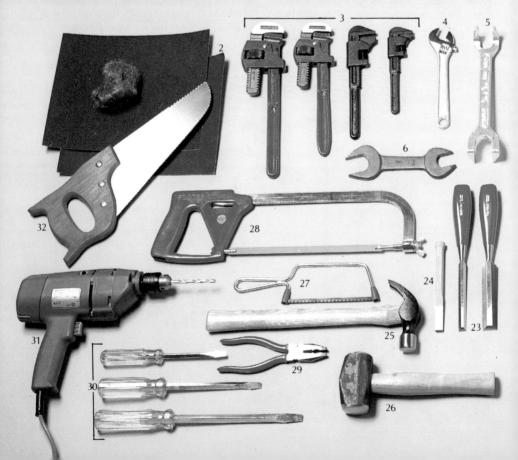

TOOLS AND FITTINGS FOR PLUMBING WORK 167

available so they can readily be connected into copper systems; because most plumbing systems are now run in copper pipe — it is easy to work with and all plumber's merchants stock it — this is what you'll be using for most of your plumbing jobs.

Copper pipe can be joined in one of two basic ways. 'Compression' joints consist of a brass or gunmetal central body with a 'capnut' at each end or outlet, which, when tightened, compresses a brass or copper ring called an 'olive' against the pipe end to form a watertight seal. Avoid the type termed as 'manipulative', which requires the pipe ends to be specially shaped to

The Plumber's Toolkit
1 Fine-grade steel wool. **2** Abrasive paper. **3** Adjustable wrenches (Stilsons). **4** Adjustable spanner. **5** Basin wrench (crowsfoot spanner). **6** Open-ended spanner. **7** Second-cut files – flat, round, half-round and tapered. **8** Spirit level. **9** PTFE sealing tape. **10** Degreasing fluid and solvent-weld cement. **11** Heat-resistant mittens. **12** Flux and brush applicator. **13** Flame-proof sheet. **14** Solder. **15** Blowlamp with gas canister. **16** Internal pipe bending spring. **17** External pipe bending spring. **18** Pipe bending machine with 15mm and 22mm formers. **19** Extendable steel tape. **20** Swarf brushes. **21** Torch. **22** Wheel tube cutter. **23** Wood chisels. **24** Cold chisel. **25** Claw hammer. **26** Club hammer. **27** Junior hacksaw. **28** Hacksaw. **29** Pliers. **30** Screwdrivers. **31** Electric drill. **32** Floorboard saw.

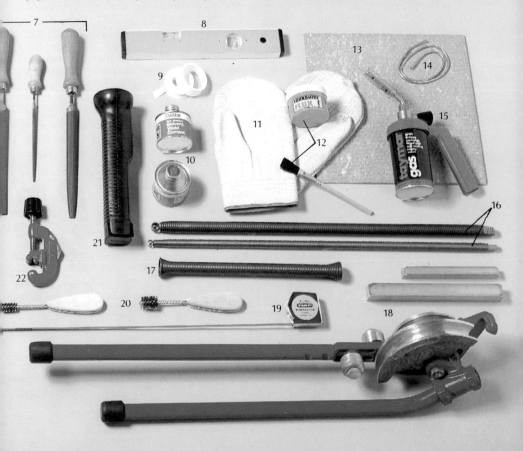

accept an internal cone fitting.

'Capillary' joints are neater looking in exposed pipe runs. They consist of a copper sleeve with outlets to take the pipe ends. 'Yorkshire' fittings have an integral ring of solder inside the sleeve which, when melted with a blowtorch, spreads around the pipe end by capillary action and forms a seal. With 'end feed' types of capillary fitting, the solder is applied separately and drawn into the space between sleeve and pipe end by capillary action. The minimum of solder should be used with these so that it doesn't flow inside the pipe. Wash out the pipes as soon as possible after making a soldered joint to remove all traces of flux.

There is a variety of fittings to enable you to join lengths of pipe: commonly straight couplers (end-to-end fixings); elbows (right-angle curves); and tees (branching into a length of pipe). Variations of these are also made for use in special situations, such as connecting pipes of differing diameters.

You will have to use plastic pipe, however, for the waste runs. If you've got a very modern system you may even find plastic hot and cold supply pipes or polythene cold water supply pipes. Again, the techniques involved in dealing with these materials are quite straightforward; if anything, they are even easier than working with copper.

Planning a pipe run
Probably the most disruptive part of any plumbing job comes when you've got to install a new pipe run. Floorboards have to be raised and exposed pipework boxed in or set in channels in the wall. Consequently, it's important to plan the route carefully and to work out exactly how you are going to proceed *before* you start. Normally, it's best to begin at the end, at the site of the new appliance, and then work towards a convenient point on the existing system where you can connect the branch. This will normally be on the pipes leading away from the cold water storage cistern and the hot water cylinder. If you work in this order, you'll only have to turn off the water supply to the rest of the house for a short time while you make the final connections between the new pipes and the old ones.

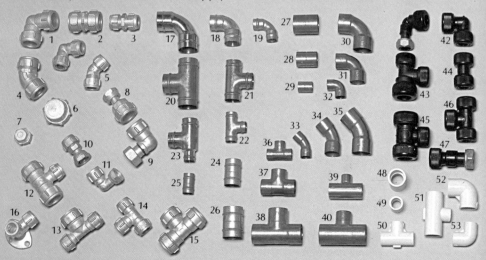

Try to plan the run so that there are as few bends as possible. A lot of right-angle bends, for example, will affect the smooth flow of the water inside and could give you a problem with air locks. Furthermore, if you use special fittings (see photographs) to make the bends then you increase the number of potential sites where leaks may occur. Once you are happy with the route, measure the length of pipe you are going to need, remembering to add extra for bends. Then check the existing pipework as it may affect the type of pipe you use to make up the new branch.

What pipework to use
There's a good chance that the main system will be copper pipe, in which case copper for the branch pipe is the obvious choice. But there is one factor you have to take into account: if the plumbing was installed before 1970, it is likely to be in imperial sized pipe — $\frac{1}{2}$in, $\frac{3}{4}$in and 1in, for example, as measured across the internal diameter. Since 1970, copper pipe has been manufactured to a metric specification, but the new sizes are not direct equiva-

Common Plumbing Fittings
Compression fittings: **1** 90° elbows. **2&3** Straight couplings. **4&5** 135° bends. **6&7** Blanking-off plugs (stop ends). **8-11** Tap connectors. **12** 22 × 22 × 15mm reducing tee. **13** 15 × 15 × 22mm reducing tee. **14&15** Equal tees. **16** Elbow with backplate.
Capillary fittings (integral solder rings): **17-19** 90° bends. **20-22** Equal tees. **23** 22 × 15 × 22mm reducing tee. **24-26** Straight couplings.
Capillary fittings (end feed): **27-29** Straight couplings. **30-32** 90° bends. **33-35** 135° bends. **36-38** Equal tees. **39** 22 × 22 × 15mm reducing tee. **40** 28 × 28 × 22mm reducing tee.
Polybutylene plastic push-fit fittings: **41** Bent tap connector. **42** 90° Elbow. **43** 22 × 15 × 15mm reducing tee. **44** Straight connector.
45&46 Equal tees. **47** Straight tap connector.
CPVC plastic solvent-weld fittings.
48 28 × 22mm reducer. **49** 22 × 15mm reducer. **50** Equal tees. **51** 22 × 22 × 15mm reducing tee. **52&53** 90° Elbows.
Solvent-weld waste systems: **54&55** Swept tees. **56&57** Straight couplings. **58&59** 90° bends.
Push-fit (ring seal) waste systems: **60&64** straight couplings. **61** Tee. **62&63** 90° bends. **65** Swept tee.
Types of pipe: **66** Pliable corrugated copper pipe, one end plain, the other with a tap connector. **67** 15mm and 22mm copper pipe. **68** CPVC plastic pipe. **69** Polybutylene plastic pipe. **70&71** Two types of plastic waste pipe.
Various types of pipe clip are also illustrated.

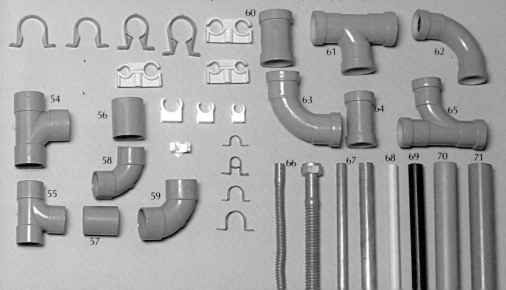

170 **WORKING WITH PIPES**

lents of the old because they refer to the outside diameter of the pipe. What this means, from your point of view, is that when you are connecting into ½in or 1in copper pipe you can use 15mm and 28mm compression tees, but with ¾in pipe you have to use a 22mm compression tee fitted with larger olives where it connects to the imperial pipe. With capillary fittings you can use straight adaptors to convert a short length of imperial pipe to metric and then connect metric fittings into this section.

This may all sound complicated, particularly if you have difficulty in deciding whether you have metric or imperial pipe. Therefore, because you'll be connecting mainly into 15mm (½in) or 22mm (¾in) pipe, use compression tees. They will save you a lot of time and aggravation.

If you still have dull-grey lead or clanking iron pipes, you'll know instantly that you're dealing with an old plumbing system that is nearing the end of its life. So if you are going to the trouble of installing a new branch supply, you should also consider replacing the entire system. It may sound like drastic action, but what is worse — taking this preventative measure or cleaning up after a burst pipe?

However, you may have to install,

1 Cutting copper pipe. Mark the length needed and hacksaw down the edge of tape wrapped round the pipe for a square cut.

2 Use a half-round file to remove the burr from the inside edge of the pipe and clean out any swarf from inside.

3 Remove the burr from the outside edge, then file a slight bevel so the pipe will slip smoothly into the fitting.

4 Rotate a wheel tube cutter round the pipe, gradually tightening the jaws to give a clean, square cut.

5 Insert the attached reamer into the end of the pipe and rotate it to remove any burr on the inside edge.

6 Burnish the end of the pipe with steel wool so it's ready to accept a capillary or compression fitting.

WORKING WITH PIPES 171

say, a washbasin, in which case you'll have to lay the branch as a temporary measure. If you are connecting into lead, you can use copper pipe for the branch, although stainless steel and polythene are also suitable. First, you'll have to set a tee into a short run of copper pipe and then fit this length into the lead supply pipe using a type of connection known as a 'wiped soldered' joint. There's an art to making these joints, and special tools are required, so it may be best to call in a plumber to complete this part of the job for you. Likewise, connecting into iron pipe can cause problems as threads have to be cut on the ends of the iron pipe. Again, it is wise to call in a plumber. What you must also remember with iron pipe is that you can't connect copper pipe to it because it sets up an electrolytic action that will eventually cause the iron pipe to fail. Alternatively, you can use stainless steel or polythene pipes.

Connecting into polythene pipe is virtually the same as connecting into copper. Polythene pipe isn't yet produced in metric sizes, so you will have to ask for ½in and ¾in (which refers to the inside diameter) instead. The compression tee you use to make the connection is similar to the one used for copper except that it incorporates

1 Bending copper pipe. Smear petroleum jelly on the spring, fit it in the pipe, and centre it on the bend's apex.

2 Pull the pipe round your knee, moving it slightly to prevent too tight a bend. Overbend a little, then return to the correct angle.

3 Remove the spring. If it sticks, insert a metal bar through the eye and rotate it clockwise to free the spring.

4 With a bending machine, set the pipe on the correct former under the pipe stop. Place the back guide on top.

5 Draw the two levers together so the roller works the pipe round the former until it reaches the correct angle.

6 Pliable corrugated pipe can be bent simply by hand with little effort. Don't overwork it or it will split.

1 Making a compression joint.
Slip the capnut and olive over
one pipe end, then offer up the
body of the fitting.

2 Mark the capnut and body
as a guide to the number of
turns you give the capnut when
tightening the joint.

3 Hold the body with a wrench
while rotating the capnut about
1½ turns with a second. Then
make up the other side.

special larger olives. The fitting also
has to be used in conjunction with
metal liners that are pushed into the
open ends of the pipes to prevent them
collapsing when the capnuts on the
fitting are tightened. The liners are
supplied with the fitting.

With some types of plastic pipe you
have to 'stick' the tee and sections of
the branch in place using solvent-weld
cement — in fact, this melts the contact
surfaces so that they bind together as
they dry. Consequently, you have to
work fairly quickly when making the

joins, but it is probably the easiest way
of getting a watertight seal. The same
technique is used to join plastic soil
pipes together.

Another type of plastic supply pipe
uses pushfit connections. These look
like plastic compression fittings, but
instead of an olive they contain an

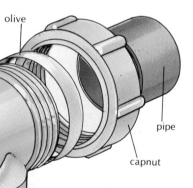

Making a compression joint
As the capnut is screwed on to
the body of the fitting it
compresses a metal ring – an
olive – against the end of the
socket and the pipe so forming
a watertight seal. Although
more expensive than a capillary
joint, it is much easier to use. It
may be made of brass or
gunmetal.

WORKING WITH PIPES 173

Capillary joints

The pipe must fit tightly into the socket of the fitting to ensure a good soldered seal which will be watertight.

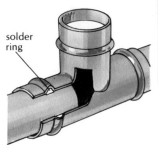

solder
ring

On heating, the solder flows round the pipe and bonds the contact surfaces on cooling.

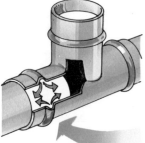

1 Making a capillary joint Apply flux to the prepared ends of the pipes and inside the sockets of the fitting.

2 Slip the fitting over one of the pipe ends, rotating it to get an even spread of flux. Then offer up the other section of pipe.

3 If the fitting has integral solder rings, play the blowlamp on the pipe and fitting until solder appears at the fitting's lip.

4 With end feed fittings, heat the pipe and fitting first. Then work solder round the joins until no more is drawn in.

O-ring seal, which forms the watertight connection. The joint is prevented from being pulled apart by a ring grip that bites into the plastic pipes.

Assembling the run

You should now be in a position to decide on the type of pipe you are going to use, how much you need and where you are going to lay it. Next comes the installation.

If you are taking the pipework under the floor, you'll obviously have to lift a few floorboards. Where the run is to be parallel to the supporting joists, clip the pipework to the side of one of them about 50mm (2in) from the top edge, so

they are well out of the way of stray floorboard nails. To avoid raising too many floorboards, you should be able to feed lengths of pipe underneath some of the boards and then lift boards at each end to give access for making any connections. Plug the end of the pipe with a rag before you slide it into position so that it doesn't scoop up any debris. Make sure, too, that you don't inadvertently damage any electricity cables.

Where the run crosses the joists this should be at right-angles. You can notch the pipes into the tops of the joists below the centres of the floor-boards or drill holes for them through

174 **WORKING WITH PIPES**

1 Joining into a pipe run. Find the pipe stop positions with a dowel and mark them on the casing. Transfer the distance between them to the pipe.

2 Cut the first section of branch pipe to length. Prepare the ends and slip over the capnuts and olives before offering it up into position.

3 Turn off the supply, cut out the section of pipe and prepare the ends. There should be enough play on the run to spring the tee into place.

4 Use an adjustable wrench to hold the body of the tee secure while you tighten the capnuts to make a watertight seal.

5 Connect one end of the first section of branch pipe to the branch itself. Then manoeuvre the other end into the tee.

6 Make sure the branch is pressed tightly against the pipe stop. Screw on the capnut and tighten with a wrench.

the joists about 50mm (2in) from the top so they are clear of fixing nails. Any notches should be 12mm (½in) wider and 6mm (¼in) deeper than the pipe diameter to allow for movement and expansion of the pipework. Holes, likewise should be slightly larger than the pipe diameter. On the ground floor, though, if you have a sprung timber floor, you may be able to clip the pipe to the underside of the joists. This is preferable to notching or drilling since this can weaken the joists. As a well-ventilated ground floor is likely to be cold you'd be wise to insulate the pipework in this position with a proprietary lagging material. Similarly,

insulate any pipes that run through the roof space.

Taking pipework across solid concrete floors causes more of a problem. You could channel the pipe into the surface and take it round the perimeter of the room but this is a laborious and messy job. A much simpler solution is to run the pipes on the surface at skirting level where they can be boxed in unobtrusively. You face similar problems when taking a pipe run up a wall. On a brick or block wall you could channel or 'chase' the run, but this will damage any decorations, so it is not really worth considering unless you plan to redecorate. You may also

1 Polybutylene push-fit joints. Cut the pipe with a hacksaw and insert the stainless steel sleeves into the ends.

2 Apply a bead of silicone lubricant round the pipe end and also coat the O-ring seal in the socket of the fitting itself.

3 Push the pipe end firmly into the body of the coupling. It is prevented from coming out by a grab ring inside the socket.

find that heat from a buried hot water pipe might cause the plaster to crack. The answer, again, is to run the pipe on the surface, ideally in a corner where it will be least conspicuous.

Avoid long, unsupported pipe runs as these may cause knocking as the water flows through them. Clip the pipe at regular intervals — 1.2m (4ft) for 15mm pipe and 1.5m (5ft) for 22mm pipe. Too high a mains pressure may also cause knocking, and this can sometimes be prevented by partially closing the mains stopvalve.

Working with pipe
Regardless of the material the pipework is made of, the first thing you'll have to do with it is to cut it to the required lengths. Accurate measuring is important, as is cutting squarely. A good hacksaw with a sharp blade will handle most types of pipe, but with copper you'll find a wheel tube cutter a good investment, particularly if you have a lot of cutting to do.

Joining and connecting Joining lengths of pipe is a straightforward task. Use compression fittings for copper, stainless steel and polythene. You can also use capillary fittings for copper and stainless steel. When you are working with certain types of plastic pipes (such

as UPVC and CPVC), you'll need to make solvent-weld joins. Pushfit fittings are used on plastic waste pipes, and for one particular type of plastic hot and cold supply pipes. You can also use conventional compression fittings for the latter, but in addition you need to insert a metal liner into the mouth of the pipe. Most connections to waste traps and to appliances are made with screw fittings.

Bending pipe No pipe run is perfectly straight; sooner or later it will have to change course. Lengths of copper pipe can be bent using a bending spring — the internal type that slips inside the pipe is now the most common — or a pipe bending machine, but you can also use special angled couplings. Polythene pipes can be bent by hand but they need to be firmly clipped in position to prevent them springing back. With stainless steel, it's best to use the special fittings.

Draining the pipes
Before you install any new branch pipe, you will have to drain that section of the supply pipe you intend to cut into. Most connections will be made on the supply pipes that leave the cold water storage cistern and the hot water cylinder. Don't forget that you must not

176 WORKING WITH PIPES

1 Solvent-welding waste pipes
Cut the waste pipe to length with a hacksaw, using a paper template to get a square end.

2 Use a file to remove any rough edges, then chamfer the ends so the pipe can be slotted easily into the fitting.

3 Rub the ends of the pipes and the insides of the sockets on the fitting with steel wool to give a key to the contact surfaces.

4 Wipe degreasing fluid over the contact surfaces with a cloth so that they are thoroughly cleaned.

5 Use the brush applicator in the can to apply solvent-weld cement liberally to the pipe and the inside of the sockets.

6 Push the pipe into the socket, twisting it to spread the cement. Clean off surplus cement and allow it to set.

connect into the cold pipe that feeds the hot cylinder or the primary circuit that runs between the boiler and the hot cylinder.

With luck, there should be gatevalves on the supply pipes leading away from the cold cistern. Just close these off and open the hot and cold taps in the bathroom and the hot tap over the kitchen sink. The hot water pipes will only flow for a very short while because the draw-off point is at the top of the cylinder, and with the cold feed turned off there is little pressure in the system to generate the flow. Consequently, you won't empty the cylinder of water. If you have to drain the cylinder, there should be a

draincock (tap) near the bottom so you can run a hose from this to an outside gully.

Once the water in the pipes has stopped flowing, you can insert the branch, but be prepared with some old rags to catch the inevitable small trickle of water as the pipe is cut. When you restore the supply, make sure all the joins are watertight before concealing the pipework.

If there are no gatevalves, you'll have to drain the cold water cistern. First of all, you've got to cut off its supply. Rather than turn off all your water by closing the main stopvalve, it's best to tie the cistern's ballvalve to a length of wood spanning the tank so it cannot

WORKING WITH PIPES 177

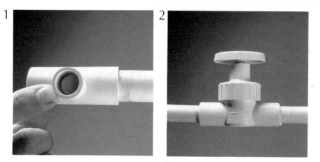

Solvent welds in CPVC pipe
Basically this is the same operation as that used for waste pipes. Chamfering is unnecessary, nor do you have to remove surplus cement. **(1)**. Allow this to set for 1 hour before running cold water and 4 hours before running hot. You can fit gate valves **(2)** provided they are fitted with stubs of CPVC pipe.

open when the taps in the house are turned on. By only draining down through the cold taps, you won't waste expensively-heated hot water.

You may also want to connect into the rising main above the stopvalve. This won't cause any problems if there is a draincock directly above the valve. If there isn't, then the job is a little more complicated. Turn off the supply as normal, and then release the top nut making the compression fitting between the valve and pipe leading to the

cold water cistern. You should be able to spring the pipe from the body of the valve and quickly put a funnel connected to a length of hose under it. Lead the hose to a bucket nearby to catch the water as it drains out. Re-make the compression joint when the branch is complete; then you can restore the supply. But before doing this, why not take the opportunity to fit a draincock — the type with a straight compression coupling — into the run to make draining easier in future.

Push-fit joints in waste pipe
This process is slighty more involved than making similar connections in plastic supply pipe, because this pipe expands when heated by hot water and this has to be allowed for.

When making a join, first clean all the contact surfaces with special cleaner. Chamfer the pipe ends and apply a coating of petroleum jelly **(1)**. Check to see that the sealing ring is correctly positioned in the socket, then push the pipe in firmly so that it butts up to the pipe stop **(2)**. Make sure the pipe is positioned squarely before marking the position of the socket mouth on it **(3)**. Now withdraw the pipe so that the pencil mark is about 10mm (³⁄₈in) from the socket **(4)**. This should provide sufficient room for the pipe to expand.

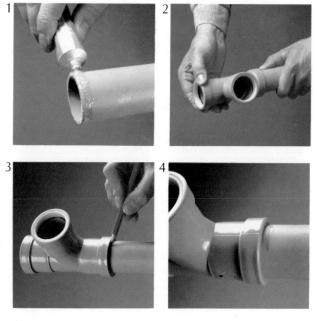

178 THE KITCHEN SINK

The kitchen taps and sink are probably the most used part of a domestic plumbing system. The sink, particularly, takes a battering, being used to wash everything from dishes and clothes to paint brushes. The waste system, too, has to deal with all kinds of debris that it would be best off without.

It is remarkable how well a sink — whether enamelled pressed steel or stainless steel — will stand up to this treatment. Eventually, however, the scratches will show, the enamel will chip and hard water scale will build up. The net result is a rather un-hygienic-looking sink. The answer is to fit a new one.

You may even have an old glazed earthenware sink with bib taps projecting from the wall instead of being fixed to the sink itself. While these sinks have their charm, they are not really practical as they have no attached drainer. If

Types of inset sink top

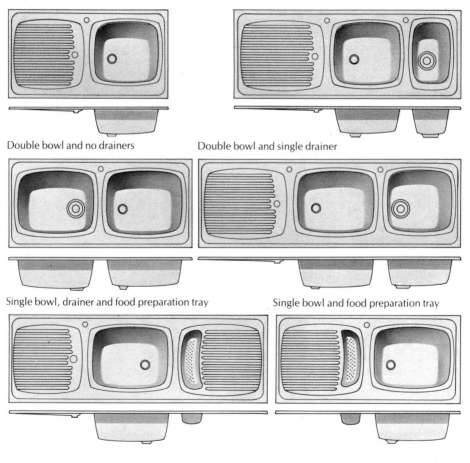

Single bowl and drainer

Bowl and half bowl with single drainer

Double bowl and no drainers

Double bowl and single drainer

Single bowl, drainer and food preparation tray

Single bowl and food preparation tray

How a mixer tap works

The flow of hot and cold water into the body of the mixer is controlled by individual taps. But the supplies are not actually mixed here. Instead, they are conducted along separate channels in the spout and only come together as they leave its nozzle. The reason for this is to prevent hot water from being siphoned into the rising main.

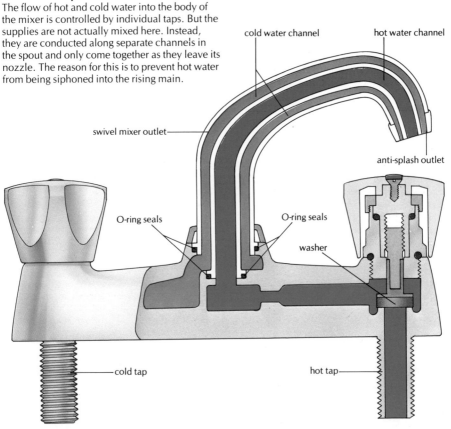

cold water channel

hot water channel

swivel mixer outlet

anti-splash outlet

O-ring seals

O-ring seals

washer

cold tap

hot tap

you are modernising your kitchen, such a sink is something you'll almost certainly want to replace.

There is a wide variety of sink tops from which to choose. These range from a traditional one-piece sink and drainer that fits over the top of a kitchen unit to an inset sink with double bowls, or just inset bowls where the surrounding worktop acts as the drainer. Stainless steel is still popular, but modern chip-resistant enamel and plastic sinks are becoming common and are available in a choice of colours. Likewise, ceramic sinks are making a comeback.

New taps?

If you're replacing an old sink, the chances are that you'll also need new taps; and if you're replacing bib taps with taps fixed to the sink, you'll also have to modify the plumbing to take the pipework under the sink. Taps vary in price enormously, but basically you have the choice between individual pillar taps and mixers with a swivel spout — the most practical type to get. The most modern are known as 'monobloc' taps and they often incorporate a useful rinsing brush to remove suds from dishes.

180 INSTALLING A NEW SINK

Firstly remove the existing sink top, but don't do anything until you've turned off the hot and cold supplies to it and drained the pipes (see page 175); then you can undo the connections. With the old sink out of the way, you'll be able to see if the hot and cold supply pipes and the waste outlet match the new sink. If they don't, you'll have to adjust their positions. This could lead to some awkward pipe bending, so as an alternative try using pliable copper pipe to bridge the gap between the supply pipes and the tap inlets. This may mean cutting the supply pipes back a little so you can get a smooth run on the bendable pipe.

Fortunately, much of the installation work can be done before the sink is put in position — which makes the job easier and quicker. You then have to set the top on its unit or over the hole in the worktop if it's an inset sink. When it's fixed in place, you can reconnect the supply pipes and screw on the trap and waste. The trap should be a 'P', bottle or dip-partition type (see page 165). Finally, restore the water supply and check for leaks.

If you previously had a glazed earthenware sink, it will probably have had a lead trap and waste pipe. You will have to replace this in its entirety using a 38mm (1½in) diameter trap and pipe, which is usually made of UPVC. As the waste will discharge into a gully, make sure that the end of the new pipe is carried below the grille but stops short of the water level. You can cut the grille to admit the pipe or simply buy a replacement grille with a suitable hole in it.

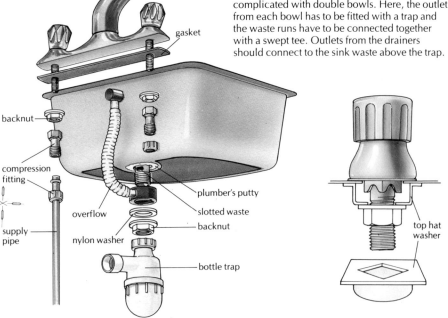

The plumbing connections for a single bowl sink are relatively straightforward and are shown in the diagram. They are somewhat more complicated with double bowls. Here, the outlet from each bowl has to be fitted with a trap and the waste runs have to be connected together with a swept tee. Outlets from the drainers should connect to the sink waste above the trap.

mixer

gasket

backnut

compression fitting

supply pipe

overflow

nylon washer

plumber's putty

slotted waste

backnut

bottle trap

top hat washer

INSTALLING A NEW SINK 181

1 Wind PTFE tape round the waste outlet thread and apply plumber's putty beneath the flange, unless a plastic or rubber washer is supplied.

2 Insert the waste into the sink's outlet. Smear jointing compound on the washer and slip it over the outlet thread, compound side down.

3 Align the outlet in the collar of the overflow hose with the slot in the waste. Then fit and secure the backnut to hold everything in place.

4 Attach the other end of the overflow hose to the outlet at the top of the bowl by screwing it to a small grate and chain stay, attached to the plug.

5 Next, position the mixer tap and slip top hat washers over the inlet tails. Screw on the backnuts, then connect lengths of pliable pipe.

6 Set the inset sink on a rubber gasket or clear mastic bed when positioning it over the hole in the worktop. Clip it so it cannot move.

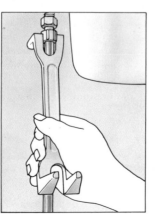

7 Bend the pliable pipes so that they will meet the supply pipes. Screw on the bottle trap and connect the waste pipe.

A crowsfoot spanner, also known as a basin wrench, is little more than an open-ended spanner with the ends bent at 90°. This means that it doesn't have to be held at right angles to a nut in order to turn it. Consequently, it is ideal for loosening those seemingly inaccessible connections at the back of a bath or basin when you want to remove the taps. If backnuts are difficult to shift, apply extra leverage to the free end by slotting in a spanner and putting pressure on that.

182 WASTE DISPOSAL UNITS

A waste disposal unit is a boon to the modern, efficient kitchen because it disposes of kitchen waste — which usually ends up in the dustbin — hygienically and quickly. You simply tip the waste down the sink, turn on the cold tap and the unit, and steel grinders reduce the matter to a slurry that's safe to flush into the waste system.

Obviously, the unit can't deal with all kitchen waste. Large bones, cartons and fibrous matter which will bind round the grinding blades still have to be thrown in the bin.

A waste disposal unit must be connected to the waste outlet of the kitchen sink before the trap, and to accommodate the unit the sink needs a larger outlet hole than normal — one with a diameter of 89mm (3½in) instead of 38mm (1½in). However, there is a model available which does connect to the normal-sized outlet.

If you are replacing a sink, you can buy a replacement with the correct sized opening, but if you've got a stainless steel sink which you are keeping, you can cut a larger hole using a special tool. It's not possible to cut a larger hole in a ceramic sink or an enamelled sink, so replace both.

When you've connected the unit to

1 Remove the old waste from the sink and check that the diameter of the outlet is big enough to take the new sink bush of the disposal unit.

2 The waste disposal unit is attached to the sink bush via a clamp seal and suspension plate. These are held together by a circlip.

3 First, apply a layer of water-resistant sealant under the flange of the sink bush, then set the bush in the sink outlet, bedding on the sealant.

4 Slip the seals and plates over the bush, fit the circlip and slightly tighten the grub screws on the suspension plate.

5 Fit the seal over the outlet bend and locate the bend in the top housing. Secure it by screwing on the outlet plate.

6 Set the flat seal in the recess in the top of the housing and smear it with a silicone lubricant.

WASTE DISPOSAL UNITS 183

Right: Waste disposal units consist of three sections: a clamping system which holds the unit securely round the sink waste outlet; a top housing where the waste is ground to a slurry; and a sealed motor unit to which the grinding blades are connected.

the new outlet, screw on the trap. Use an ordinary 'U' or 'S' trap rather than a bottle trap, as the latter is more prone to blockages. The waste pipe should slope at about 15°, and if it discharges into an open gully it's important the pipe ends below the grille so there is no chance of the slurry creating a blockage. Otherwise, the waste pipe can be connected to a single stack system.

The unit also needs an electric power supply. You can run this as a spur from a ring circuit to a switched fused connection unit with a neon indicator. The flex from the disposer has to be wired to this. Never undertake any electrical work unless you're sure you know what you're doing. Follow the maker's instructions, and consult a qualified electrician regarding any cross-bonding required with the pipework.

Site the connection unit in an accessible place but away from the sink unit. On some disposers you have to fit a magnetic cap into the sink outlet before the unit will operate.

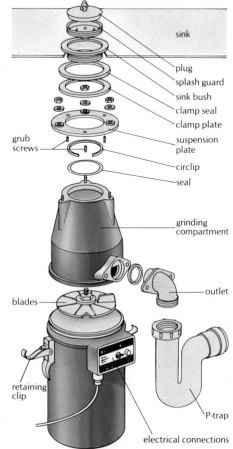

sink
plug
splash guard
sink bush
clamp seal
clamp plate
grub screws
suspension plate
circlip
seal
grinding compartment
outlet
blades
retaining clip
P-trap
electrical connections

7 Offer up the top housing so that the studs locate in the suspension plate grommets. Then bolt the unit to the plate.

8 Swivel the housing to align the outlet pipe with the trap. Tighten the grub screws to prevent further rotation.

9 Fit an O-ring seal to the motor housing and clip it to the top housing, making sure that the switch panel is accessible.

184 **WASHING MACHINES AND DISHWASHERS**

Although you can still buy twin tub washing machines, front- and top-loading automatics that include a spinner are now considered a necessity in many households. The convenience of having a washing machine permanently connected to your home's plumbing system, ready for use at the touch of a button, is obvious and many people are also realising the benefits of an automatic dishwasher.

Because they are usually stationed in the kitchen or utility room where there are hot and cold supply pipes and a waste system to hand, plumbing in these appliances is a job you can easily tackle yourself.

The plumbing connections
Washing machines and dishwashers are plumbed in similarly. Most need a supply of hot and cold water, although some just need a cold supply, which they heat internally to the required temperature. Ideally, the pressures of the hot and cold supply should be the same. However, when putting a machine in the kitchen it's usual practice to take the cold water from the supply to the kitchen tap, which is

under mains pressure, and the hot water from the hot supply to the kitchen hot tap, which is under lower gravity pressure. Most machines can cater for the pressure difference, but check the manufacturer's instructions.

When you are teeing off the hot and cold supplies, you're almost certain to need 15 × 15 × 15mm compression or capillary fittings to start the branch. You'll also need to install 'mini-stop-valves' on the individual runs, which will enable you to screw the flexible rubber hoses of the appliance directly to their outlets. When the machine needs to be serviced, all you have to do is to turn off the valves and disconnect the hoses.

The waste outlet hose of the machine simply hooks into the end of a 'stand-pipe'. This is a 600mm (2ft) long vertical pipe with an internal diameter of 35mm (1⅜in). It should have a 75mm (3in) 'deep seal' trap at its bottom end, which is then connected to the drainage system. Sometimes, the trap comes as part of the standpipe itself. This arrangement prevents water being siphoned out of the machine while it's in operation.

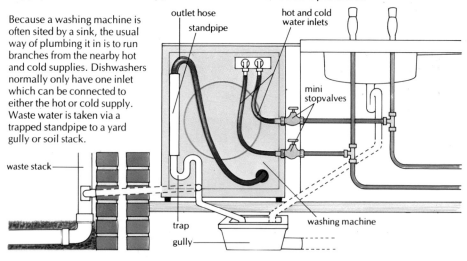

Because a washing machine is often sited by a sink, the usual way of plumbing it in is to run branches from the nearby hot and cold supplies. Dishwashers normally only have one inlet which can be connected to either the hot or cold supply. Waste water is taken via a trapped standpipe to a yard gully or soil stack.

outlet hose

standpipe

hot and cold water inlets

mini stopvalves

waste stack

trap

gully

washing machine

WASHING MACHINES AND DISHWASHERS 185

1 Knock a hole in the outside wall and feed through the waste pipe from the standpipe position inside. Then fit a 90° bend to the end.

2 Direct the waste pipe into a nearby gully so that it stops below the level of the grille, which you will have to cut to fit round the pipe.

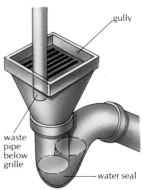

The waste pipe should end above the water.

3 Make up the standpipe and connect the trap to the waste run. Bracket the pipe to the wall and check the top is 600mm (2ft) above floor level.

4 Run 15mm branch pipes to the site of the appliance from suitable hot and cold supplies. The pipes should stop just to one side of the machine.

5 Fit washing machine or mini-stopvalves to the branch pipes. Some have a backplate for wall fixing. Make sure they are easily accessible.

6 Fit the machine's inlet hoses directly to the outlets of the stopvalves. (Note: dishwashers only have a hot or cold fill.)

7 Feed the outlet hose 150mm (6in) into the standpipe. The hose must never be immersed when the appliance empties.

8 Adjust the feet of the appliance so that it's level. Then plug it into a 13 amp socket and test the system.

186 DEALING WITH HARD WATER

When you look at a glass of water it's difficult to believe that this seemingly inoffensive liquid could actually be attacking your plumbing system. But if you live in a hard water area — and about two-thirds of homes in Britain have such a supply — this may be happening.

The visible signs of hard water are all too apparent: scale builds up round the element in an electric kettle; soap is difficult to lather; and baths, sinks and basins have to be cleaned constantly to remove the tide marks that remain when water drains away. So just think what is happening on the inside of pipes and boilers as scale begins to accumulate. The plumbing system has to work harder to achieve the same results as the flow of water is gradually reduced. Sooner or later, something is bound to fail, and often it's the element of an immersion heater that burns out fighting to overcome the blanket of fur.

What is hard water?

Hardness in water is due to the presence of certain magnesium and calcium mineral salts. However, there are two types of hard water: temporary and permanent. If temporary hard water is heated to above 60°C (140°F) scale is deposited and the water starts to lose its hardness. It is this form of hard water that can play havoc with a hot water system. This doesn't happen with permanent hard water — heating it doesn't cause the fur deposits that block the pipes, yet the water still retains its other hard qualities.

Dealing with the problem

There are several things you can do to alleviate the effects of hard water. First, you can set the boiler or immersion heater thermostat to 60°C (140°F) — in soft water areas it can be 10°C (18°F) higher — and, if you haven't already got one, install an indirect hot water

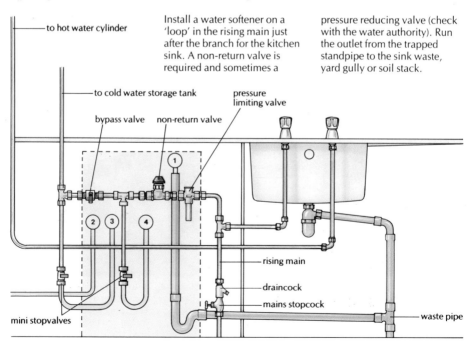

to hot water cylinder

Install a water softener on a 'loop' in the rising main just after the branch for the kitchen sink. A non-return valve is required and sometimes a

pressure reducing valve (check with the water authority). Run the outlet from the trapped standpipe to the sink waste, yard gully or soil stack.

to cold water storage tank

pressure limiting valve

bypass valve   non-return valve

mini stopvalves

rising main

draincock

mains stopcock

waste pipe

DEALING WITH HARD WATER 187

1 Connect the flow and return pipes into the rising main together with any bypass valve, non-return valve and pressure reducing valve supplied.

2 Run the drain pipe from the unit to a trapped standpipe, which in turn can either discharge into a yard gully or soil pipe via a strap boss.

3 Run the overflow pipe sloping downwards to a visible point on an outside wall where you will be able to see any water flowing from it.

4 Next, cut the flow and return hoses to length and fit connectors to the ends. Do not forget to incorporate their sealing washers.

5 Connect the other ends of the hoses to mini-stopvalves on the branch pipes. Fit a filter washer on the 'flow' to stop debris entering the unit.

6 Wire the softener directly to a switched fused connection unit fitted with a 3 amp fuse, or connect it to a socket via a plug with a 3 amp fuse.

cylinder (see page 213). Scale inhibitors can then be added to the water in the primary circuit. You can also put water softeners in your washing water; indeed, many cleaning agents already contai them.

Hov ever, the most effective way of dealin₃ with hard water is to install a chemical mains water softener, which will take all the hardness out of your supply. It does this by converting the offending magnesium and calcium salts into sodium salts, which do not form scale. Normally, it is plumbed into the rising main after the branch to the cold

tap over the kitchen sink, as it's thought healthier to drink hard water in preference to soft. The unit also needs an electric power supply and a connection to a drain. Given these requirements, probably the easiest place to install it is in the kitchen, but it doesn't have to be there; you can install it anywhere convenient.

Water softeners are expensive and some people see them as something of a novelty. However, they may reduce household bills — for soap and the like — and so pay for themselves in about six to seven years.

188 **FITTING A NEW HANDBASIN**

The other major area in your home where water is required is the bathroom, and often this may include a WC. Plumbing jobs in the bathroom range from the simple — dealing with a leaking tap — to the more complicated tasks of installing a new shower or a completely new bathroom suite. In the latter case, if you are putting the new bath, basin or WC in the same place as the old one, you are unlikely to breach any building regulations. However, if you want to alter the position of any of the appliances you should consult your local building inspector, who will be able to advise you on whether your plans meet the various regulations. Mostly, he'll be interested in how you intend to run the waste pipes and connect into the drainage system.

Replacing the handbasin

One of the most common jobs in the bathroom is to replace the handbasin, which may just be old fashioned or, worse, cracked.

Obviously, the first job is going to be the removal of the old basin. Once you've turned off the water supplies, use a special 'crowsfoot' spanner to undo the tap connectors, then unscrew the waste. This will leave the basin free to be unscrewed from the wall and lifted clear of any mounting brackets. As with a kitchen sink, you may now have to alter the position of the supply pipes and waste to accommodate the new basin. If you are lucky, everything will match up but don't forget that the shanks of new taps are shorter than those of old ones. Fortunately, you can buy specially extended tap connectors to get round this problem.

The step-by-step photographs show you how to go about fitting a new basin. As you can see, much of the work — fitting the taps and outlet — can be done on the floor. If you are

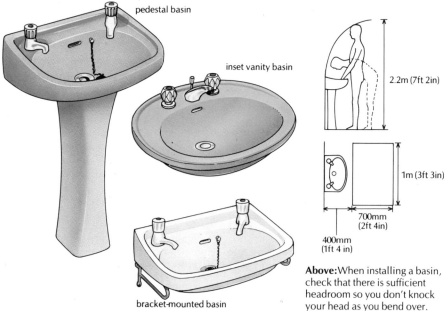

pedestal basin

inset vanity basin

2.2m (7ft 2in)

1m (3ft 3in)

700mm
(2ft 4in)

400mm
(1ft 4 in)

bracket-mounted basin

Above: When installing a basin, check that there is sufficient headroom so you don't knock your head as you bend over.

FITTING A NEW HANDBASIN 189

1 Mark the position of the special support studs on the wall. Drill and plug the fixing holes, then screw the studs in place with a wrench.

2 Before mounting the basin, attach the taps. Bed them on gaskets or plumber's putty, then tighten up the backnuts to hold them securely in place.

3 Unscrew the heads of the studs, allowing you to slip the basin over the shanks. Check for level, then secure with the nuts set on the studs.

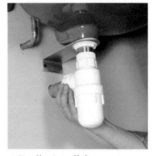

4 Insert the waste, bedded on plumber's putty or any gasket supplied. Sandwich the angle bracket between washers and loosely screw on the backnut.

5 Fix the bracket to the wall, then tighten the backnut fully. At this stage, you can also connect up the hot and cold water supply pipes.

6 Finally, install the new waste run, taking it to a suitable outlet point such as a gully or soil stack. At the basin fit a bottle trap to the waste outlet.

installing a basin in a new location, there are a few other points you've got to bear in mind.

First, you've got to decide how you are going to dispose of the waste water. The waste run to the soil stack or downpipe shouldn't be longer than 2.3m (7ft 6in) and should contain as few bends as possible; and on single stack drainage systems the gradient of the branch should be between 1° and 2½°. If the waste run is less than 1.7m (5ft 6in) long, you can use 32mm (1¼in) waste pipe; anything longer than this should be run in 38mm

(1½in) diameter pipe. In both cases, these must run from a 75mm (3in) deep seal P-trap. On basins it's common to fit a bottle trap.

The final task is to connect the waste run into the drainage system. If the basin is upstairs and you've got two-pipe drainage, the waste can discharge into a hopper head. With single stack drainage you'll have to break into the plastic soil pipe using a special 'strap boss' (see page 208). If the basin is on the ground floor, the waste can either discharge over a yard gully or be linked to the soil stack.

190 **REPLACING A BATH**

Despite the convenience of showers, many people still like to relax in a bath. Yet if you install a bath/shower mixer tap, instantly you have the advantages of both. Lately, there have been some new developments that have aroused more interest in baths. Not least of these is the spa bath, in which a 'whirlpool' (created by streams of air and water fed into the bath through a series of inlet ports) certainly provides a bath with a difference.

If you have an old cast iron bath, you may want to change it because the enamel has started to wear away — a problem that occurs particularly below the spouts of taps and round the waste outlet. Probably the main reason for changing the bath, however, is because you want to modernise the bathroom completely.

If you're doing this, there's the opportunity to change the position of some or all of the fittings. A word of warning here: always bear in mind the space you need to use the bath, basin and WC, and how you are going to run the plumbing.

To help solve the planning problem, one manufacturer produces a special bathroom planning kit. It incorporates a grid on which you can position scale outlines of bathroom fittings, allowing you to double check that everything you want will fit in the room with space to use it. You can also plan the hot and cold supply runs and the route for the waste pipes. The irony is that you may find the original layout was, after all, the most logical for the space available and so end up simply replacing everything in situ.

The techniques of replacing a bath are much the same as those for a basin, except that you're dealing with a larger fitting and all the plumbing is likely to be less accessible. The best plan, therefore, is to complete as much of the

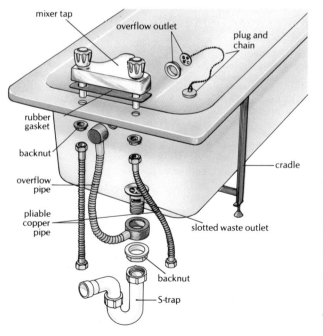

mixer tap
overflow outlet
plug and chain
rubber gasket
backnut
overflow pipe
pliable copper pipe
cradle
slotted waste outlet
backnut
S-trap

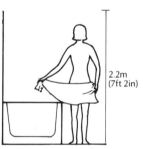

2.2m (7ft 2in)

Make sure you have space to stand upright by the bath when drying yourself.

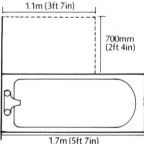

1.1m (3ft 7in)
700mm (2ft 4in)
1.7m (5ft 7in)

REPLACING A BATH 191

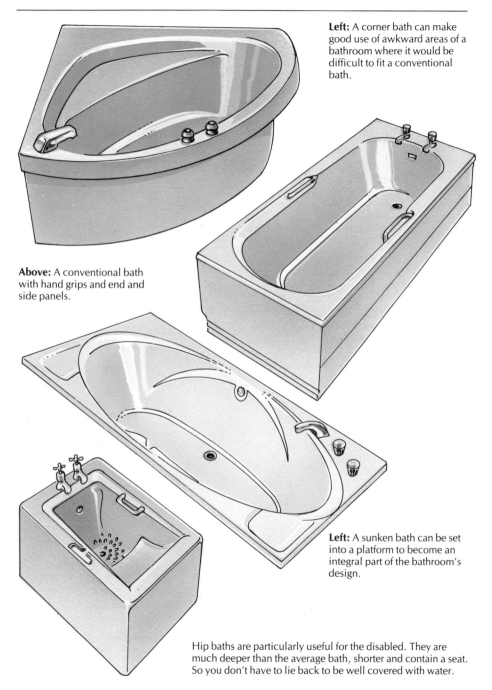

Left: A corner bath can make good use of awkward areas of a bathroom where it would be difficult to fit a conventional bath.

Above: A conventional bath with hand grips and end and side panels.

Left: A sunken bath can be set into a platform to become an integral part of the bathroom's design.

Hip baths are particularly useful for the disabled. They are much deeper than the average bath, shorter and contain a seat. So you don't have to lie back to be well covered with water.

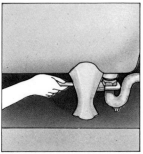

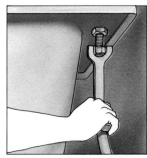

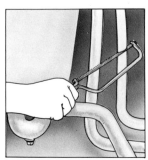

1 Removing an old bath First, turn off the water supply, then deal with the lead trap. Unscrew the nut holding the trap to the bath with an adjustable spanner.

2 Use a crowsfoot spanner to get to the tap connectors, but there should be space to use an adjustable spanner on other couplings.

3 If the nuts won't move, you'll have to cut the pipe, yet this won't matter if you have to re-route the runs to the new bath.

work as you can on the new bath before you have to turn off the water and take out the old one.

Preliminary work

As you'll probably be fitting new taps to the new bath, this is one of the first jobs you can do. Individual pillar taps or a mixer normally sit on rubber gaskets. You have to slip a deep 'top-hat' washer over the shank beneath the tap to bridge the unthreaded section. Then, the backnut can be wound tight to hold the tap firmly in place. With individual taps, grip each spout while you are turning the nut so the tap isn't tightened up crooked. At this stage, it is also worthwhile connecting lengths of hand-bendable corrugated pipe to the tap tails, making it much easier to connect to the supply pipes later on — rigid lengths of pipe can be difficult to connect up if there's even a slight misalignment.

Next, you can fit the bath outlet. Its rim, or 'flange', should be bedded down on a rubber washer, so place this round the underside of the flange. Push the outlet into place and screw up the backnut. The final job is to connect the overflow to the bath and link a special collar sometimes called a 'banjo unit',

on the other end of the flexible plastic overflow pipe, to the waste outlet. Align the hole in the collar with the slot in the waste outlet.

Removing the old bath

Disconnecting the old bath from the plumbing may prove something of a problem, particularly if it's been there for a good many years; the tap connectors may be impossible to free even with a crowsfoot spanner. Some penetrating oil may do the trick, but if not, the simplest solution is to cut through the pipes. There should be enough room to use a mini-hacksaw, but if there is not, use a file saw. Don't be too worried about making the cuts square; you can tidy up the ends later.

Check to see if there is a separate overflow and if there is, disconnect it. As the overflow on a modern bath is connected to the waste outlet just above the trap, you can remove this pipe and block up the hole through the wall. Remove any screws attaching the bath to the floor and walls.

You should be able to remove the old bath and dispose of it now, but if it's cast iron you're going to need help — it will be very heavy. The alternative is to break it up where it stands so you

REPLACING A BATH 193

1 First mount the bath in its cradle, then fit the mixer. Bed it on a gasket, slip the tails through the fixing holes and secure the backnuts.

2 Fit the slotted waste to the bath outlet. Slip on the overflow collar and screw on the backnut. Connect the other end to the bath overflow.

3 Fit pliable copper pipe to the mixer inlet tails so that connections to the hot and cold supplies will be easier when the bath is positioned.

4 Position the bath and adjust the cradle's feet to get it level. Screw through the feet and bracket to the wall.

5 Join the pliable pipes to the supply pipes using compression couplings. This avoids any scorching of the bath.

6 Finally, screw on the P-trap to the bath's waste outlet. Link the trap to the waste pipe with a ring-seal, push-fit connection.

can carry it out piece by piece. You'll need a club or sledge hammer to do this, but you must cover the bath with an old carpet or blanket to prevent shrapnel flying in all directions.

With the old bath out of the way, there will be plenty of space to make any alterations to the supply pipes, but if you are using flexible copper pipe you may not have to do this. You might just have to cut back a small section of supply pipe so you can get a smooth bend on the flexible pipe. Now is also a good time to install a new plastic waste run in 38mm (1½in) diameter pipe.

When you are happy that all the pipes are in the right place, you can install your new bath. Check that it's level, evenly supported by its cradle and that there is sufficient clearance underneath for the P-trap, which should have a 75mm (3in) seal.

Join the supply pipes to the flexible pipes using compression fittings; if they are the old imperial ¾in pipes all you have to do is fit larger olives to the fittings. It may be a bit awkward wielding spanners in the restricted space available, but if you were to use a blowlamp to make a solder coupling you would risk damaging the bath, particularly if it is made of plastic.

194 FITTING A NEW WC

Browsing through the glossy brochures of any manufacturer of bathroomware will immediately bring home to you just how far bathroom design has advanced in recent years. Although the shapes of baths and basins have been refined, if not dramatically altered, it is in the design of WCs that the changes are most apparent. Nowadays, one of the main reasons for fitting a new WC suite is because the existing one is conspicuously old-fashioned, bulky and noisy when it's flushed. The old type of high-level cistern with its pull chain is ungainly when compared with a modern low-level, streamlined design operated by a neat handle or plunger.

Replacing a WC is not as difficult a job as at first it may appear, particularly if you intend to connect the pan to the same waste outlet. In fact, one of the most common jobs is to convert a high-level set-up into a low-level one. You needn't change the pan to do this, so simplifying matters even further. All you'll need is a slimline cistern known as a 'flush panel', which will only stand out 115mm (4½in) from the back wall. You need this type of cistern because with a high-level arrangement the pan is set close to the wall; if you installed an ordinary cistern low down you wouldn't be able to raise the seat fully.

After you've turned off the water supply and drained the cistern, disconnect the pipework attached to it. You may find it quicker to cut through it if the nuts on the connectors are encrusted in paint and difficult to turn. The cistern can then be removed.

Next, fix the flush panel in place — the top should be at about waist height. When you are happy with its position, you can install the internal flushing mechanism and the operating handle. The ballvalve can also be attached at this stage. All that remains then is to connect up the new pipework. The 15mm cold water supply could be an

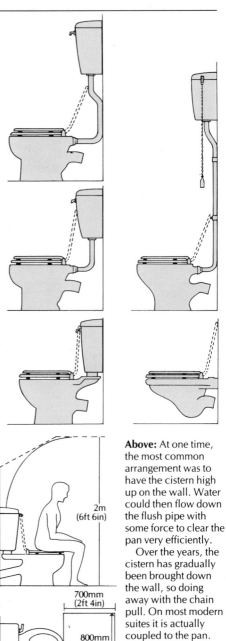

Above: At one time, the most common arrangement was to have the cistern high up on the wall. Water could then flow down the flush pipe with some force to clear the pan very efficiently.

Over the years, the cistern has gradually been brought down the wall, so doing away with the chain pull. On most modern suites it is actually coupled to the pan. **Left** Make sure you have enough room around the suite.

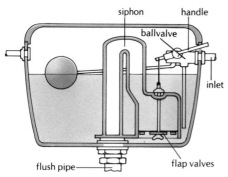

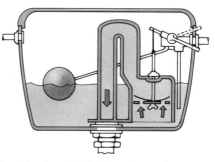

On a modern piston-type cistern, when the lever is pulled down, the plunger in the cylinder is drawn upwards to lift water over the siphon bend. Siphonic action continues the flow, with water passing through the flaps in the plunger until the cistern empties.

Different types of WC pan

Right: In a conventional flush-down pan, it is the force of water entering from the cistern that enables the pan to be cleared of waste and the trap replenished with clean water. The water flows in two streams around the rim of the pan, meeting at the front, efficient operation depending on correct cistern capacity and length and diameter of the flush pipe.

WASHDOWN WC

Below: In a single-trap siphonic pan, it is the gravity pressure of water that starts the flow through the trap. But the outlet is designed to create a siphonic action which further helps to draw the water through.

SINGLE-TRAP SIPHONIC WC

Below: With a double-trap siphonic pan, when water flows into the pan, air is drawn out of the chamber between the traps through a valve. This, combined with the gravity flow of water, sets up a strong siphonic action to clear the trap.

DOUBLE-TRAP SIPHONIC WC

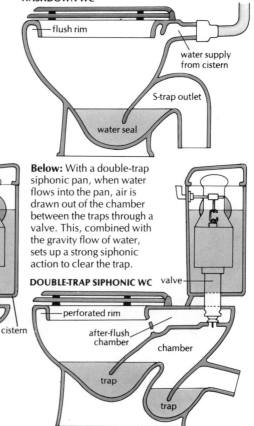

extension of the feed to the old cistern. As this may provide you with a somewhat conspicuous and ugly pipe run, however, you may choose to branch off the cold water network in a more convenient and less noticeable place. Now is also a good time to install a stopvalve on the pipe run just before it enters the cistern to connect to the ballvalve. This will enable you to isolate the cistern to make repairs without the need to turn off all the cold water supply.

Finally, you'll have to link the pan and cistern with a new plastic feed pipe and drill a hole through the outside wall to take the overflow pipe.

Installing a close-coupled WC

If you're going to install a completely new close-coupled suite, you will have to deal with the pan as well as the cistern. Start by removing the cistern (as previously described), then turn your attention to the pan, which you can bail out now or wait until later.

First of all, you've got to break the seal between the integral trap of the pan and the waste outlet. The pan may have a P-trap, in which case the waste pipe will probably go straight back through the outside wall — the usual arrangement with an upstairs WC — or

it may have an S-trap, with the waste pipe rising up through the floor. After you've broken the seal with a club hammer and bolster chisel, check to see if the pan is screwed to the floor. If it is, remove the screws and you should then be able to lift clear the pan and the feed pipe from the old cistern.

When you've cleaned and prepared the rim of the waste outlet, you can stand the new suite in place and mark the fixing holes for the cistern and pan. These can be drilled and plugged (for wall and solid floor fixing) when the suite is taken away. The easiest way of connecting the trap to the collar of the waste pipe is to use a flexible plastic connector. This can be fitted before the pan is finally screwed to the floor.

Next, you can slot the cistern into the coupling at the back of the pan and fit the flush mechanism and ballvalve. All that remains is for the 15mm cold water supply pipe to be connected up, for a new hole to be drilled for the overflow, and for the overflow pipe itself to be laid in.

Changing the position

If you want to change the position of the WC, it's important that you don't contravene the Building Regulations. So it's a good idea to contact your local

1 Turn off the supply to the cistern, then flush to empty it. Disconnect the pipes, cutting them free if necessary.

2 Remove any fixing screws driven through the back of the cistern so you can lift the tank carefully off the brackets.

3 Unscrew and take out the pan. Block up the outlet socket on the soil pipe while you drill and chisel out the old mortar.

building inspector to check that your plans are in order. There are a number of points that you ought to consider. The most important of these are concerned with the waste run, which should always be in 100mm (4in) UPVC plastic pipe.

Most WCs are situated on an outside wall and you won't run into too many problems if you just want to move the suite along that wall. You can extend the waste along the skirting from where it enters the room and then use a 90° connector to take it into the back of the pan. The waste pipe branch should not be longer than 6m (20ft), should incorporate a 100mm (4in) fall and should contain as few bends as possible. Usually, the pipe can be neatly boxed in to conceal it.

If you want to install a completely new WC and waste branch, you'll have to make a new connection into the drainage system either at the soil stack or, if the WC is on the ground floor, at an inspection chamber. This is a somewhat ambitious job and one where it is worth taking professional advice — particularly if you have a two-pipe drainage system with a cast iron soil pipe. See page 208 for more information about work involving soil stacks.

1 Here, the cistern and soil pipe will be hidden behind a false wall. Join the pan to the soil pipe with a 'Multikwik' connector.

2 Mark the position of the cistern within the framework. It needs to be screwed to the back wall as well as being supported on brackets.

3 Connect the overflow pipe to the top of the cistern, then run it at a slight downward gradient to a place where it will be visible on an outside wall.

4 Set the siphon over the outlet in the base of the cistern, then assemble the linkage for the flushing mechanism.

5 Run in the 15mm cold water feed pipe attaching it to the ballvalve assembly. Make sure the capnut is tightened fully.

6 Connect the flush pipe to the bottom of the siphon and the pan. Test the system, adjusting the float arm if necessary.

198 INSTALLING A BIDET

Until recently, the bidet was regarded as something of a curiosity in the bathroom. But it is, in fact, a useful and versatile appliance.

There are two types of bidet to choose from. The over-rim or wash-basin bidet operates, as its name implies, like an ordinary basin. In fact, it is plumbed in identically, often sharing the hot and cold supplies to the basin. This bidet can have individual pillar taps or a mixer, and the most up-to-date version of the latter has a spray at the end of the nozzle.

The second type of bidet is known as a rim supply bidet with ascending spray, and is somewhat more difficult to install than the basin type. When you turn on the taps, warm water is first directed round the underside of the rim, so making it more comfortable to sit on. The supply can then be switched to a spray in the bottom of the bidet, which works like a fountain. This means that the rose is covered in water

when the pan is filled. So in order to reduce the risk of soiled water being siphoned back into the plumbing system, the hot water supply must be taken directly from the hot cylinder and the cold from the cold cistern. This is where the extra plumbing work comes in, and how much you have to do depends on where the tanks are situated. The base of the cold water cistern should also be 2.75m (9ft) above the inlet of the bidet.

When you come to deal with the waste, you'll need to fit a 75mm (3in) deep seal trap if you've got single stack drainage, and the 32mm (1¼in) waste pipe — 38mm (1½in) if the run is between 1.7m (5ft 6in) and 2.3m (7ft 6in) maximum — must connect directly into the stack. For information about this, see page 208. On a two-pipe drainage system, you need only fit a 50mm (2in) shallow trap, and the waste can discharge directly into a gully or hopper head.

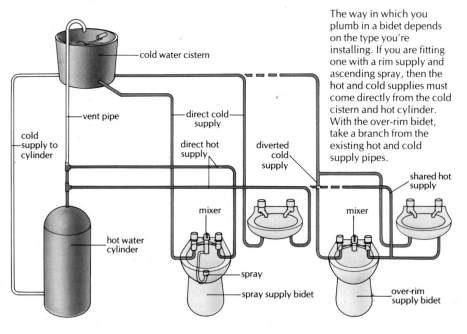

The way in which you plumb in a bidet depends on the type you're installing. If you are fitting one with a rim supply and ascending spray, then the hot and cold supplies must come directly from the cold cistern and hot cylinder. With the over-rim bidet, take a branch from the existing hot and cold supply pipes.

cold water cistern

vent pipe

direct cold supply

cold supply to cylinder

direct hot supply

diverted cold supply

shared hot supply

mixer

mixer

hot water cylinder

spray

spray supply bidet

over-rim supply bidet

INSTALLING A BIDET 199

1 Link the mixer unit, incorporating the pop-up waste control, to the tap headgear and screw on the flange to hold it firmly in place.

2 Screw on the nuts to hold the taps in position, making sure there are washers on both sides of the bidet, then fit the decorative covers.

3 Work a layer of plumber's putty round the flanges of the slotted waste outlet and spray rose and set them in the base of the bowl.

4 Slip a washer over the waste outlet and screw on the waste extension piece. On some types you have to fit a backnut before doing this.

5 Next, connect the bendable metal hose to the bottom of the rose and take the other end to the spray outlet on the mixer control unit.

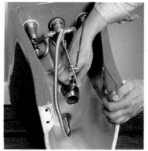

6 Link the control rods of the pop-up waste. Connect one end to the plunger and insert the other into the waste outlet, where the plug is fitted.

7 Make up a P-trap and screw it to the waste outlet. You may need to offset it slightly to avoid the waste mechanism.

8 As with a bath, you will find it easier to connect the water supply to the bidet if you fit pliable pipe to the tap tails.

9 Fit the waste pipe to the trap. Connect the hot and cold supplies and finally screw the pan to the floor.

200 INSTALLING A SHOWER

To many people, there are few pleasures that come near to relaxing in a hot bath; indeed, in many homes a bath is still the only means of providing a complete wash, but the increasing popularity of the shower is steadily changing that.

Baths do have a number of drawbacks and it is these that shower manufacturers have been able to capitalise on. Baths take up a considerable amount of space; they take time to fill; and they use a lot of expensively heated hot water.

Showers, on the other hand, are more hygienic, they are easier to control, and quick to use. The other main benefit is that the average shower uses only 20 per cent of the water a bath would. Furthermore, because a shower cubicle doesn't take up much room — about 760mm (2ft 6in) square is all that's required — it doesn't have to be sited in the bathroom. Providing you can meet the plumbing requirements, you can put a shower in a bedroom, on a landing, in a downstairs utility room or cloakroom, or even under the stairs. In fact, by not installing the shower in the bathroom you could avoid the usual bathroom traffic jams first thing in the morning!

The simplest shower

If you don't want to go to the trouble (and expense) of installing an independent shower, the easiest alternative is to make use of the bath and its plumbing. You're probably familiar with the basic rubber hose shower attachment, together with its limitations, but you can buy a bath/shower mixer that simply replaces the bath taps. This has a spout which is used to fill the bath and a flexible hose leading to a shower rose, which you can hook on the wall. A plunger mechanism lets you decide whether you want to work the shower or run water into the bath. As you can

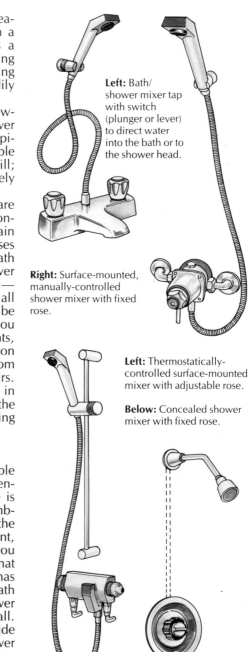

Left: Bath/shower mixer tap with switch (plunger or lever) to direct water into the bath or to the shower head.

Right: Surface-mounted, manually-controlled shower mixer with fixed rose.

Left: Thermostatically-controlled surface-mounted mixer with adjustable rose.

Below: Concealed shower mixer with fixed rose.

If you have a conventional plumbing system with a cold water cistern in the loft and a hot water cylinder, say, in an airing cupboard, feeding the hot taps, then fitting a shower mixer in a cubicle or over a bath is virtually the same as installing any tap outlet. But to minimise the problem of the water running cold or scalding hot when the bath taps are operated, take the cold supply direct from the cistern and the hot from the feed and expansion pipe above the main draw off point.

Since the supply of water to the shower will be under gravity only, you should also check that there is a pressure head of at least 1m (3ft 3in) between the bottom of the cistern and the shower rose. This will ensure a good strong flow of water to the rose when the tap is turned on.

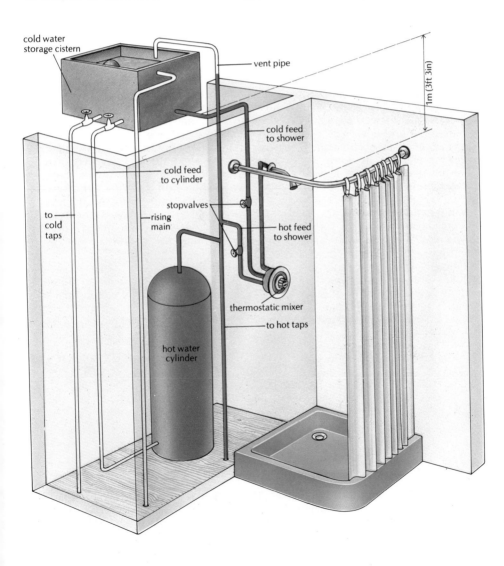

cold water storage cistern

vent pipe

1m (3ft 3in)

cold feed to shower

cold feed to cylinder

stopvalves

to cold taps

rising main

hot feed to shower

thermostatic mixer

to hot taps

hot water cylinder

see, this arrangement provides an easy and cheap shower. The only extras you'll need are a shower screen or a curtain to prevent water splashing over the bathroom floor.

As with all showers, there must be sufficient pressure in the water supply in order to get a good flow of water through the rose. With the basic bath/shower mixer you will also have to adjust the taps delicately to obtain the water pressure and temperature you require for a comfortable shower.

But because of the way your bath plumbing is likely to be organised, someone may only need to flush a WC or run the hot tap over the kitchen sink to cause sudden variations in the temperature and flow. You could even scald yourself as a consequence. The simplest way of avoiding these unpleasant occurrences is to buy a thermostatic mixing valve.

An independent shower

If you want to install a shower in its own cubicle, or a separate shower over the bath, you have a choice of two methods. You can either use your home's hot and cold water system to supply the water or, if this isn't possible, you can install a new electric shower. So before you go out and buy a

shower unit, you must first check out the plumbing system.

Fortunately, the design of most domestic plumbing systems is such that you should have few problems in fitting an ordinary mixer shower (see page 201). Because the cold water cistern is normally in the loft, in all probability its base will be at least 1m (3ft) above the shower rose which will give sufficient 'head' of water. The cold water supply to the mixer is taken from a new 15mm pipe, which you'll have to run from the cold water cistern. The hot water supply should be taken from the vent and draw-off (expansion) pipe that leaves the top of the hot water cylinder.

You may be tempted to take an easier alternative by branching off the bath or basin hot and cold feeds, but don't. The mixing valve works most efficiently if the water supplies have an equal and constant pressure. By connecting the pipes directly to the cold water cistern and hot water cylinder outlet, you will ensure the minimum of temperature fluctuation.

Mixer taps

Once you've got the water to the site of the new shower, you can connect the pipes to an array of different styled controls and shower roses — some

1 Fitting a shower rose. Fit the glide, which incorporates a rose holder, to the runner, then screw this bar to the wall.

2 Mark the position of the hose outlet on the wall and run the pipe from the mixer to this point behind the cubicle.

3 Connect the pipe to the hose union with a compression joint concealed by a plate. Screw the other end to the rose.

1 A surface-mounted mixer. Screw the backplate to the wall. Fit the unit, mark the pipe entry points and run them in.

2 You will find it easier to make the supply connections at the mixer if you first disconnect the chrome stubs.

3 Screw the hose on to the mixer outlet and take the other end to the rose, which can either be fixed or adjustable.

mixers can be recessed into a wall; others are surface mounted. Looks will play an important part in deciding what you choose because the unit is going to be visible, but on the practical side make sure the mixer can deliver about 4.5 litres (1 gal) of water a minute at about 43°C (109°F) — a typical good, soaking shower.

There are two types of mixer from which to choose: manual and thermostatic. There are two controls on the manual mixer, one for the rate of flow and the other to set the temperature of the water. However, the mixer will still be affected by fluctuations in the supply, so it's important that you run the

supply pipes as previously described. For ease, you could branch off the hot system close to the shower but then you've got to put up with the shower suddenly going cooler when someone turns on a hot tap. This is where the more expensive thermostatic mixer scores, because it allows you not only to control the flow but also to set the temperature of the water and maintain it at that level despite fluctuations in the supply. These mixers usually incorporate a cutout device which shuts down the shower if, for example, the cold water supply pipe bursts, leaving only very hot water flowing through the mixing valve.

1 The shower tray. Fit the waste outlet to the tray and connect a shallow-seal P-trap to it. This should have an inspection eye.

2 Temporarily set the tray in place so you can work out where the waste pipe needs to be run in relation to the trap.

3 The tray should be set level on a brick or timber plinth if it does not incorporate its own mounting frame.

204 INSTALLING A SHOWER

You may be unlucky and not have a typical plumbing system, in which case you'll have to make some modifications, install a shower pump or fit a mains pressure electric shower (see page 206 for details).

The commonest problem you'll have to deal with is a cold water cistern that isn't high enough above the shower rose to give a sufficient 'head' of water. If the cistern is already in the loft, you could raise it up on a platform. In itself, this isn't a difficult plumbing job — just fiddly. Similarly, if the cistern is above a hot water cylinder in the airing cupboard, then it is a quite straightforward job to transfer it to the loft to give the head of water you need.

However, moving the cistern into the loft is out of the question if you have a flat roof. The easiest solution, here, is to install a shower pump, and this will also involve you in a small amount of electrical work. If you are not confident that you can do the electrical work, consult a qualified electrician.

You might have a combination hot and cold water storage unit. With this, you've got another problem apart from low water pressure, because the cold water capacity of the unit is only large enough to supply the hot cylinder and not any taps or other outlet points. In fact, the other taps will probably be supplied direct from the mains. What you have to do, therefore, is to install a new small cold water storage cistern, which will be used exclusively for the shower, and a shower pump. The alternative is to install an electric shower, virtually bypassing the entire plumbing system.

If you've got a multi-point gas heater, and so no storage cylinder, you should still be able to fit a shower, but take professional advice on this because you may have to fit a 'pressure governor' on the cold water supply to the heater and shower.

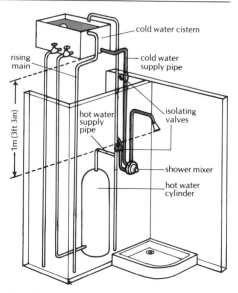

cold water cistern

rising main

cold water supply pipe

hot water supply pipe

isolating valves

1m (3ft 3in)

shower mixer

hot water cylinder

It may be necessary to raise the cistern in the loft (see above), otherwise there are alternative shower arrangements using shower pumps. These need to be wired to a ring circuit via a double-pole, switched fused connection unit.

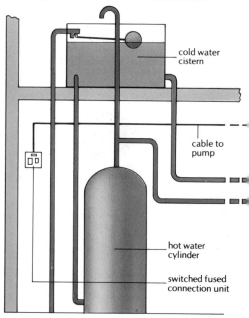

cold water cistern

cable to pump

hot water cylinder

switched fused connection unit

Right: On packaged hot and cold water systems, install a small cold water cistern to feed the shower and take the hot water direct from the cylinder. You'll also need to install a shower pump (see below).

Below: Depending on the type, shower pumps can be located either somewhere convenient outside the shower cubicle (on the floor under a bath, for example) or within it, protected by a waterproof casing. If the pump is operated by a flow switch, so that it comes on when the shower is turned on, it should be plumbed into the outlet side of the mixer running to the shower rose.

However, there are pumps that can be turned on and off independently of the flow by a 12 volt switch or a cord-operated switch which takes its power from the pump itself. The pump is connected to the hot and cold supplies before they reach the mixer.

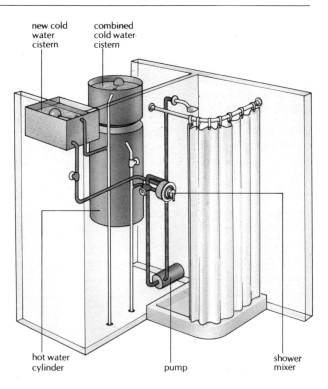

new cold water cistern

combined cold water cistern

hot water cylinder

pump

shower mixer

Pump concealed behind cubicle wall.

Pump inside cubicle in waterproof casing.

Pump outside cubicle on the floor.

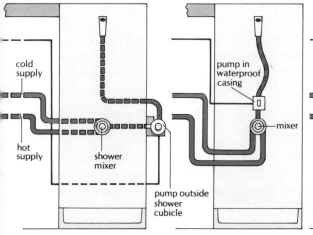

cold supply

hot supply

shower mixer

pump outside shower cubicle

pump in waterproof casing

mixer

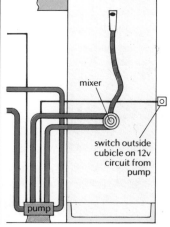

mixer

switch outside cubicle on 12v circuit from pump

pump

206 ELECTRIC SHOWERS

If you can't run a shower easily from your existing plumbing system, it may be worth considering fitting an electric shower. This is economical to run as you only heat the water you use. All it requires is a 15mm cold water feed, branching from the rising main, and a separate 30A electrical circuit. Because all the workings are concealed behind a waterproof cover, the unit can even be installed inside a shower cubicle.

As the shower contains its own heating element, you don't have to worry about a hot water supply, but the need to heat the water instantly reduces the flow through the unit. Therefore, because it emits less water than an ordinary shower, it's considered less 'wet', but still adequate for giving a refreshing spray of water.

When you buy one of these showers, it's best to buy one with a temperature stabiliser so that the temperature of the water doesn't fluctuate if the pressure in the rising main drops. Normally, if the pressure drops too low, a pressure sensor will turn off the shower before the water has a chance to overheat and scald you.

Containing the water

Perhaps it is stating the obvious to say that a shower cubicle must be waterproof, but it is a point worth reiterating. Water has a way of seeping through the tiniest of gaps and can give rise to all sorts of problems if not checked.

If you are installing a shower over a bath, the majority of cubicle problems are solved immediately, as you're using a ready-made system to dispose of the waste water. All you need is a waterproof curtain or a plastic or safety glass screen to provide the sides of the shower cubicle.

Installing a new cubicle requires a

Types of shower cubicle

Left: A shower can be fitted in a small alcove. **Right:** Freestanding units are quickly installed. **Below:** A simple screen turns a bath into a shower cubicle.

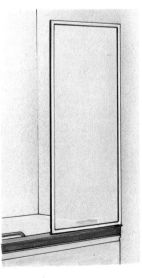

ELECTRIC SHOWERS 207

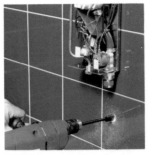

1 Mark the fixing holes for the unit and the cable entry hole. Drill these holes and mount the shower at about chest height on the cubicle wall.

2 Drill an access hole for the cold water feed. Use a flat bit on cubicles lined with laminate and a masonry bit on a ceramic tiled surface.

3 Connect up the 15mm cold feed to the inlet of the shower. Do not forget to protect tiles from a blowlamp when making capillary joints.

4 Next, screw the shower hose on to the outlet. The connector must incorporate a washer in order to make an effective watertight seal.

5 Connect the 6mm^2 2-core and earth cable to the terminals of the unit. Run the other end to a 30 amp double-pole cord-operated switch.

6 Fit the rose to an adjustable glide. Then screw on the casing, checking that the fingerplates link correctly to the controls behind.

little more work, particularly in deciding how you're going to run the waste pipe to the domestic drainage system. You can get round some of the installation work by using a shower cabinet with a combined tray and sides, but in most cases you'll be installing a ceramic or plastic tray and erecting one of the vast selection of proprietary screens round it. It's vital that the join between the two is waterproof and this is usually ensured using mastic.

You could, if you wish, build your own solid surround to a shower tray, facing it with ceramic tiles or laminate.

In all cases, make sure you leave enough space under the tray to attach the 50mm (2in) shallow seal P-trap. This may mean raising the tray on bricks, wooden blocks or metal brackets. A shower tray with a corner outlet will improve access to the trap in case of blockage. The waste pipe should have a diameter of 38mm (1½in) and it should run with as shallow a fall as possible to connect into a soil stack or to discharge over a hopper (see page 208). Don't position your shower so that you have to cut through any joists in order to install the waste pipe.

208 DEALING WITH THE WASTE

When you start dealing with soil stacks, and waste systems generally, plumbing work can get more involved. This is not so much because of the techniques required — plastic waste systems, after all, have either solvent weld or pushfit joints — but because of the type of system you may have and the building regulations regarding how waste pipes should be run. Consequently, it's worth restating that before you start to modify or add to your plumbing system you should make sure you know what you are going to do with the waste.

Single-stack drainage
If you've got single-stack drainage (either a system that was installed when the house was built, or a properly carried out conversion from a two-pipe system), your problems are reduced considerably. The diagram opposite shows exactly what your system should conform to, but there are a number of points to bear in mind if you are carrying out any modifications.

If you are installing a new WC upstairs, try and connect it into the existing soil waste branch with a 'running swept tee' joint so you don't actually have to make a new connection into the stack. If this isn't possible and the waste pipe comes from the other direction, you'll have to insert a 'double equal branch' into the stack so that both runs can join at the same level. This may prove difficult if the soil pipe is inside the house and boxed in, as you may be limited for space. Even if the pipe is on the outside, you may still have problems when trying to manoeuvre the junction into place after you've cut the pipe.

The waste from a new shower or basin could also be linked to a convenient waste pipe, but with a basin you may be able to arrange the waste run so that it can connect directly to the stack. Here, you can use a fitting known as a 'saddle' or 'strap boss' (a curved plastic plate with a socket inlet in the centre).

Before you begin work on modifying or installing a new above-ground drainage system, however, you should draw up plans of the system and submit them to your local building inspector. It is essential that any work you do is with his approval and complies with local building regulations.

The same type of connection problem exists at ground floor level, but here you can link a new WC directly to the underground drain, either at an existing inspection chamber or at a new one which you'll have to build. However, this is a job which goes beyond basic domestic plumbing, and you will definitely have to consult your local authority for advice and approval.

Two-pipe drainage
Because the soil stack of a two-pipe system is likely to be made of cast iron, you should not try to make additional connections to it. Instead, organise your new waste runs so that they will connect into existing waste branches inside. There are plastic pushfit connectors to link old cast iron pipes to new plastic runs; if the old pipe is bigger than the 100mm (4in) diameter pipe now used, there's an offset connector that will make the conversion. New shower and basin wastes can discharge into the hopper at the top of a downpipe, or they can be taken to a downstairs gully.

However, if you intend making alterations in a two-pipe system, you should consult your local building inspector. Hopper heads, for example, are considered unsanitary and are no longer encouraged; it may be better, therefore, to modify the system or to convert it to a single-stack layout, depending on where the appliances are sited. In turn, this may mean replacing the traps and waste and soil pipes.

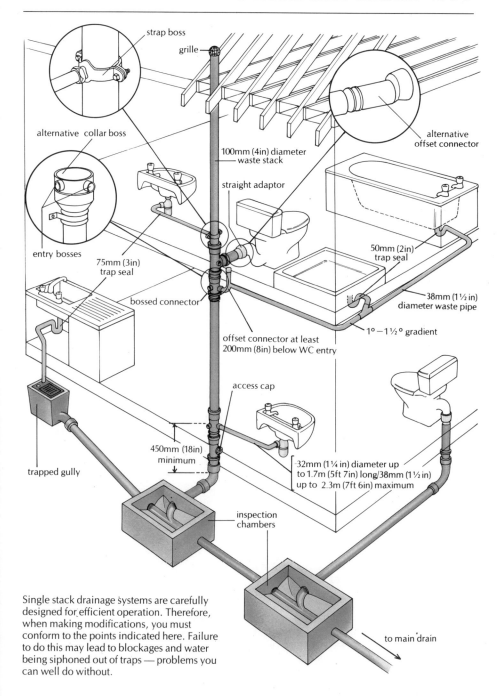

strap boss

grille

alternative collar boss

alternative offset connector

100mm (4in) diameter waste stack

straight adaptor

entry bosses

75mm (3in) trap seal

50mm (2in) trap seal

bossed connector

38mm (1½ in) diameter waste pipe

1° − 1½ ° gradient

offset connector at least 200mm (8in) below WC entry

access cap

450mm (18in) minimum

trapped gully

32mm (1¼ in) diameter up to 1.7m (5ft 7in) long/38mm (1½ in) up to 2.3m (7ft 6in) maximum

inspection chambers

to main drain

Single stack drainage systems are carefully designed for efficient operation. Therefore, when making modifications, you must conform to the points indicated here. Failure to do this may lead to blockages and water being siphoned out of traps — problems you can well do without.

210 COLD WATER CISTERNS

Most domestic plumbing work entails installing or repositioning fittings — a basin may need to be moved or a new shower fitted — but to carry out most of this work, you won't have to touch the cold water cistern. Usually, if you want a new supply of water, all you have to do is run a branch from a convenient point on the pipe network. Only if you are installing a shower will you need to run a new cold feed from the cistern; and then there are alternative plumbing arrangements which mean you don't necessarily have to do this.

Modern cold water cisterns are usually made from plastic, although you may well find that you've got one made from glassfibre, asbestos cement or zinc coated (galvanised) steel. The cistern is normally sited in the loft, but if your house has a flat roof it's quite likely to be over the hot water cylinder in the airing cupboard. In fact, as stated previously, there are package systems where the cold water cistern and the hot water cylinder are incorporated in the same unit.

Basic maintenance
Although you won't have much call to get to the cistern, it still requires periodic checks, say, about two or three times a year.

Plastic and asbestos cement cisterns don't corrode, but if you've got a grey galvanised steel tank then this is something worth looking for. These cisterns do have a long life, but the increasing use of copper pipe can lead to problems. Copper and zinc in the same system, with a slightly acid mains supply of water, can set up an electrolytic action which causes the zinc to dissolve. Without its protective coating the steel cistern is defenceless against the effects of corrosion.

However, you can still use copper pipes with this type of cistern if you suspend what's known as a sacrificial

anode (a piece of magnesium) in the water. As this is more prone to electrolytic action than zinc it will slowly dissolve instead, so leaving the zinc layer intact and the cistern protected. If you do find that the zinc has started to wear away, drain down the cistern, scrape off any rust and then treat the inside with a couple of coats of bituminous paint. Make sure it's the type made for use in cisterns as this won't taint the water.

The other item to check is the ballvalve. Although this may be working, it only takes a small piece of grit brought up in the rising main, or a speck of hard water scale, to stop the valve opening and closing properly. If the taps aren't being used too regularly, you may not notice that anything is wrong until you draw off a lot of water and suddenly the taps go dry because the cistern hasn't been filling properly. Repairing the ballvalve, however, is a simple job (see page 225), and all it may need is a good clean or the washer replaced. At worst, replacing the entire ballvalve is a straightforward job.

Installing a new outlet
Making a new outlet in your cistern to feed, say, a new shower shouldn't cause any real problems, although you may find working in the restricted space of a loft a bit awkward.

With plastic and galvanised cisterns, you can use an electric drill fitted with a special tank cutter accessory or a hole saw of the appropriate size to make the outlet 50mm (2in) up from the bottom. Then, install the outlet fitting and screw up the swivel connector to secure the pipe. Remember, when working with plastic cisterns, never to use jointing compound — only PTFE tape — to make watertight seals. Always use compression fittings instead of capillary types when working in a roof space, as the flame from a blowlamp could ignite

COLD WATER CISTERNS 211

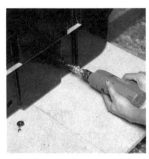

1 Set the new cistern on an 18mm (¾in) platform. Drill all the outlet holes 50mm (2in) above the base using a hole saw cutter fitted to a drill.

2 Wind PTFE tape clockwise round the thread of the tank connector. Slip on a washer and push the thread through from inside the cistern.

3 Slip another washer over the thread, then tighten the connector nut to form a watertight seal. Repeat this operation for all outlets.

4 Connect short stubs of pipe to the connectors using compression fittings. You can wrap PTFE tape round the pipe ends for a good seal.

5 Connect gatevalves to the ends of the pipe stubs before continuing the runs. These are better than stopvalves, as they help prevent hammering.

6 When cutting the inlet hole at the top of the cistern, support the flexing wall with a block of wood held against the inside face.

7 Fit a high-pressure ballvalve to the inlet as you would a tank connector. Then connect the rising main to this.

8 Similarly, drill a hole and fit a plastic tank connector to the overflow outlet. Run this pipe to discharge at the eaves.

9 Fit the lid and make a hole in it to take the expansion pipe from the hot water cylinder. Then lag the tank and pipes.

212 COLD WATER CISTERNS

the dust there and cause a major fire.

Making an outlet in an asbestos cistern may be a little more difficult because of the nature of the material and the extra thickness of the walls. However, by marking the hole on the side, at least 100mm (4in) up from the bottom, and drilling a series of small holes round the inside of the perimeter, you should be able to tap out the centre and clean the edges with a half-round or round file. You'll find drilling this material much easier if you first grind the tip of the bit to a sharp point. When you fit the connector, make sure you use soft washers against the asbestos surface to get a really watertight seal.

Installing a new cistern

Just because you've got an old cistern doesn't necessarily mean you've got to replace it, but if the existing one is badly corroded, or too small for your present needs, a new one is called for. You may be able to repair holes in a galvanised cistern with epoxy resin filler, but this is only a stopgap measure and it is best to cut your losses and replace the cistern entirely.

You will also have to install a small cistern as a feed and expansion tank for the boiler if you're converting a direct hot water system into an indirect one. If you have a combined cold water cistern and hot water cylinder unit, the capacity of the cistern is usually only great enough to serve the cylinder, so if you want to install a conventional shower, you'll have to put in another small cold water cistern to serve it.

Plastic cisterns are the best to use; and one with a capacity of 228 litres (50 gal) is sufficient for household needs. Because the plastic is flexible, such cisterns can usually be manipulated even through small trap doors to the loft. However, if access to the loft is a problem, take up two 114 litre (25 gal) cisterns and connect them together in series. The ballvalve inlet should go at the top of one of the tanks and the outlets should be taken from the bottom of the other. The cisterns are connected by a length of 28mm pipe.

You can also use this 'tandem' arrangement if, when you've pushed the old cistern to one side, there's not the space to install a new larger one. You're in luck if the old cistern can be lowered through the trap door because most cisterns were installed before the roofs that cover them.

You may find it easier to drill the holes for the pipe connections to the cistern before setting it on a chipboard or timber platform. The expansion pipe from the hot water cylinder should discharge over the rim, while the inlet pipe from the rising main should be installed as high on the side as possible. The overflow pipe should be fitted 25mm (1in) below the outlet point of the ballvalve, which should be the high-pressure type. The supply pipes must be connected 50mm (2in) up from the bottom of the cistern.

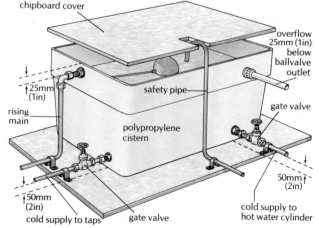

chipboard cover

overflow 25mm (1in) below ballvalve outlet

25mm (1in)

rising main

safety pipe

polypropylene cistern

gate valve

50mm (2in)

50mm (2in)

cold supply to taps

gate valve

cold supply to hot water cylinder

REPLACING A HOT WATER CYLINDER 213

Replacing a hot water storage cylinder is a job you'll be forced to do only if the existing one develops a leak; there is no alternative. Of course, you may want to put in a larger cylinder if the present one can't cope with the demands of a family first thing in the morning and again in the evening. If there are two adults and two children, for example, a cylinder with a capacity of 140 litres (30 gal) or 160 litres (35 gal) should be sufficient to prevent running out of hot water.

The other main reason for changing the cylinder is to install an indirect version in place of a direct type. It's certainly worth doing this if you live in a hard water area, as it prevents scale building up in the boiler.

However, before you jump in with your spanners, you've a little investigating to do to find out exactly how the existing system operates; it's not a bad idea to label the pipes next to the hot cylinder so you know where each goes. When you've decided whether you've got a typical direct or indirect cylinder, a self-priming indirect cylinder or a packaged hot and cold system (which could be direct, indirect or self-priming), you can decide on the type and size of cylinder you want to replace it and how you are going to deal with the pipework. Remember, if you want to install a new indirect cylinder you'll also need to fit a new feed and expansion cistern (header tank), unless you use a 'self-priming' system, which doesn't require one (see diagram). However, some plumbers don't like using these because they consider that the air bubble inside doesn't effectively separate the primary circuit from the domestic hot water.

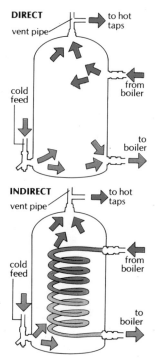

Types of hot water cylinder

With a direct cylinder (A), cold water from the cistern is fed into the bottom of the tank and then passes to the boiler for heating before being returned to the cylinder. In contrast, an indirect cylinder (B) contains a heat exchanger which heats the water in the cylinder. Self-priming cylinders (C) work on a similar principal, but the water in the heat exchanger is kept separate from the water in the cylinder by an airlock. You can also get a self-priming packaged system (D) which incorporates a cold water cistern on top to feed the hot cylinder below.

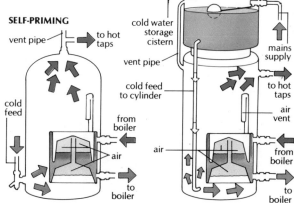

214 REPLACING A HOT WATER CYLINDER

The first, and obvious, thing to do is to turn off the boiler. Before you disconnect the immersion heater (if there is one) from its switch, you must turn off the electricity supply. Then you can drain the cylinder. Close the gatevalve on the cold water feed pipe and open the hot taps. Unfortunately, if there is no gatevalve, you'll have to tie up the ballvalve in the cold water cistern and then drain this, too. However, if you fit a rubber bung in the mouth of the outlet in the cistern, you can restore the cold water supply.

The hot water cylinder should have a draincock on its side near the bottom, so you can run the water out of this and through a hose feeding into a yard gully. Alternatively, if there is no draincock, you'll have to siphon the water out. To do this, disconnect the outlet on the top of the cylinder and fill a length of hose completely with water; put your thumbs firmly over the ends. Insert one end of the hose through the outlet and deeply into the cylinder, taking the other to a yard gully. Take your thumb off the end, and the cylinder should empty itself.

If you've already got an indirect cylinder, you will have to drain the primary circuit as well, and you can do this from the draincock by the side of the boiler. It's important that you allow the system to cool before attempting this. Don't forget to tie up the float arm of the ballvalve in the feed and expansion cistern, otherwise you'll never drain the circuit! You may be lucky and have a stopvalve on the cistern feed.

With the system drained, you can undo all the connections linking pipes to the cylinder. You may have to bend the pipes slightly so that you can work

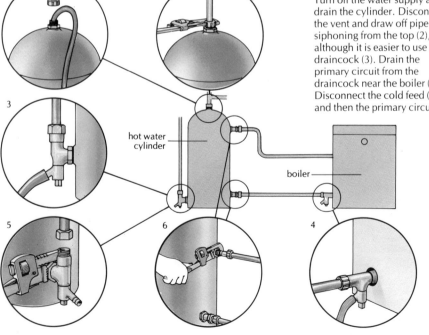

Removing an indirect cylinder
Turn off the water supply and drain the cylinder. Disconnect the vent and draw off pipe (1) if siphoning from the top (2), although it is easier to use the draincock (3). Drain the primary circuit from the draincock near the boiler (4). Disconnect the cold feed (5), and then the primary circuit (6).

hot water cylinder

boiler

REPLACING A HOT WATER CYLINDER 215

1 Set the cylinder on timber battens to allow air to get underneath. This will prevent condensation forming when cold water enters the cylinder.

2 Wrap PTFE tape round the connector that will link the feed and expansion pipe to the top of the cylinder. Straight versions are also available.

3 Screw the connector into the boss on top of the cylinder, making sure it is tight, and then join the pipework to it with a compression coupling.

4 Similarly, make up the male connector for the cold water inlet. Screw this into the female socket, making the final turns with a spanner.

5 Install a draincock just before the feed from the cold water cistern enters the bottom of the cylinder, so the hot water system can be drained.

6 The flow and return pipes to the boiler are joined to the cylinder with female/male connectors. Check these are tight in their sockets.

7 If fitting an immersion heater (see page 65), use the bosses provided in the top or side of the cylinder.

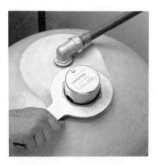

8 Use an immersion heater spanner to fix the unit firmly in place. Remove the cover to expose the wiring terminals.

9 Unless the cylinder is already insulated, fit a separate insulation blanket, leaving the heater control panel exposed.

216 REPLACING A HOT WATER CYLINDER

them free. This should enable you to drag the cylinder clear.

Before standing the new cylinder in place, check the 'tappings' of the inlets and outlets to make sure they haven't worked loose. Then, when in position, check that the tappings align with the pipework. It's quite likely that you'll have to adjust the runs, and often it's easier to do this by cutting back a short length of pipe and inserting a new section bent to the required angle.

You will certainly have to make some modifications if you're replacing a direct cylinder with an ordinary indirect one. The boiler flow and return pipes will have to be connected to the primary circuit heat exchanger in the cylinder. Just before the hot flow from the boiler enters the top of the heat exchanger, you'll have to 'tee' in an expansion pipe which leads up to a new feed and expansion cistern in the loft. The feed from this to the primary circuit is connected to the boiler return pipe taking water from the heat exchanger back to the boiler.

Now you can make up the cylinder connections and join the pipework. If you're not going to fit an immersion heater, you'll have to screw a blanking plate over the boss. With all this done, you can start to fill the system.

In order to prevent air locks, it's best to do this from the bottom up. If you are filling a direct cylinder or the primary circuit of an indirect cylinder run a hose from the cold tap over the kitchen sink to the draincock by the boiler. Make sure the plug is unscrewed and turn on the tap. The water entering will force the air back through the system. With a direct cylinder when water flows out of the vent pipe into the cold water cistern, you'll know the cistern is filled. Turn off the tap and close the draincock, then restore the cold feed to the cylinder either by turning on the gatevalve or by removing the bung

from the outlet in the cold water storage cistern.

With a primary circuit, when the water begins to flow through the feed outlet into the feed and expansion cistern this indicates that the system is filled. Turn off the tap, close the stopcock on or near to the boiler and then turn on the stopvalve controlling the flow of water into the cistern via a ballvalve, or release the float arm. If the boiler is connected to a central heating system, the radiator bleed valves should be left open when filling; close them as soon as the water begins to flow from them.

All that remains is to fill the rest of the cylinder, which you can do in exactly the same way as for a direct cylinder, connecting the hose to its draincock. Now, turn on the boiler or immersion heater to check the system; the expansion of the pipes caused by hot water flowing through them may weaken a joint, resulting in a leak. When you're happy that all is in order, you can lag the cylinder with a suitable proprietary jacket.

Refilling the system
By filling the system from the bottom through the draincocks, you'll reduce the risk of air locks forming. Connect one end of a hose to a tap supplied from the rising main, and the other end to the draincock. When the tap is turned on, the pressure of water will drive the air before it right back through the system.

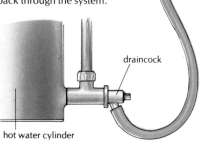

draincock

hot water cylinder

IMMERSION HEATERS 217

Many people frown on using an immersion as a means of heating water, primarily because they think it is expensive to run. But if used wisely with a well-lagged storage cylinder, an immersion heater is an easy, clean and economical way of providing a hot water supply. It's also an ideal back-up system, particularly in summer when you may not want to go to the trouble, say, of lighting a solid fuel backboiler to get hot water.

An immersion heater fits into a special tapping usually provided in the cylinder, although you can cut your own access point. For the utmost economy, it's best to install a heater with a dual element or two separate units, one at the top of the cylinder, the other at the bottom. This way, if you only want a small amount of hot water you don't have to heat the whole cylinder; you simply switch on the upper element. Furthermore, if you connect the heater to a time switch, you can limit its operation automatically to periods just before peak demands are normally put on the hot water system.

If you are replacing a burnt out immersion heater, you should already have a suitable, nearby electricity supply to connect into. However, if

1 Wrap PTFE tape round the thread of the immersion heater, slip on a washer smeared with jointing compound and screw the heater into the boss.

2 Once the heater is in place, on some models, you will have to fit the thermostat in a separate operation. First remove the cover.

3 The thermostat consists of a control unit set on top of a long rod, which passes down through the casing into the cylinder.

4 Set the temperature to which you want the water heated, say 60°C, by turning the dial on the control unit with a screwdriver.

5 Wire the element to the thermostat, then connect 1.5mm² 3-core heat-resisting flex to the terminals as shown.

6 Connect the flex to a switched fused connection unit fitted with a 3 amp fuse and run on a 15 amp radial circuit.

218 **IMMERSION HEATERS**

you are putting one in for the first time, it's probably best to run a new 15A radial circuit from the consumer unit or fuse box to a 20A fused double-pole switch. Then, you can connect the heat-resisting flex from the control panel on the heater to this.

Alternatively, if you're installing a 3kW heater or one of a lower rating, you can plug the heater into a 13A socket on a ring or radial circuit. If you choose this method, consider installing a fused connection unit to supply it. This will ensure that the outlet point is only used for the heater so it cannot be disconnected inadvertently.

Again, don't attempt any electrical work unless you know exactly what you're doing.

Types of immersion heater
Probably the most common immersion heater is the type that protrudes down into the hot water cylinder, either vertically or at a slight angle, from a boss at the top. Sometimes these units run almost the full depth of the cylinder, and they are often used as a back-up hot water heating system, particularly to a coal-fired back boiler. A thermostat that is also inserted into the cylinder can be set to control the water temperature by switching the unit on and off.

However, this type of immersion heater has the costly disadvantage that all water in the cylinder is heated by expensive electricity, even though only a little may be required. To overcome this you can fit two smaller elements instead, one at the top, the other at the bottom, perhaps keeping the top one on permanently and only turning on the second to supply bath water. For this system to work efficiently the cylinder must be well lagged.

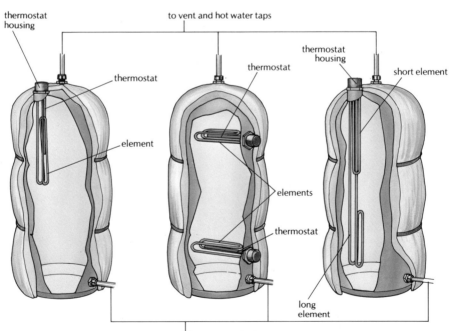

thermostat housing

to vent and hot water taps

thermostat

thermostat housing

short element

thermostat

element

elements

thermostat

long element

cold supply to cylinder

INSTANTANEOUS WATER HEATING 219

The commonest way of heating water for household needs is to have some form of hot water storage system with a boiler of some description that may also be powering a central heating system. You may have an immersion heater as well. However, there is an alternative, and that is some form of instantaneous water heating system that heats the water just before it flows out of the tap.

Gas systems are the most versatile of all. At the top of the range is a 'multipoint' heater which, as its name implies, will supply hot water to various outlet points round the house — over baths, basins and sinks, for example, and even showers. The heater is normally connected to the rising main and has to be sited against an outside wall because it has a balanced flue: the burners use air taken from the outside and not from the room where the heater is situated. You can also get small single point heaters to fit over a sink or basin.

Of the electric heaters, only the instantaneous showers operate in the same way as the gas heaters; that is they only heat the water when the tap is turned on. Other heaters operate like a very small storage system. Each comprises a small cylinder which incorporates two heating elements.

The smaller electric heaters come into their own when you need to provide water at an outlet point that would be difficult to supply by any other means. They are easy to install and they don't require an outside wall.

With an instantaneous gas water heater, when the cold water supply is turned on, water is conducted through a series of channels. These are heated by powerful burners which are ignited simultaneously. Some models also incorporate a cold tap so that cold water can be mixed with the hot on leaving the heater to give the temperature of water required.

Most of these heaters need a balanced flue (below) because the air for the burners has to be drawn from outside and not from the room where it is installed. Similarly, the exhaust gases must not be discharged into the room.

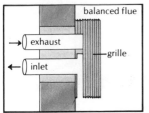

balanced flue

→ exhaust
← inlet
grille

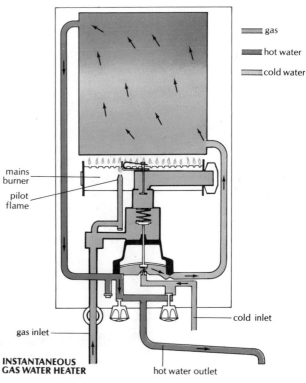

gas
hot water
cold water

mains burner
pilot flame

cold inlet

gas inlet

INSTANTANEOUS GAS WATER HEATER

hot water outlet

220 A GARDEN WATER SUPPLY

When a house is built and the plumbing installed, it's rare that provision is made for an outside water supply. Considering that you need water for the garden and perhaps to wash a car, it's a pity at least the beginnings of a system — an outside tap fixed to the house wall — are not provided. Providing a garden water supply is one of the easiest plumbing projects you can carry out, but you must first get approval from your local water authority; you'll have to pay a higher water rate, and in some areas the garden supply may need to be metered.

Because an outside tap is likely to be used infrequently, take the supply from the rising main. Normally, it's most convenient to do this under the kitchen sink by teeing off the supply leading to the cold water tap. You then have to drill a hole through the outside wall, feed the pipe through and connect a tap to the other end. It's essential to install a stopvalve in the branch just after the tee so the pipe can be drained in winter — a vital safeguard that prevents water freezing in it and so damaging the run. Make sure that you use a suitable outside tap as well. The

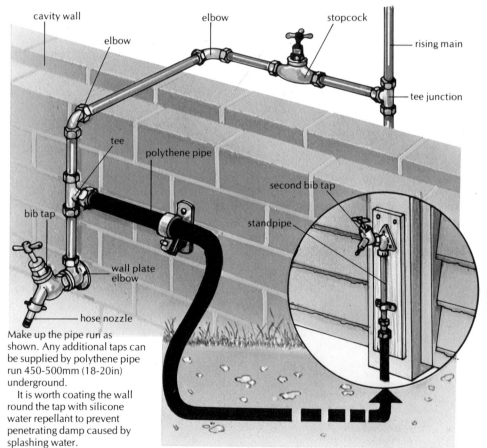

Make up the pipe run as shown. Any additional taps can be supplied by polythene pipe run 450-500mm (18-20in) underground.

It is worth coating the wall round the tap with silicone water repellant to prevent penetrating damp caused by splashing water.

A GARDEN WATER SUPPLY 221

type to buy is an inclined bib tap, which screws into a backplate connector. The headgear of the tap slants outwards so that you can turn the simple crutch handle without grazing your knuckles on the wall. The tap should also have a removable hose union so a garden hose can be fitted easily.

Of course, the garden tap doesn't have to be set against the house wall. It could be positioned against a nearby garage wall, and even inside an outbuilding if needed to supply a washing machine. You could also install a standpipe further down the garden to save having a hose snaking down the path ready for everyone to trip over it when in use.

To give the supply pipe as much protection as possible against frost and even the accidental blow from a spade, it's best to run it underground. For this, use either polythene or plastic pipe. The beauty of polythene is that you can buy it in long, coiled lengths so you shouldn't need any joins underground. Furthermore, the pipe connects easily to copper with compression fittings; it is not so susceptible to frost damage, and has good impact resistance, preventing damage by garden tools.

1 Insert a tee in the rising main above the main stopvalve after turning off the latter. Then connect in the 15mm branch to the garden tap.

2 Fit a stopvalve into the new run inside the house so the branch can be drained easily in winter to prevent freezing and when repairing the tap.

3 Chisel or drill a hole through the outside wall as near to the site of the tap as possible. Keep it small to reduce the amount of making good.

4 Use a 90° elbow to take the run down the outside wall to an angled tap connector incorporating a backplate.

5 Install an inclined bib tap fitted with a removable hose union. Wrap PTFE tape round the thread before fitting.

6 Use a 15 × 15 × 22mm tee to run a 12mm (½in) polythene pipe to other garden taps. This can be run underground.

222 DEALING WITH LEAKING TAPS AND PIPES

Signs
Tap fails to turn off properly.
Tap drips from spout, resulting in un-sightly scale.

Cause Worn washer or worn seating.

Action — pillar and bib taps.
● turn off the water supply to the tap.
● unscrew and lift up the cover to expose the headgear nut.
● hold the tap's spout and undo the nut with a spanner.
● lift out the headgear and remove the jumper unit. The washer is usually attached to the bottom.
● undo the nut holding the washer in place, or prise the washer free.
● if the washer is difficult to remove, replace the jumper unit.

● bath taps require a ¾in washer, basin and sink taps a ½in washer, but you can turn the old washer over as a temporary measure.

If the washer is in good condition, the seating of the tap is worn:
● regrind the seating with a reseating tool (hire rather than buy one, but they are not that common).
● alternatively, fit a washer and reseating set.
● another easy solution is to fit a domed rubber washer that will push well down into the seating when the tap is closed.

After repair:
● replace the headgear and partially close the tap.

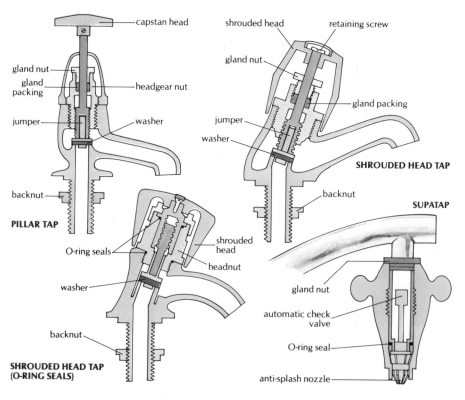

capstan head

gland nut
gland packing
headgear nut
jumper
washer

backnut

PILLAR TAP

shrouded head — retaining screw
gland nut
gland packing
jumper
washer

backnut

SHROUDED HEAD TAP

O-ring seals
washer
shrouded head
headnut

backnut

**SHROUDED HEAD TAP
(O-RING SEALS)**

SUPATAP

gland nut
automatic check valve
O-ring seal
anti-splash nozzle

DEALING WITH LEAKING TAPS AND PIPES 223

● restore the water supply with the tap runing to prevent airlocks.

Action — shrouded head tap.
This type of tap is a more modern design than the previous taps, but the procedure for rewashering and reseating is similar. The biggest problem is in deciding how to remove the shrouded head itself.
● turn off the water supply to the tap.
● prise off the hot or cold indicator cap to reveal the retaining screw.
● undo the screw and remove the shrouded head.
(Alternatively, the retaining screw may be on the side of the head, or the head may just pull off.)
● hold the spout and release the headgear nut, then take out the headgear.
● undo the screw holding the washer in place and secure a new washer.
● reverse the procedure to reassemble the tap and restore the water supply.

Action — Supatap.
With this design of tap there is no need to turn off the water supply.
● turn on the tap a little so there is an even flow of water.
● hold the nozzle in this position and undo the head-nut.
● turn on the tap fully and continue to unscrew the nozzle.
● a cut-off valve will stem the flow of water as the nozzle comes away.
● tap the nozzle upside down in your hand to release the anti-splash device; the washer is attached to its end.
● prise the washer unit free and fit a new one.
● reassemble the tap.

Signs
Water oozing round spindle, or from under shrouded head, with the tap fully closed.
Juddering in the plumbing system when

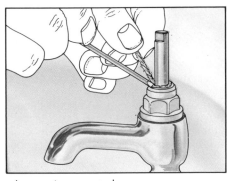

the tap is operated.
Tap turns on too easily.
Cause Worn gland packing on old taps, worn O-ring seals on new taps.

Action — old pillar and bib taps.
● remove the handle and cover from the tap.
● try tightening the gland packing nut.
● if this doesn't work, replace the packing round the headgear with graphite-impregnated string (above), which is specially made for the purpose. Make sure you pack it down well. You could use wool steeped in petroleum jelly as a stopgap measure.
● replace the packing nut.
● reassemble the tap and restore water supply.

Action — modern pillar and shrouded head taps with O-ring seals.
● turn off the water supply.
● remove the headgear (see above).
● remove the circlip on top of the headgear to reveal the seals.
● prise off the seals with a small screwdriver, but be careful not to damage their seatings.
● slip on seals of the correct size.
● reassemble the tap and restore water supply.

Action — Supatap.
If water seeps from round the top of the nozzle, you will have to fit (or replace)

224 DEALING WITH LEAKING TAPS AND PIPES

an O-ring seal underneath the head-nut. To do this, remove the nozzle as if you were rewashering.

Action — mixer taps.
Treat the hot and cold controls as shrouded head taps. The O-ring seals on a swivel spout may sometimes need replacing. The spout can be released either by turning it to one side and pulling it from its mounting, or by releasing a grubscrew.

Leaking pipes
Cause Frost, corrosion, mechanical failure resulting from a drill or nail being driven through the pipe.

Action
● if any electrical equipment is affected by the leaking water, or caused the leak in the first place, turn off the power supply immediately. Remove the offending equipment and check nearby ceiling roses and sockets to make sure no water has seeped behind them. After making sure that all electrical accessories are dry, you can turn on the power again.
● turn off the water supply to the damaged pipe. Drain down that section.
● cut out the damaged section of pipe and insert a new short length. If it's only a small hole you're mending, you may only need a straight coupling.
● restore the water supply and check the repair for leaks.

Proprietary emergency repair kits are also available:
● plastic putty that has to be mixed with a hardener before being packed over the hole or into a leaking joint.
● sticky waterproof tape that has to be wound round the pipe or fitting.
At best, these products are a temporary measure. They are not 'instant' because you still have to drain the pipe. The most effective immediate repair is to use a pipe clamp.

One of the main advantages of the tape repair kit is that it can be used on leaking joints as well as punctured pipes. It is a two-part system consisting of a base tape (**1**), which is wound tightly round the pipe or fitting for 25mm to 35mm (1in to 1½in) each side of the leak. The second tape (**2**) is applied over this and continued for a further 25mm to 35mm (1in to 1½in) each side of the first tape, being stretched slightly as it is wound round the pipe.

Where space permits on pipe runs, a pipe repair clamp (**3**) makes an effective seal. It is an 'instant' repair that does not need the pipe to be drained beforehand. But it is not suitable for use on leaking fittings. Clip the pad and metal plate together round the pipe and then tighten the wing nut (**4**) to stem the flow.

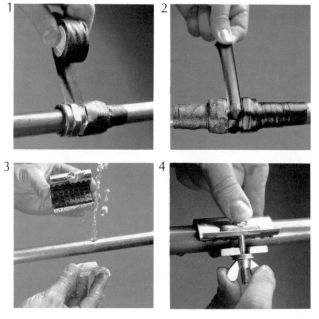

PROBLEMS WITH BALLVALVES AND WCS 225

Signs

Water continues to enter the storage cistern even though the float arm appears fully raised. The problem usually comes to light when water is seen discharging from the overflow pipe.

Action

● check the float at the end of the float arm. If it's perforated and water is seeping into it, the ballvalve won't cut off when the water reaches the correct level, resulting in an overflow. In this event, all you have to do is replace the float with a new one; simply unscrew the old float and screw on the new one.
● check the position of the float arm. By bending (or adjusting) it slightly downwards, you can apply more pressure to the valve mechanism to make sure it cuts off the supply of water before the cistern overflows.

If, after you've made these checks and adjustments, water still continues to flow into the cistern, the problem rests with the ballvalve itself. Use the information given below to identify the type fitted to your cistern and the repairs you may have to carry out.

Croydon pattern

This is the oldest type of ballvalve and is now fairly rare. Because it tends to be noisy in operation, you would be better off replacing it with a newer type rather than repairing it.

Portsmouth pattern

● first check the metal body for the initials stamped on the side:

HP = high pressure. This type should be used on main cold water storage cisterns.

LP = low pressure, fed from a storage cistern. This type should be used on WC cisterns and the like. If an LP valve is fitted to a main storage cistern, the valve will not shut off properly. There-

An equilibrium valve copes with mains pressure fluctuation by admitting water to a sealed chamber at the end of the valve. This ensures that an equal pressure bears on both ends of the sealing plug and only movement of the float arm will open it. A rubber disc stops the flow in a diaphragm valve, and a Torbeck valve combines facets of both designs.

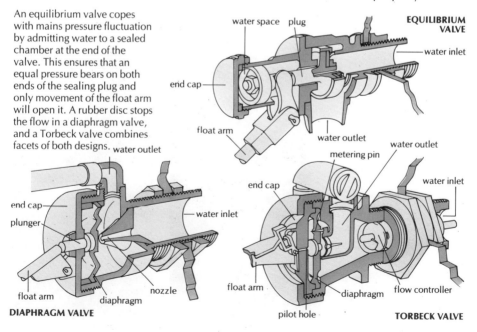

EQUILIBRIUM VALVE
water space plug
water inlet
end cap
float arm
water outlet

DIAPHRAGM VALVE
water outlet
end cap
plunger
water inlet
float arm
nozzle
diaphragm

TORBECK VALVE
metering pin
water outlet
water inlet
end cap
float arm
diaphragm
flow controller
pilot hole

226 *PROBLEMS WITH BALLVALVES AND WCS*

fore, you should change the valve for the correct type.

● If the correct type is fitted, the problem is either a worn washer, a build up of scale or a corroded ballvalve seating. In the latter case, replace the valve.

To change the washer:
● turn off the water supply to the cistern.
● take out the split pin and remove the float arm.
● unscrew the retaining cap.
● insert a screwdriver blade into the slot where the float arm sits and push out the piston.
● unscrew the piston cap to release the washer. If the cap is difficult to undo, hold one end in a pair of pliers and hold the other under a hot tap. Alternatively, prise the cap round with a screwdriver.
● if you still can't remove the cap, use a nail to dig out the old washer and

work a new one into the seating.

If the valve is badly scaled:
● remove the valve by undoing the tap connector and the outer back-nut. This will allow you to withdraw the valve from the cistern.
● dismantle the valve and clean it with a wire brush and steel wool. Make sure the nozzle isn't obstructed by scale.
● smear the piston with petroleum jelly before reassembling.
● reassemble the valve.

Diaphragm valve (also known as the BRS or Garston pattern. Often, they have an overhead spray-type outlet for silent operation).

If this fails to cut off properly, check:
● the adjusting screw on the float arm which may be preventing it closing.
● the rubber diaphragm to see if it's been perforated. Sometimes, the diaphragm jams against the nozzle.

Rewashering a Portsmouth ballvalve

This is a job that can be done with the valve remaining attached to the cistern. The water supply, however, first needs to be shut down. If the valve controls the main cold water system, this means turning off the main stopvalve; if it is on a WC, close the gate valve on the supply pipe.

Once you have removed the float arm by taking out the split pin, and have unscrewed the retaining cap, you should be able to lever out the piston (1). This needs to be dismantled (2) to give access to the washer (3). After pushing this out, a new one can be worked into the seating and the valve reassembled in the reverse order. Lubricate the piston with petroleum jelly (4) before replacing it.

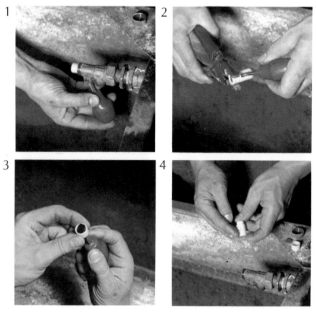

PROBLEMS WITH BALLVALVES AND WCS 227

● the nozzle to see that it isn't blocked by grit.

Noisy ballvalves
At one time, a silencer pipe, extending from the ballvalve outlet to below water level, was commonly fitted to reduce the gushing noise of the cistern filling up. However, because of the possibility of 'contaminated' water from the cistern being siphoned back into the mains supply, these devices are no longer permitted. So if you have a noisy valve, you'll have to consider replacing it with an equilibrium Portsmouth or diaphragm (Torbeck) pattern. This gives a quiet, fast refill, and also prevents water hammer.

A fluctuating water supply?
If the pressure in the mains supply varies with demand during the day, it could affect how well the ballvalve on the main cold water storage operates. To overcome the problem, fit an equilibrium valve.

Faulty WC cistern flushing mechanism
Signs
It takes several pulls in quick succession to start the water flowing through the siphon and into the pan.

Causes In a modern piston-type cistern, failure is due to worn siphon washers or flap valves covering the inlet holes in the base of the piston (see above right).

Action
● tie up the float arm to prevent water entering the cistern, then empty the cistern.
● disconnect the lever from the piston rod.
For a low-level cistern with flush pipe to pan:
● disconnect the flush pipe from the cistern by undoing the back-nut.
● undo the siphon retaining nut,

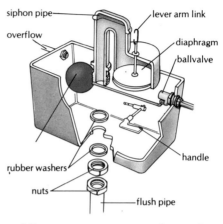

siphon pipe — lever arm link
overflow — diaphragm — ballvalve
rubber washers — handle
nuts — flush pipe

enabling you to remove the siphon from the cistern.

For a close-coupled suite:
● undo the retaining nuts on the underside of the cistern to release the siphon.
● separate the base of the piston from the siphon. You'll see the old flaps resting on top.
● replace these flaps with new ones, which are usually made of rubber or plastic that can be trimmed to size.
● make sure the new flaps move freely against the sides of the siphon (they shouldn't quite touch).
● reassemble the cistern in the reverse order.

Note
You may have an old Burlington pattern (bell-type) high-level cistern. In all probability, this will be nearing the end of its life. It is noisy in operation, and rust may be affecting its workings. Water continually entering the pan, even though the chain hasn't been pulled, is a sure sign of this. This type of cistern also attracts condensation. Rather than repair it, you would be better off installing a new modern type of cistern.

228 DEALING WITH BLOCKAGES

Signs
Water fails to flow from a sink, basin, bath or shower tray.

Action
● check that the outlet is not blocked by hair, soap, or kitchen waste.
If the outlet is unobstructed, the blockage is likely to be in the trap. This can be cleared either by using a plunger or by dismantling the trap.

Using a plunger:
● partially bale out the water.
● hold a damp rag over the overflow outlet.
● place the rubber or plastic cup of the plunger over the main outlet and work it up and down to force water through the trap.

Dismantling the trap:
● an old lead trap will have an access eye at the bottom which can be unscrewed with a spanner (support the rest of the trap so that it doesn't buckle or twist).
● push a length of wire (an opened-out coat hanger will do) into both sides of the U-bend and rake out the debris. You can also push the wire through from the outlet.
● make sure you place a container under the trap to catch the water and blockage material.
● replace the eye and flush the system.

For a modern plastic P-trap:
● this usually unscrews in two places. Loosen both nuts, remove the bend and flush out under a tap. (Don't use the taps over the sink or basin you are working on.)
● replace the bend and flush the system.

For a modern plastic bottle or dip partition trap:
● unscrew the bulb and flush it out.

If you find that the trap is clear, the blockage has probably worked its way round into the outlet pipe. Usually, this is quite short so you can poke a length of wire along it to free the blockage before you replace the trap. On longer runs, check that the pipe doesn't sag, providing a collecting point for a blockage.

Signs
WC pan fails to clear after cistern is flushed, and water level is much higher than normal.

Cause
Blocked WC pan U-bend. Blocked main drainage run, causing a backlog in soil stack.

Action
● use a special plunger (which is similar to, but larger than the one used for sinks) to force the blockage through to the main drainage run.
● alternatively, try and work the blockage free, using a piece of wire.
If this fails, the blockage is likely to be in the soil stack or underground drainage run.

Note
A double trapped siphonic pan will block repeatedly if an object such as a full-length pencil or ballpoint pen gets into the second trap. To clear this, it may be necessary to remove the pan and use a string passed through the waterway to pull a ball of cloth through from the outlet to inlet.

Blockages can occur in the main drainage run at the foot of the soil stack, in the trap of a yard gully, or in the pipework and inspection chambers (manholes) linking the house to the main sewer. Don't forget to check rainwater hopper heads as well, as these sometimes become blocked with leaves.

DEALING WITH BLOCKAGES 229

To unblock a yard gully:
● use a trowel or a gloved hand to clear out the debris.
● rinse the gully — a jet of water from a hose will be far more effective than running in water from a tap.

If the drain is blocked at the foot of the soil stack or just a little way down from a yard gully, no waste will reach the first manhole on the run.
● check the manhole, and if the blockage is where you suspect, use drain clearing rods to free it (below).
● as these rods are fairly expensive, hire them instead of buying.
● screw the rods together to form a flexible pole, and attach the appropriate head to the front end.
● from the manhole, push the rod up the pipe towards the house to break down the blockage.
● always turn the rods clockwise so they don't come undone in the pipe. Retrieving them can be difficult.

● cover the outlet of the manhole so that when the debris from the blockage flows into the chamber it can be scooped out.

If the blockage is in the branch pipe just before it joins the main sewer, the manholes are likely to overflow.
● work at the lowest manhole on the branch. The outlet will be trapped to prevent sewer smells entering the chamber, and it may be this which is blocked.
● if the trap is clear remove the disc or plug covering the rodding eye (see diagram), allowing drain rods to be pushed into the pipe.
● by plunging and twisting the rods, you should be able to work the blockage so that it passes into the sewer.
● when the blockage has been removed, flush the system thoroughly. Make sure the rodding eye plug is refitted properly and replace the manhole cover.

Various cleaning heads can be screwed on to the end of the rods to break up the blockage in the pipe.

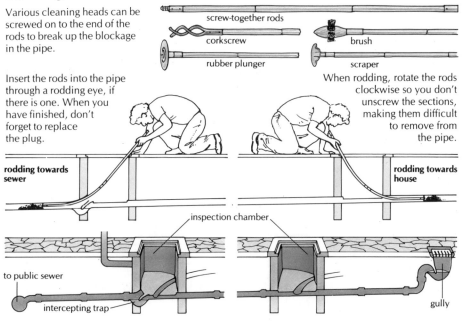

screw-together rods

corkscrew

brush

rubber plunger

scraper

Insert the rods into the pipe through a rodding eye, if there is one. When you have finished, don't forget to replace the plug.

When rodding, rotate the rods clockwise so you don't unscrew the sections, making them difficult to remove from the pipe.

rodding towards sewer

rodding towards house

inspection chamber

to public sewer

intercepting trap

gully

230 PROBLEMS WITH GUTTERS

Signs
Gutter overflows during heavy rain.

Cause Blockage in gutter due to build up of debris. Also sagging gutter run, or a blockage in the downpipe.

Action Clear any debris into a bucket. If this isn't the cause, check for sagging with string lines between ends of gutter. Replace any loose brackets.
    You may be able to scoop out a blockage at the top of a downpipe, but . if it has passed into the eaves offset, or further down, you may have to dismantle the downpipe from the bottom up. Sometimes it's possible to ease the eaves offset from its sockets without disturbing the pipe.

Signs
Water leaking at gutter joint.

Cause On cast iron and asbestos-cement guttering, this is probably due to the putty seal between sections of gutter having worn away. On PVC guttering, the sections may not have been clipped together tightly.

Action — cast iron and asbestos-cement guttering.
● unbolt joint (cut away rusted bolts).
● clean up contact faces.
● apply bed of mastic between faces.
● rebolt sections together.

Action — PVC gutters
● check that sections are fully clipped into connectors.

Signs
Water leaks through hole in gutter.

Cause Rust in cast iron guttering, and particularly where ogee sections have been screwed to the fascia board.

Action
● Remove all traces of rust with a wire brush.
● Paint the affected areas with bitu-mastic paint.
● Use a proprietary repair kit to patch up hole or insert a length of plastic guttering.
(If gutters are generally in a poor state then it's worth replacing the entire system.)

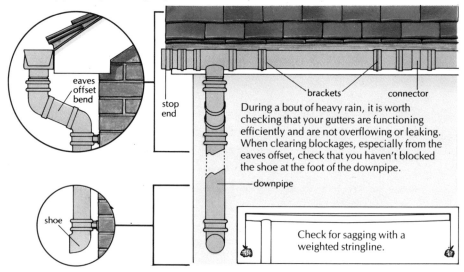

eaves offset bend

stop end

brackets   connector

During a bout of heavy rain, it is worth checking that your gutters are functioning efficiently and are not overflowing or leaking. When clearing blockages, especially from the eaves offset, check that you haven't blocked the shoe at the foot of the downpipe.

downpipe

shoe

Check for sagging with a weighted stringline.

Central Heating & Insulation

Ned Halley
Consultant Editor Richard Wiles

234 Central heating explained 1

Half the households in Britain are centrally heated; yet to many of us the central heating system is a source of complete mystery. We prefer not to dwell on the bewildering jumble of pipes, the strange sounds emitted by boiler and radiators, the robot-like way in which the whole works switches itself on and off.

Perhaps the only time our interest is aroused is when a large fuel bill arrives. We may wonder whether *all* that extra cost over last year's bill is due to higher energy charges — or might the cause be more local? Is there anything we can do to reduce heating bills to a more affordable level?

In most cases, the answer is 'yes'; there are many ways in which we can and should make more of our central heating systems, not only for improved economy, but also for greater comfort. The first step is to understand what central heating is and how it works.

What is central heating?

In a typical domestic system, water is heated at a central point, the boiler, and then pumped round a circuit of pipes leading to radiators. The hot water remains in each radiator long enough to emit a calculated amount of heat before returning to the pipe which carries it back to the boiler.

How does it work?

By dividing a central heating system into 'circuits' of just a few radiators each, the designer ensures that the heated water travels the minimum distance; therefore, the water will be able to heat up the last radiator on the circuit just as efficiently as the first. Because the water is pumped along pipes with a small surface area, it reaches the radiators quickly with minimal heat loss on the way.

It's an efficient way of distributing heat, so only a modest boiler is needed for the typical domestic system. Progressive refinements in central heating have meant that every room in the house can be kept comfortably warm for a fraction of what it would cost with individual appliances.

There's further economy from the combining of the hot water supply with the room heating system. In today's systems, the boiler also heats the cylinder which supplies the hot taps; when the central heating is operating at the same time, this represents a very cheap source of hot water.

Designing and installing these advanced central heating systems demands a good deal of technical knowledge and skill. It's not a job for an untrained

The most common form of central heating is known as a 'wet' system, in which hot water is used as the heating medium for the house and often the domestic hot water supply as well. The water is heated at a central point, the boiler, and then pumped through a series of pipes to heat emitters. The water then returns to the boiler for reheating and recirculation through what is effectively a 'closed' system of pipes. In most cases, an expansion or 'header' tank will be situated in the loft, and a vent pipe from the boiler will be arranged to discharge any steam or boiling water into it should the boiler overheat; the tank also keeps the system topped up and receives a direct supply from the mains. An overflow pipe is fitted to warn of a faulty ballvalve. Some systems have a sealed expansion vessel in place of an expansion tank, notably those in flats or flat-roofed buildings. The pipework in a modern installation will be of small diameter and is easily concealed beneath floors.

radiators

to hot water cylinder and vent pipe

enthusiast. However, it's entirely up to us, to see that we get value for the considerable amount of money we spend on our systems.

This book deals with the aspects of central heating that householders will be able to cope with, given certain levels of skill. Routine maintenance, proper use of controls or the addition of new controls, extending the system — all are feasible, sometimes at considerable savings in contractors' charges as well as wasted fuel.

The typical system
Central heating systems vary in many respects, but for the purposes of this book, a typical setup is taken to be a modern, forced-flow, small bore, indirect system. The term 'forced-flow' indicates that water is pumped round the system; 'small bore' simply means that the pipes are small; 'indirect' refers to systems in which the boiler also heats the tap water by sending a supply of heated water into a coil immersed in the cylinder, thus 'indirectly' producing domestic hot water.

The typical arrangement is described as a 'two-pipe' system, whereby the heated water is fed to the radiators by one pipe and the cooled water leaving the radiators is returned to the boiler through a separate pipe. The purpose of this two-pipe layout is to supply consistently hot water to all the

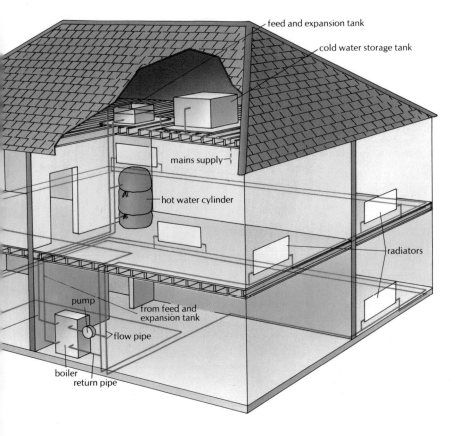

236 Central heating explained 2

radiators; no cooled water enters the hot pipe on its way round.

The two-pipe system costs more to install than the earlier 'one-pipe' arrangement, but it does not call for larger radiators at the ends of the circuits, as the latter does. In the one-pipe system, cooled water leaving a radiator goes on to the next radiator instead of into a second 'return' pipe. Consequently, a large area of radiator is needed at the end of the pipe run to emit sufficient warmth. In addition, a two-pipe system is more straightforward to design, so that part of the installer's charge is reduced.

Two-pipe systems account for the vast majority of new installations. One item, however, is difficult to typify: the boiler. Fuel, methods of ventilation, and sizes and shapes of appliance vary radically. These aspects, which don't affect the system at any point other than at the boiler itself, are discussed later (see pages 238 to 241).

Warm air systems
While most central heating is 'wet' (based on heated water), there are some systems that can be termed 'dry'. A common dry system is based on a heat emitter which pushes warmed air along ducts under the floors or inside the walls. The warm air passes into each room through grilles, which can be closed when the room does not need to be heated.

In most cases, warm air systems are built into new homes during construction; it would be very expensive to

A two-pipe heating system
The pipes in a two-pipe central heating system are arranged into 'flow' and 'return' circuits. The former carries hot water to the inlet of each radiator, while the latter carries the cooler water away from each radiator outlet. This ensures that the water reaches each radiator at a similar temperature, unlike an older single-pipe system where the water had to pass through each radiator in turn before going on to the next, losing heat all the time.

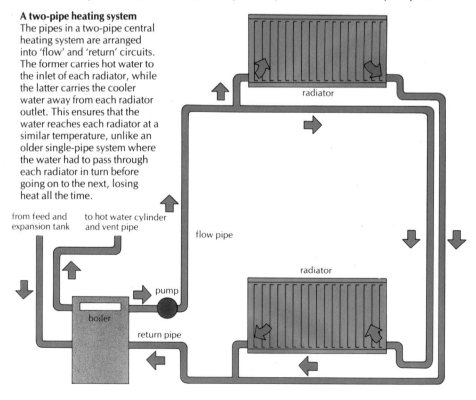

from feed and expansion tank

to hot water cylinder and vent pipe

radiator

flow pipe

radiator

pump

boiler

return pipe

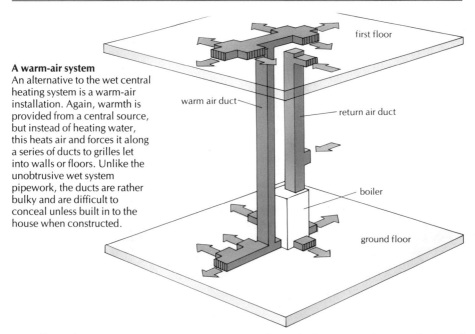

A warm-air system
An alternative to the wet central heating system is a warm-air installation. Again, warmth is provided from a central source, but instead of heating water, this heats air and forces it along a series of ducts to grilles let into walls or floors. Unlike the unobtrusive wet system pipework, the ducts are rather bulky and are difficult to conceal unless built in to the house when constructed.

first floor

warm air duct

return air duct

boiler

ground floor

install such a system in an existing building. For similar reasons, ducted systems are difficult to extend to new areas of a house.

Another dry system is underfloor heating. Again, this needs to be incorporated during construction. It makes use of a lengthy electrical element built into the subfloor to give off enough heat to warm the air above without making the floor itself too hot for comfort.

Solar heating
Neither ducted air heating nor underfloor heating enjoy any great reputation for fuel economy, but one form of heating that certainly does is the solar-power system.

'Active' solar heating (the type that involves special equipment) can, it is claimed, supply up to 50 per cent of domestic hot water needs, central heating included. In the system for which this claim is made, the sun's energy is 'collected' by way of special glazed panels, usually mounted on the roof, and converted into heat.

Solar heating only works in tandem with a conventional system, and installation costs for the overall setup are therefore higher than those for a 'typical' system.

Electric storage heaters
Because the term 'central heating' means heating from a central source within the home, and a typical system is taken to be a boiler-powered 'wet' setup, electric storage heaters don't fall within this category. This is not to imply that the electric storage method of heating should not be considered when planning your room heating. Such 'total heating' systems operate on the 'Economy 7' tariff (night-rate), and require the installation of a special electrical circuit. Storage heaters can be economic where the house is well insulated (see pages 274 to 291).

238 The boiler 1

Compact, safe and efficient, today's domestic boiler — the powerhouse of a central heating system — is unobtrusive and, if properly used and maintained, will run trouble-free for many years. The water serving your central heating and hot water system is first heated at the boiler, which may burn oil, gas or solid fuel, and it's here that the water returns for reheating.

In addition to fuel inlets, the boiler also incorporates a chimney called a 'flue', which carries unwanted combustion gases from the house.

Among the wide range of boilers available are wall-mounted, freestanding or backboiler models. Gas and oil boilers may have either a conventional flue (where combustion air is drawn from the room in which the appliance is sited and exhaust gases pass up a vertical chimney), or a 'balanced' flue (which supplies combustion air and removes exhaust gases along a single duct passing through an outside wall). Solid fuel boilers always have a conventional flue.

Boilers with conventional flues must be located in rooms with chimney access; a backboiler fitted into a fireplace behind a roomheater is a good example — and a neat way to conceal the equipment. In most cases, a flue liner, which is a length of flexible metal tubing, must be run from the boiler exhaust up the chimney to the outside air. This is to prevent any leakage of the boiler gases. Also, any room containing a conventionally-flued boiler must be ventilated to the outside.

There are fewer limitations on the use of the balanced flue. So long as the boiler is positioned close to an outside wall through which the flue's short duct can be fixed, the boiler can go in any kind of room. No special ventilation of the room is necessary, and this type of appliance is often described as 'room sealed'; but the balanced flue outlet must not be near a window, door or pathway.

Wall-mounted and freestanding balanced flue boilers can be conveniently fitted into most kitchens, taking up no more space than a single cupboard unit and often quite inconspicuous.

Choosing a boiler
If you're planning to install a central heating system, or intend to replace an existing boiler, how do you decide on the right appliance for your needs? There are three vital factors to bear in mind when choosing. These are:
● the types of fuel available.
● where you wish to install the boiler.
● what capacity of boiler you need.
The fuel Most households have ready access to all types of fuel. As the fuel cost chart on page 241 clearly shows, gas central heating appears cheaper than its rivals. Also, it has the advantage of needing no storage facility, and

Boilers for a wet central heating system may be gas- (left), solid-fuel- (centre) or oil-fired (right). A gas-fired unit is the most convenient provided there is ready access to a gas supply, but if none is available you will need to choose between the

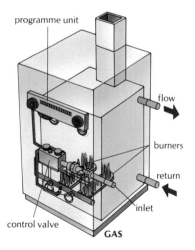

programme unit

flow

burners

return

inlet

control valve

GAS

gas customers enjoy the benefit of paying for their fuel after they've used it, whereas stored-fuel users must pay cash on delivery.

A cost argument that might be made against gas is that its customers pay standing charges, whereas oil and solid fuel users do not. This would be a fair point, however, only if no other gas installation — a cooker, for example — was in use so that the full cost of the standing charge had to be put down solely to the central heating and hot water system.

This is not to say that other fuels are without merit. To begin with, only oil and solid fuels are universally available. Because only those homes within 23m (25yd) of a main have the right to gas, about three million households have no access to a supply.

Oil, as the chart shows, seems to be the most expensive of fuels. As a commodity much affected by the

vagaries of politics, oil's price is likely to remain unpredictable at best. This is something to bear in mind when choosing a boiler you expect still to be using in ten or more years' time.

Solid fuels are more competitive in price with gas, and refinements are being made to both appliances and fuels that, in some cases, show coal products to be a cheaper source of central heating than gas. It does no harm, therefore, if you're uncertain about your choice of boiler, to obtain from your local gas showroom the *Guide to Fuel Running Costs* and to ask at your local Solid Fuel Advisory Service branch for their information on comparative costs.

An important aspect of solid fuel boilers is that they need more regular attention than gas or oil models. The hopper, for instance, has to be filled with fuel regularly (once a day at least, as a rule) and the ash removed; the

other two. Both require outdoor storage for the fuel; oil is more expensive than solid fuel but the latter needs regular topping up and ash removal. It is normal to fit a safety valve and draincock to the flow and return pipes in every case.

All types of boiler are available in freestanding form, as shown below, but room heaters (with a radiant portion in front of a back boiler) are also made for gas or solid fuel. Compact gas-fired wall-mounted boilers are also available.

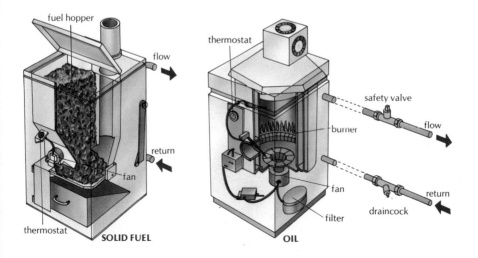

boiler flueways must be kept clean. Although these tasks have been simplified through good boiler design, it may be that some users would still find such jobs unappealing or overstrenuous.

If you're seeking quotations for a new boiler or system, but are undecided about which fuel to choose and need some independent advice, your installer should help. To be sure you only deal with reliable installers, use members of dependable organisations such as the Heating and Ventilating Contractors' Association or the Confederation for the Registration of Gas Installers.

Positioning the boiler Your choice of appliance is affected significantly by where you want to put the boiler. If you'd like to put it out of the way in, say, the living room fireplace, you'll need a backboiler; but note that a backboiler burning solid fuel will have a limited output because of the restricted space. Elsewhere, conventionally flued boilers must be connected to existing or purpose-built chimneys.

If you want to install the boiler in the kitchen or utility room, as most householders installing new systems now do, you can use a balanced flue type mounted on or next to an external wall. Precisely where you position the boiler will, of course, determine whether you choose a wall-mounted or a freestanding model.

Capacity The output of the boiler should be related to the needs of the system. Heating designers work this out mathematically, taking into account the level of heat required throughout the house. The designer also calculates heating demand in relation to the size of each room, the materials which compose the floor, ceiling and every wall — and what is on the other side of each wall, floor and ceiling.

In short, it's a complicated business! To be sure your new system has the correct boiler, your best bet is to obtain about three different quotations, all from reliable contractors, and if you find any dramatic discrepancy in recommended boiler size, confront your preferred installer with it.

Because metrication in this area has made slow progress, heating experts tend to talk in a confusing mixture of terms. The traditional measure of heat output from boilers, radiators and heaters has long been expressed in British thermal units per hour, or Btu/h. The metric measure is in kilowatts, or kW. To convert Btu/h to kW, divide by 3,412, the number of the former to 1kW. Therefore, a 40,000Btu/h boiler is known metrically as an 11.7kW boiler.

If a conventional chimney is used as the boiler flue (right), it should be fitted with a metal liner to reduce the flue diameter to the optimum size for the boiler and to prevent condensation attacking the brickwork. Some gas- and oil-fired boilers have what is termed a 'balanced' flue (below). This is a short duct, which passes through an outside wall; it removes combustion gases and provides fresh air to allow combustion to take place.

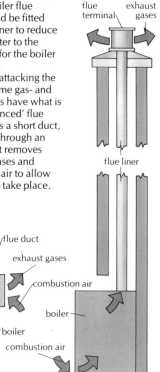

flue terminal
flue exhaust gases

flue liner

flue duct

exhaust gases

combustion air

boiler

boiler

combustion air

Domestic heating fuel cost comparisons

SOUTHERN	**3-bedroom semi**	16,470/2,130* units 880 therms 2,362.88 litres (520 gallons) 2.8 tonnes
	2-bedroom terrace	9,160/1,240* units 470 therms 1,317.76 litres (290 gallons) 1.6 tonnes
MIDLANDS & NORTHERN	**3-bedroom semi**	19,230/2,470* units 945 therms 2,703.68 litres (595 gallons) 3.2 tonnes
	2-bedroom terrace	10,670/1,420* units 540 therms 1,522.24 litres (335 gallons) 1.8 tonnes
SCOTTISH	**3-bedroom semi**	20,350/2,640* units 1,005 therms 2,885.44 litres (635 gallons) 3.4 tonnes
	2-bedroom terrace	11,390/1,510* units 580 therms 1,613.12 litres (355 gallons) 1.9 tonnes
WELSH	**3-bedroom semi**	17,520/2,260* units 865 therms 2,499.2 litres (550 gallons) 2.95 tonnes
	2-bedroom terrace	9,730/1,310* units 495 therms 1,408.64 litres (310 gallons) 1.65 tonnes

Electricity   Gas   Oil   Anthracite

*First figure denotes night-rate units; the second, day-rate units.
Note This cost comparison chart is based on official Department of Energy figures and takes into account standing charges and routine maintenance costs. It should be used as a guide only since fuel prices fluctuate constantly.

242 The pump

The introduction of the pumped, or forced-flow, method of hot water circulation has been largely responsible for making domestic central heating a practical proposition. Before pumped installations, systems worked on the gravity principle: water from a cold tank flowed down large pipes to a massive boiler, which heated it, causing it to rise in the system, as the heated water was lighter than the unheated. Pipes had to run at carefully calculated slopes, carrying great volumes of water sufficient to give off some heat as it flowed through bulky radiators.

The pump changed this expensive method by allowing smaller quantities of water to be rushed at speed to smaller radiators capable of holding the water for a calculated period of time. Shorter routes could be taken along the system, as smaller pipes were now possible and were much easier to install. In turn, all this improvement in efficiency meant that a smaller boiler was needed.

Pumps may be built into some makes of boiler, but it's more usual for a

The electric circulating pump has improved the efficiency of the wet central heating system considerably. Its cast body houses a powerful electric motor, which drives a centrifugal rotor to push the heated water round the pipes. A valve is incorporated to allow any air to be bled from inside the pump.

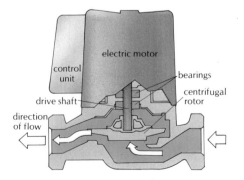

electric motor

control unit

bearings

centrifugal rotor

drive shaft

direction of flow

separate unit to be mounted on the flow (outlet) pipe close to the boiler at a point conveniently accessible for maintenance work. In this position, the pump pushes the heated water along the flow pipe, into the circuits and through the system under 'positive pressure'.

It exerts 'negative pressure' on the water in the short length of flow pipe connecting it to the boiler.

The size of the pump is determined by the 'duty' it must perform: that is, the amount of water it must force through the system to distribute the necessary amount to each circuit. Pumps may be either of the single-speed type or the 'variable head' type, which must be adjusted to match the system in which it is installed.

In domestic systems, the maximum desirable flow rate through the pipes is 1.2m (4ft) per second right round the system, because water travelling any faster can produce unwelcome noise. Modern pumps do this work at a very economical rate, using about the same amount of electricity as a 60 watt light bulb. A pump in good running order should be virtually silent.

Efficient and dependable as today's pumps are, they're still regarded as the Achilles' heel of central heating systems. It's not unusual for a pump to be replaced at least once during the life of a system (see page 255). Your pump should, therefore, be fitted between isolating valves (see opposite), so that you can maintain or remove it by closing them down, rather than having to drain the whole system.

In a combined indirect system, where the water cylinder is situated some distance from the boiler, the 'primary' circuit carrying the boiler-heated water into the cylinder coil may require a pump. This will be a separate unit in no way connected with the central heating pump.

Positioning the pump

The best position for the circulating pump is in the flow pipe of the system (below), close to the boiler. From here, it can push the water round the system under positive pressure, and there is only a short amount of pipework from the boiler under negative pressure.

If the pump is positioned in the return pipe, as shown below, it will exert suction on the entire radiator circuit. This could cause air to be drawn into the system through gaps at pipe joints, which are too small to allow water to pass.

The circulating pump should be fitted between two isolating gate valves so that if it needs removing at any time for replacement or repair, the valves can be shut off and the pump removed without the need to drain the entire system.

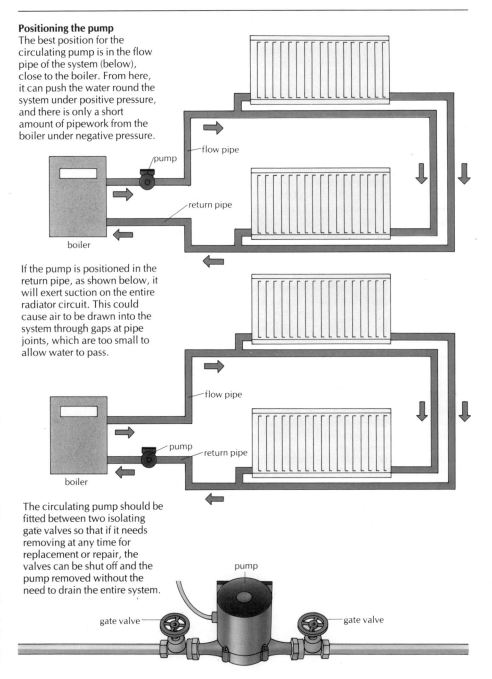

244 Pipework

Domestic heating pipework is now usually of the small bore type, made in copper and supplied only in metric sizes. As a rule, 15mm pipe is used over the greatest part of the system, with 22 or 28mm pipe connecting boiler and pump to the points at which circuits divide. These three metric pipe sizes correspond approximately with the ½in, ¾in and 1in sizes used when small bore piping was first introduced.

Because the bore, or inside, of copper pipe is very smooth, friction with flowing water is minimal and the pump's job is made easier. Copper does not rust and it's ideal to solder for simple, secure jointing. Using the right equipment, small pipes can be bent quite easily by hand.

Small bore pipes are comparatively easy to conceal. Underfloor runs, for example, can be made without the risk of weakening the supporting joists because the holes necessary to take these small pipes present no hazard. Where it's necessary to run pipes along the surface, small bore lengths can be fixed discreetly round window frames and along skirtings. They can be boxed in behind chipboard or plasterboard fixed to timber battens as a false wall. With small bore pipes, this need not encroach significantly on room space.

Another type of heating system makes use of 'microbore' pipework. At 8 and 10mm sizes, these pipes are small enough to be produced in a flexible form and supplied in a coil. This means that the pipe can be fed into cavities (such as those beneath floorboards) with little disruption to the household, and it can be run round corners without the need for joins.

But, such narrow pipes can't carry sufficient water to heat more than one radiator per circuit, so the system must be designed on a 'starfish' basis, with a number of pipes branching from a main flow. In addition, a more powerful pump is needed. Special fittings and valves must also be used, and neither these nor the pipework are as readily available as conventional materials.

Plastic systems

Some suppliers offer plastic piping and fittings as an alternative to traditional copper systems for central heating. Plastic systems are either joined using solvent cement — a simple, effective

A wet central heating system using small bore pipework will be divided into a number of circuits so that hot water does not have to travel all over the house to reach its destination. A simple installation, as shown, may be broken down into upstairs and downstairs circuits, but a larger one may have more than one circuit per floor. An unobstructed vent pipe runs from the boiler to the header tank and supplies heated water to the coil inside the hot water cylinder. Cool water from the cylinder coil passes back to the boiler via the feed pipe from the header tank. This may run direct to the boiler or radiator circuit return pipe.

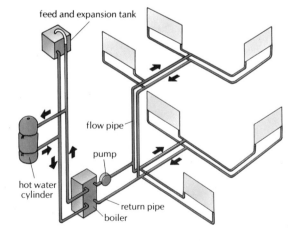

feed and expansion tank

flow pipe

pump

hot water cylinder

return pipe

boiler

In a microbore system, each radiator has its own mini circuit of feed and return pipes, which are connected to a 'manifold'. This is a section of larger diameter pipe, which is divided internally into feed and return sections, each with a number of connectors for the microbore pipework. Conventional small bore pipework is used to join the manifolds to the boiler and to provide a boiler vent pipe and feed pipe from the header tank. Connections to the hot water cylinder may be made in either small bore or microbore pipework.

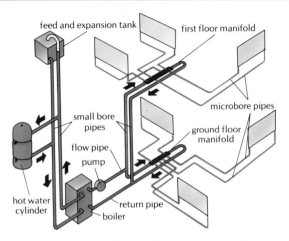

method, but with the disadvantage that separating and remaking the connection is difficult — or push-fit connectors. Supplied in standard 15, 22 and 28mm sizes, plastic pipes and fittings are usually high-density CPVC, capable of coping with high-temperature flow. Some makes come in coils and can be bent to avoid the need for many joints. They are price-competitive and can be connected up to existing copper pipework by using special fittings.

Plastic systems can certainly be installed by a competent do-it-yourselfer — indeed, they are intended for this market. This type of pipe should not, however, be connected directly to the boiler or other heat-generating source. Note also that plastic pipes will expand much more than copper pipes, and they have a greater tendency to soften when very hot: this means that you will need to fit more support brackets on lengthy pipe runs.

Draincocks
Occasionally, it may be necessary to empty all the water out of your central heating system, and special 'draincocks' (right) are fitted for this. One will be fitted at the boiler and, should any radiator be lower in the system

than the boiler, another draincock should be fitted nearby at the lowest point in its pipework.

Some systems with 'inverted loops' of piping, in which pipes drop from above ceilings to radiators and then rise up again, should have additional draincocks at their lowest points. Without pump action, water can't otherwise be emptied from these loops.

Central heating installers should provide special keys to operate draincocks. Keep a key and a length of hose to connect the draincock to the nearest drainage point, somewhere handy.

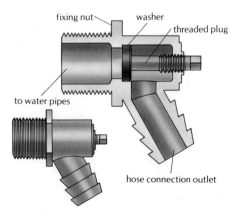

246 Radiators and convectors 1

Hot water central heating systems emit heat into rooms either through radiators or convectors. Radiated heat effectively warms the surfaces it touches and when the surfaces in a room are all thus heated, the warmth is then extended to the air. Convected heat directly warms the air itself.

A radiator is simply a steel container into which very hot water flows — the maximum temperature in domestic systems is 82°C (180°F) — gives off a proportion of its heat — usually 11°C (20°F) in domestic systems — and then escapes out of the valve at the other end. The container's panels, through which the water moves by a combination of gravity and pump action, transfer the heat into the room. Although this device is called a radiator, only about half of the heat it emits is by radiation; the rest is by convection as it warms the surrounding air.

The convector heater is equipped with a large number of 'fins', which conduct heat from the hot pipe. Cold air reaching these fins by way of the natural air circulation in the room is heated and rises into the room, causing more air to be drawn in.

A refinement of the convector heater is a fan-assisted version, which sucks in cold air and blows it, warmed, into the room. Fan convectors can warm up a room quickly, but they do require an electricity supply.

Radiators and convectors can be mixed in a central heating system, offering a large range of shapes and sizes from powerful two- or three-panel radiators big enough to heat a spacious room to ingeniously inconspicuous convectors for fixing to skirtings.

Radiator valves

Radiators are connected to the pipework by valves. These control the flow of water in and out, and thus regulate the amount of heat given off. The valves at each end of the radiator differ in one particular respect: the 'flow' (inlet) valve can be turned on or off by

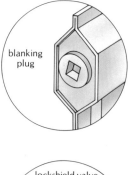

bleed screw

blanking plug

A radiator normally has a 'tapping' (threaded hole) at each corner, and these provide the means of attaching the various fittings to it. Each bottom tapping is fitted with a valve connected to the pipes. The lockshield valve regulates the flow of water through the radiator and the wheel or hand valve allows you to turn the radiator off and on. An air bleed valve is screwed into one of the top tappings and a blanking plug into the other.

lockshield valve

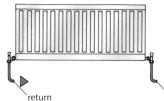

return

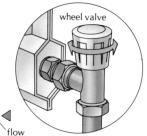

wheel valve

flow

hand, but the 'return' (outlet) valve cannot.

To turn the radiator off, simply close the flow valve; the hot water then bypasses the radiator and no heat is given off. To reduce the temperature without turning off the radiator completely, you can close the valve down and then open it slightly.

The return valve is adjusted to keep the water in the radiator for just the time it takes to shed 11°C (20°F) of its heat. This 'lockshield' valve is set by the system's installer.

Every radiator also has an air vent valve, which is operated with a special key to 'bleed' air out if it becomes trapped, or when the system has been drained and refilled. Radiators with double or triple panels will have separate bleed valves in each panel.

How much heat do you need?

The size and number of radiators per room depends on the temperature you desire and the ability of the room to retain heat. Unless you make a special request for particular temperatures, your system designer will usually seek to heat each type of room as follows:

Room	°C	°F
Living room or dining room	21	70
Bathroom	18-22	64-72
Bedroom	16-18	61-64
Hall/landing	16	61
Kitchen	16-18	61-64

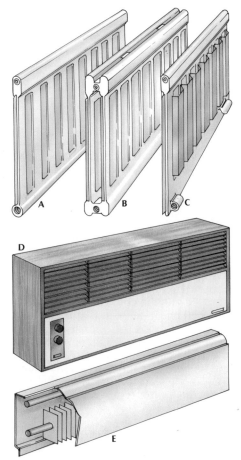

Heat emitters single-panel radiator (**A**); double-panel radiator (**B**); convector radiator (**C**); fan convector (**D**); skirting heater (**E**).

According to the type of walls each room has — whether they're external, what materials they comprise and what area of window they contain — and what type of ceiling and floor, the designer will work out how long the room is capable of keeping in heat. Making some allowance for the fact that any exposed pipework will give off heat, the designer can then determine the output needed from one or more radiators to do the job.

Radiator manufacturers state the output of each heat emitter they make, so it's only necessary to match up the known heat demand with the known output — both being measured in kW or Btu/h. As a rule, if the heat required is more than 2kW (7,000Btu/h), more

248 Radiators and convectors 2

than one radiator should be used. This avoids the use of over-large radiators and makes for a more even distribution of heat round the room.

Siting the radiators

Because it's at the window that the greatest amount of heat escapes, the best way to ensure the most even room temperature is to position the radiator at the window. In many cases, this makes good use of wall space that isn't otherwise employed, and lessens the problems of stains caused by rising hot air that tend to appear on walls behind radiators.

It's true that some of the radiator's heat does go straight out of the window, but this loss is neither critical nor avoidable. Certainly, the downdraught caused by air cooling and sinking on contact with the cold glass is effectively reduced by siting the radiator there.

The positions of radiators dictate their size and shape. Under a window, the radiator should extend ideally to the full width of the glazed area. Many long models are available for this purpose, including types which are bent specially to fit round window bays. Where space is limited, double- and triple-panel radiators with high outputs can be used.

Convectors can be fitted to extensive lengths of skirting — again, preferably under the windows. Fan-powered convectors, however, are different; as they 'push' their heat out into the room, there's no special merit in placing them under windows.

Radiators should be fixed to walls with the special brackets supplied by the maker. There should be at least 125mm (5in) clearance under the radiator for cleaning access. Only use ordinary paints to decorate a radiator, as metallic types can cut down the heat output by as much as 15 per cent.

Hanging curtains in front of any heat emitter will waste warmth, as they will shield the room from any radiated heat given off and tend to trap warm air behind them. However, if you have double glazing, the need to fit the radiator beneath the window is not so great since downdraughts and heat loss will be reduced. You can site the radiator anywhere convenient.

Despite its name, no more than half the heat provided by a radiator is by radiation; the remainder comes from natural convection as it warms the air around it. This warmed air rises towards the ceiling, causing more cooler air to be drawn in around the bottom of the radiator. As the air near the ceiling gradually gives up some of its heat it begins to sink and is displaced by fresh warmed air from the radiator. Eventually, a gentle circulation takes place, with the overall air temperature of the room rising all the time. Radiators are often sited below windows to counteract cold downdraughts.

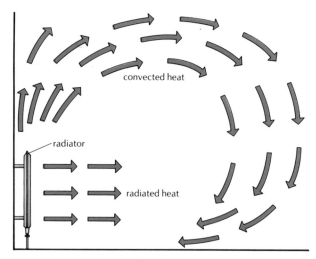

convected heat

radiator

radiated heat

Controls for central heating 1 249

Some central heating controls are built into the system to ensure that it is safe, reasonably efficient and capable of being repaired rather than completely replaced should anything go wrong.

Controls that come as extras include some that are vital to economy and comfort — and others which offer progressive degrees of temperature adjustment in different parts of the house. Some of these more refined controls are unlikely ever to pay for themselves in terms of improved fuel economy, but may be justified if they add to your comfort.

Boiler thermostat In domestic systems, the boiler shouldn't heat the water above 82°C (180°F), so all boilers are fitted with a thermostat which switches them off once the water has reached this temperature. The thermostat is fitted inside the boiler casing, and you can adjust it to lower temperatures: refer to the operating instructions.

Room thermostat This activates the heating system according to the temperature requirement set at its in-built sensor. It's usually wired to the boiler-pump circuit and switches the pump on and off according to whether the temperature has moved below or above the preset level.

The room thermostat is normally fitted in the living room, about 1.5m (5ft) from the floor and out of the way of any particularly hot or cold spots, such as radiators or draughty windows. This enables the thermostat's sensor to take a realistically representative reading of the room's temperature. The use of a 'roomstat' assumes that any rise or fall in the temperature in the room in which it is sited will be reflected by similar rises or falls throughout the rest of the house.

Cylinder thermostat In a combined system, the boiler will heat the water for the taps to the same temperature as the water for the heating system. Because domestic hot water needs to be no hotter than 60°C (140°F) and the heating water goes up to 82°C (180°F), this is a waste of fuel. There's also the real danger of scaldingly hot water at the taps.

The answer is to fit a cylinder thermostat, which operates an electric motorised valve on the primary flow circuit. When the cylinder thermostat's sensor reads any increase in temperature above the set level (which may be less than 60°C, if required), the valve closes, preventing circulation of water from boiler to cylinder.

A simpler, if less exact, method of controlling water temperature is with a self-operating (non-electric) cylinder

The illustration on the right shows the various positions for control devices associated with a wet central heating system. Not all of them would be used at once.

1 Thermostatic radiator valve.
2 Room thermostat.
3 Programmer.
4 Zone valve.
5 Time clock.
6 Modulating controller.
7 Boiler thermostat.
8 Low limit (frost) thermostat.
9 Cylinder thermostat.

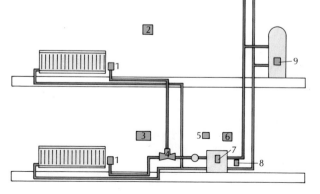

250 Controls for central heating 2

temperature controller. This is fitted in the return part of the primary circuit.

You must not fit either type if you have a solid fuel boiler, as this can't be switched off instantly and the hot water cylinder acts as a valuable 'heat sink', preventing overheating in the boiler.

Time switch This is a straightforward clock, which switches the system on and off at preset times of the day. It can be used to switch the heating on early in the morning and off late at night. Usually, just two on/off switchings are possible every 24 hours, and the clock must be reset if the power has been turned off for any reason.

Programmer A step up from the time switch, the programmer can switch the central heating and hot water systems on and off independently at different times of the day. The time settings can be overridden by an integral switch, should you have a special need for either central heating or hot water during what is normally an 'off' period. Some programmers can be wired to the room thermostat for additional flexibility of control.

Specialised controls
Devices other than basic thermostats and timers are usually economic only in special circumstances. The range of such controls includes the following:

Frost thermostat If any part of your system is at risk of freezing (such as a

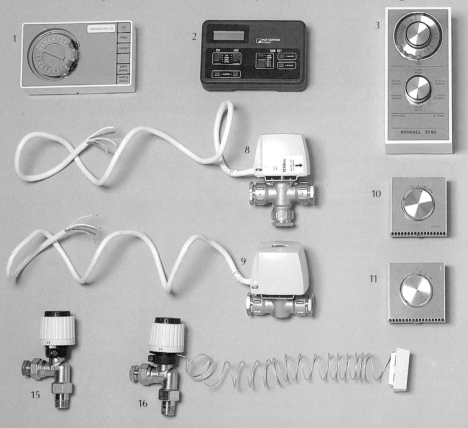

boiler located in an outbuilding), a frost (or low limit) thermostat will automatically switch on the system whenever it detects a near-freezing temperature, switching it off again when the danger has passed.

Zone valve In some cases, it's desirable only to heat one of the system's circuits, for example upstairs rather than downstairs. By fitting a motorised valve at the point where the system divides, the flow of hot water to a particular circuit can be isolated and diverted to another circuit.

Thermostatic radiator valves Fitted to radiators in place of the normal hand valves, these give individual room-temperature control — arguably the most sophisticated central heating control system of all.

Modulating controller This advanced form of control never actually switches the system off, but maintains a carefully adjusted temperature in the continuously flowing hot water. The fabric of the building is therefore never allowed to lose its heat (heat loss is monitored by the modulator's electronic sensors) and the system never has to run at full power (as ordinary systems do) to compensate for the total heat loss caused by a switch-off.

Modulators are expensive to install, but one maker claims that the cost can be recouped through fuel-saving in only two to three years.

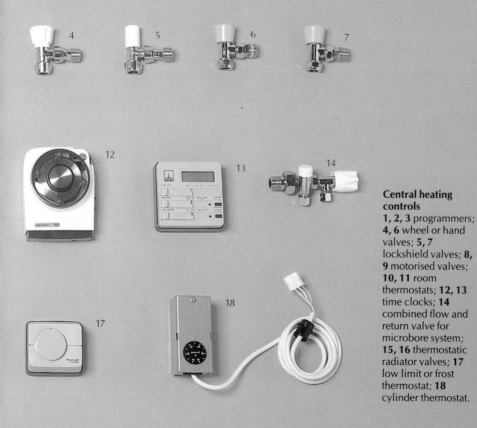

Central heating controls
1, 2, 3 programmers; **4, 6** wheel or hand valves; **5, 7** lockshield valves; **8, 9** motorised valves; **10, 11** room thermostats; **12, 13** time clocks; **14** combined flow and return valve for microbore system; **15, 16** thermostatic radiator valves; **17** low limit or frost thermostat; **18** cylinder thermostat.

252 Keeping the system going

Without regular maintenance, no central heating system can be expected to run efficiently for very long — and faults occuring during the winter can be at best an inconvenience; at worse, a hazard, especially to the young and elderly.

Breakdowns caused by neglect can be very expensive — as you'll soon discover if you ever have cause to call in a heating contractor at short notice.

Preventative measures
As always, prevention is better than cure. You can do much to forestall problems by running your system diligently. Minimise the workload on the boiler by insulating your home thoroughly (see pages 274 to 291); consider the benefits of running the system continuously during very cold weather, with a low thermostat setting during parts of the day when you need less heat — a boiler that is not continually switching on and off and intermittently running at full blast to rewarm a totally cooled house will last longer. But you can, as already described, fit special controls designed to operate your system continuously at economic cost.

The professional touch
While there is a good deal you can do yourself, given certain levels of skills, some routine jobs really are better left to the professionals.

Gas boilers, for example, should be given an annual service to ensure safe and efficient running. Special equipment is needed to adjust and correct the gas/air mix, and an experienced eye will detect approaching problems which an amateur might overlook.

Oil-fired boilers, too, need an annual service along similar lines. Solid fuel boilers don't need this type of servicing, but the chimney must be thoroughly swept once a year — by someone experienced in dealing with boiler flues (see page 257).

Self servicing
Outside of the boiler, many maintenance tasks are well within the scope of

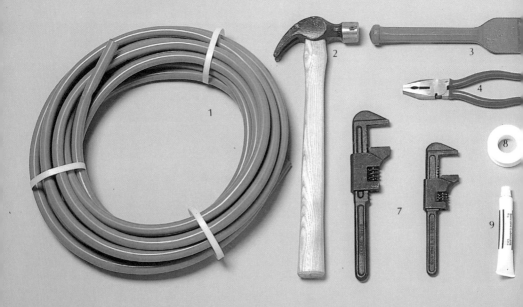

the do-it-yourselfer, given a limited number of tools and materials, and a modest range of skills, all of which this book is designed to teach you.

While the system isn't operating during the summer, there are a few simple but important ways you can prevent problems arising when it comes to switching on again. Examine each part of the system carefully.

The pump
Check that the pump is working properly. Occasionally, switch on the central heating system and run the pump. Should the pump be left unturned for too long, it could stick through a gradual build-up of impurities on its blades. Because pumps are supposed to run silently, you won't know it's running by listening to it. Place your hand on it; if you feel vibration, the pump is running.

The radiator
Turn radiator valves occasionally. In time, the hand valves that control flow into radiators may seize up, so test them every now and then. You should not, however, try to adjust the lock-shield valves opposite.

The boiler
Give the boiler a rest. If you don't have a separate hot water cylinder temperature control and you are continuing to use the boiler to supply hot water, the boiler thermostat should be turned down. The minimum setting for the thermostat should be 60°C (140°F), otherwise condensation from the boiler's flue gases can cause serious corrosion inside the appliance.

The ballvalve
Keep the feed and expansion tank ballvalve moving. At least once a year, check that the arm connecting the float to the ballvalve is not sticking. Move it gently up and down a couple of times to minimise the chance of a build-up of scale or dust from the loft space causing it to seize. Make sure the valve is not leaking.

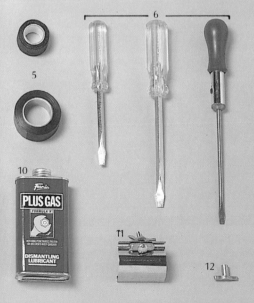

Maintenance tool kit
1 length of garden hose for draining the system; **2, 3** claw hammer and bolster chisel for lifting floorboards; **4** pliers; **5** two-part pipe leak repair tape; **6** screwdrivers; **7** adjustable wrenches for tightening compression joints; **8** PTFE tape for making watertight threaded connections; **9** silicone lubricant; **10** penetrating lubricant; **11** pipe leak repair clamp; **12** radiator bleed key.

254 Starting up

There are other routine checks you would be wise to make when starting up the system. To be safe, run the central heating for an hour or two some time in advance of switching on for the heating season itself. If any problems arise, you'll have time to deal with them before a really cold spell.

Faulty ballvalve If, after switching the system on, you notice any water dripping from the overflow pipe that runs from the feed and expansion tank to the outside (or if you notice dripping at any time for that matter), the chances are that the ballvalve is at fault. It's likely that the valve washer, which should close the valve under the pressure of the float arm rising with the water level, is so worn that it can no longer fully block the flow of water from the mains.

First, check that it's not the float which is at fault; it may have sprung a leak and be filling with water, although this is rarely the problem. Replace a faulty float with a new one if necessary; usually, they simply unscrew from the arm. Replace a worn washer as shown in the step-by-step photographs.

Leaking joints After running the system for an hour or two, check all valves and compression joints (any joint that isn't a soldered one) for leaks. Run your finger round each radiator valve at the point where it connects with the pipe as well

1 After turning off the mains water supply at the stopcock, use a pair of pliers to remove the split pin holding the float arm to the valve.

2 Remove any cap from the end of the valve body, then push the piston out with a screwdriver blade inserted through the float arm slot.

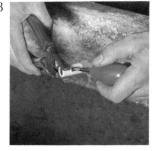

3 Unscrew the two halves of the piston by inserting a screwdriver blade in the float arm slot and gripping the other end with a pair of pliers.

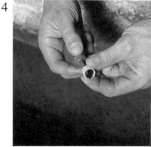

4 Push out the old rubber washer with the screwdriver blade, then insert a new washer of the correct size.

5 Screw the two piston halves together, clean off any scale or corrosion with steel wool, and lubricate with petroleum jelly.

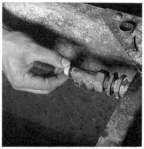

6 Slide the piston assembly back into the valve, refit the end cap and reconnect the float arm, using a new split pin.

as at the radiator itself. If you detect the slightest dampness, the joint is probably in need of tightening. Using an adjustable spanner, tighten as gently as possible. Avoid overtightening; you might damage the threads.

Bleeding the pump Immersed in water all its life, and working for thousands of hours to push and pull the weight of circulating flow, it's hardly surprising that the pump sometimes goes wrong.

If, after starting the system, you find that the pipes are not heating up, and yet you can feel the vibration of the pump, it's possible that an air bubble is trapped inside, causing the blades to spin uselessly in air instead of water;

the solution is to bleed the air out of the pump, using the special threaded spindle incorporated for this purpose.

Replacing the pump If bleeding the pump doesn't restore the flow, the unit will either need overhauling or replacing. With the appropriate tools, you can remove the pump and replace it after repairs (which must be carried out by the manufacturers). If a replacement pump is necessary, you must fit one with the same duty. This is a job you can do yourself only if the new pump is of the same precise specification as its predecessor. For a pump of different specification, the plumbing must be altered accordingly.

1

1 Prior to removing the old pump, shut down the boiler. Close the isolating valves on each side of the pump, using an adjustable wrench.

2

2 Remove the appropriate fuse from the consumer unit (keeping it in your pocket), take off the pump's inspection plate and disconnect the flex.

3

3 Have a bucket and cloths ready to mop up the water inside the pump and unscrew the nuts holding it to the valves on each side.

4

4 Fit the new pump (of the same make, size and capacity) in place, remembering to fit the sealing washers.

5

5 Reconnect the flex and refit the inspection cover. Then set the speed control (if fitted) to match that of the old pump.

6
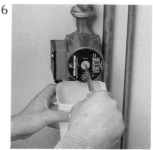

6 Open the valves, checking for leaks at the couplings, then bleed any air from the pump by opening the bleed screw.

256 Bleeding the radiators

Inevitably, in what is essentially an 'open' system, some air is bound to find its way into the water, and the most likely place for that air to collect is at the tops of the radiators. Therefore, every radiator is built with an air bleed valve at its highest point. These valves should be operated annually to release any air. If a radiator seems cooler at the top than at the bottom, the likely reason is a pocket of air. Bleed the radiator with the key supplied with the system. Do this when the system is switched off.

It's most important to turn the bleed key slowly — opening the valve too rapidly may cause it to be forced out of the radiator by the flow of water, damaging your clothes and decorations. Open the valve cautiously until the first drop of water appears; then tighten it again.

1

1 Before attempting to bleed the radiators, switch off the power to the control system.

2

2 With a suitable container handy to catch any water, open each bleed valve a quarter turn.

3

3 Any air present will give an audible hiss as it escapes. When water appears, close the valve.

4

4 Check that all compression joints are watertight with an adjustable wrench.

Servicing schemes 257

For gas and oil boilers in particular, an annual service is necessary to ensure efficient and safe operation. The particular merit of an annual servicing contract is that it prevents you overlooking necessary maintenance work — especially when the boiler seems to be running perfectly well just as it is.

Gas systems

Through their regional service centres, British Gas run a number of regular service plans. The basic scheme covers a yearly service and adjustment of the appliance and its built-in controls. Any repairs deemed to be necessary are charged separately — both for materials and labour. Additional charges are also made for any calls made between services.

A step up is a plan which offers the simple additional benefit of free labour on any repair jobs that arise from a failure of the appliance or its built-in controls, at any time of the year. This service can also be extended to cover free parts as well as labour.

Finally, there is a plan which covers all the above plus an annual check of the whole system. Your central heating as a whole is fully covered for labour and any parts that may be needed to keep it running all year.

These schemes only apply automatically to systems installed by British Gas themselves within the previous three years. Other systems will only be taken on after an inspection (for which you might have to pay). If any repairs are needed, you must make them at your own expense before the gas board will take on your system. Any system or boiler more than 10 years old may be ineligible for the service plans which offer free parts.

In effect, it is the first scheme that's only truly necessary. The others merely incorporate different types of insurance — against problems that are relatively unlikely to arise, particularly in newer gas installations looked after with reasonable care.

The saving with such a scheme is that its cost does work out cheaper than calling in a service man from British Gas to do the same job on spec.

British Gas may have a monopoly on the fuel, but there's plenty of competition with them for installation and service work. In fact, the firm which installed your system may well offer you a better deal for regular servicing; you should be offered such a facility when the system is installed. If you don't know who installed your system, but you prefer not to deal with British Gas, you'll find a large number of independent heating firms listed in your local *Yellow Pages*.

Oil systems

No monopoly exists in the oil-fired heating business, and servicing arrangements are best made with your system's installer or with your fuel distributor. Major distributors around the country offer various schemes, beginning with annual single-service contracts and ranging up to comprehensive parts-and-labour insurance schemes. Most of these plans are only offered after an inspection of your system, with the proviso that any faults are put right before the service scheme comes into effect.

Solid fuel systems

The Solid Fuel Advisory Service say that boilers run on solid fuel need an annual thorough sweeping of their flues and chimneys. So long as you operate the boiler according to its maker's instructions, it shouldn't need any other form of regular servicing.

Electric storage heaters need no regular servicing, but should be treated with the same respect as any other electrical appliance.

258 Draining and refilling the system

Draining the system is not a complicated job, but you must follow the correct procedure. Among the reasons for draining the system are: to carry out repairs to the pipework, to flush out sludge caused by corrosion in the system, to extend the system by adding radiators, or to avoid the risk of frost damage if the house will be empty for a prolonged period during winter.

The first job is to cut off the water supply to the feed and expansion tank in the loft. Do this by tying up the ballvalve float arm to a batten spanning the tank or by turning off the appropriate stopvalve.

To drain the system, you'll need to find the primary draincock, which will either be at the base of the boiler or nearby at the lowest part of the central heating return pipe. You simply attach a length of garden hose to the draincock's outlet and drain the water into a gully or soakaway.

The draincock will normally have a square shank which can be turned with a special key or an adjustable spanner.

You'll also have to open the radiator air vents to prevent water being held inside by vacuum. Open the vents in progression, starting with the radiators on the highest floor and working down to those nearest to the boiler. If the vents aren't opened in this order, there's a danger of water from the higher levels leaking out of open vents lower down. When you've opened all the vents and the flow from the hose has ceased, your system is drained.

Inverted loops

In some systems — notably in bungalows — some of the radiators may be served by pipes dropping down to them from above in what is known as an 'inverted loop' circuit. Each of these circuits should have its own draincock located at the lowest point.

Clearly, if an air vent on any of these radiators is opened before the inverted

1 Before draining the system, turn off the mains water supply to the header tank at the nearby stopvalve or by tying up the float arm to a batten spanning the top of the tank.

2 When draining down, attach a length of garden hose securely to each of the system's draincocks. Lead the free end of the hose to a convenient gully or soakaway point in the garden.

3 Open the draincock and let the water drain away. Ideally, you should have a special key to turn the draincock's square shank, but you can use an adjustable spanner if you are careful.

4 To prevent water being held in the system by vacuum, open the radiator bleed valves in progression, starting with those highest in the system. Take care not to open them too soon.

1 Tie up the ballvalve float arm or close the stopvalve on the mains feed at the header tank before draining off any water.

2 Attach a hose to one of the system draincocks, open the valve and drain off enough water to empty the header tank.

3 Close the draincock and pour the inhibitor directly into the header tank. Then restore the water supply to the tank.

loop circuit has been drained, water will flow out of the vent. The procedure is the same as for the rest of the circuit.

Refilling the system
When the time comes, refill the system by closing the primary draincock (and any draincocks on inverted loop circuits), close all radiator air vents, and restart the mains flow into the feed and expansion tank by freeing the ballvalve.

When the water ceases to flow into the feed and expansion tank, bleed each radiator (see page 256). If necessary, bleed the pump (see page 255). The system is then ready for use again.

Flushing the system
After some years of use, the central heating system may become partially clogged with corrosion sludge, which collects in its lower parts and impedes the flow of water. The corrosion occurs mostly in the steel parts of the system (boiler and radiators) but the pump carries the deposits round the pipes.

A common symptom of sludge problems is a sluggish pump. When the pump is removed for repair, it may well show evidence of a black residue.

When sludge is confirmed or suspected, flush the system through. To do

this, drain off and refill as previously described, then drain again: repeat until the water is clear.

Adding corrosion inhibitor
A build-up of sludge in the system can be largely prevented by adding corrosion inhibitor to the circulating water. This is best done when the system is newly installed or when it has for some reason been drained. But there's no need to empty the system if you want to add inhibitor at any other time.

Corrosion inhibitor is sold in liquid form, usually in 4 or 5 litre (1 gallon) containers — the quantity you need for a normal domestic system. To add the inhibitor, first close the mains water supply to the feed and expansion tank.

Switch off the boiler and pump and, as previously described, attach a hose to the primary draincock and open the valve. Drain off about 20 litres (5 gallons) of water, measured by the bucketful to empty the feed and expansion tank and part of the pipework.

Close the draincock, then pour the inhibitor directly into the feed and expansion tank, release the ballvalve and allow the inflow of water to carry the inhibitor into the pipework. When you restart the pump, the liquid will be distributed throughout the system.

260 Replacing a damaged radiator 1

In systems which have run for some years without corrosion inhibitor added to the water, there's a real risk of damage to radiators — to the point where a leak might occur. In this case, the only solution is to replace the radiator.

Assuming that you can obtain a new radiator of precisely the same specification as the one you intend to remove, this is a perfectly practicable project.

With care, it's possible even to replace a defective radiator without draining down the system.

Removing the old radiator
In order to remove the old radiator you'll have to close both the manual control valve and the lockshield valve to isolate it. When you close the latter, it's essential to note down exactly how many turns are needed to close the

1 Completely close the wheel valve and then remove the protective cap from the top of the lockshield valve.

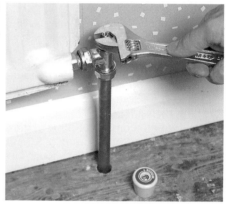

2 Close the lockshield valve, making a note of the number of turns its shank needs. Use an adjustable wrench.

5 Unscrew the valve connectors from the bottom tappings of the old radiator. They will be tight and need some force to move them.

6 Clean up the thread of each connector, using a piece of steel wool. Make sure you remove all traces of old sealant.

valve so that you can open it up by exactly the same amount when you've fitted the replacement radiator.

The valve shank has flat faces and can be turned either with a special tool or a small adjustable spanner. Alternatively, it may be possible to remove the plastic head from the wheel valve, press it over the lockshield valve's shank and turn it that way.

Once you've isolated the radiator from the system, you'll have to drain the water from one of its valves before you can disconnect it and lift it clear. Radiators are hung so that they tilt slightly upwards towards the air vent; therefore, the lowest point is at the other end — at which draining off should be carried out. Make sure you have a suitable container to catch the water as you loosen the valve connection. The radiator contains a lot of

3

3 Open the air bleed valve and unscrew the valve connector, draining the water into a suitable container.

4

4 When all the water has been drained from the radiator, disconnect it from both valves and lift it free from its brackets.

7
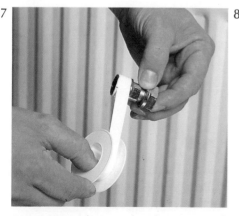

7 Wrap PTFE sealing tape about five times round each connector thread, covering it completely for a good seal.

8

8 Refit the connectors to the new radiator, making sure that they are tightened fully in each tapping.

262 Replacing a damaged radiator 2

water which will be dirty, so roll back any carpets.

So long as the valves on the pipe runs are left completely closed, it's quite safe for you to run the central heating system without the radiator.

Reconnecting the new radiator
So long as your replacement radiator is exactly the same as the old one, you should not have trouble connecting it to the pipework. Lift the radiator on to its brackets and check that the screw-threaded connectors are aligned, then screw up the retaining nuts hand tight at the lockshield and wheel valves.

When you are satisfied that the radiator is seated correctly, tighten the nuts using an adjustable spanner.

Open the wheel and lockshield valves and replace the cover on the lockshield valve.

1

1 Lift the new radiator on to its brackets, making sure that they are engaged properly behind the radiator hangers.

2

2 Align the tapered cones to the valves at each end of the radiator and start the capnuts on their threads.

3

3 Tighten the capnuts with an adjustable wrench until they are really firm, but take care not to overtighten them.

4

4 Close the air bleed valve and reopen the lockshield and wheel valves, then bleed the radiator.

Planning the extension 1 263

Adding extra radiators to your existing central heating system is a practical proposition — with two main provisos: one, that you have the skills and equipment for the job; two, that your system's present boiler can cope with the extra demand for heat.

Are you up to it?

First things first! Anyone who is capable of making an accurate measurement, wielding a saw and a spanner and who can appreciate the importance of thorough preparation of any job, should be able to tackle basic plumbing skills of the sort required for a simple heating extension.

Modern soldered joints are remarkably simple to make, and with the right equipment, a careful amateur should have no problems. Compression joints (at radiators) are also straightforward to assemble, provided you follow the correct simple procedures.

Tools and materials are not expensive. You may be able to borrow or hire several items, but the benefit of buying them is that you're then able to handle other plumbing jobs that may arise.

If you are uncertain about taking on plumbing work, follow some of the procedures described on the following pages.

Is your boiler up to it?

The answer to this question can be rather more simply reached. Nevertheless, it is an important point, because adding radiators that stretch the heat demand beyond your boiler's capacity will saddle you with enormous bills for running the appliance full-tilt whenever it's on, and you may well not have adequate heating anywhere in the house even though the boiler is straining.

You can determine whether your boiler has any spare capacity by reading the rating number of the boiler, which will be on a plate or label somewhere on the casing. It will probably read something like 'CF80' or 'B38/50'. The first means a conventional flue (CF) boiler of 80,000Btu/h; the second means a balanced flue (B) and 50,000Btu/h. Where two figures are given, such as 38/50, you can ignore the first one, which is the output when the boiler is running light — not relevant in this case.

Few boilers are yet marked with the metric equivalent rating (in kilowatts or kW), so make your calculations in British thermal units per hour.

From the output figure, subtract 10 per cent to allow for the system's heat losses in pipework. From the 90 per cent left, subtract a further 8,000Btu/h, which is the output needed to maintain the hot water cylinder supply. (If you have a large cylinder serving two bathrooms, increase the figure to 12,000Btu/h.) The figure you come up with is the maximum output available for centrally heating your house. So, if your boiler is rated CF50, the output would work out like this:

50,000 less 10%=45,000,
less 8,000=37,000Btu/h

Measure the front face of all your existing radiators and calculate the area of each in square feet. If the radiator is a single panel, its rating will be about 430Btu/h per square foot; if it's a double panel, this rises to about 730Btu/h.

These figures serve only as a rule of thumb. There's some variation in output between different makes of radiator. If you have the manufacturer's tables of radiator outputs, you can work to a more exact figure. If your radiators are not of the standard panel type, this rule of thumb will not operate; again, you'll need the manufacturer's tables.

Using the figures available, calculate the approximate output of each

264 Planning the extension 2

radiator and add them up. The difference between this total and the available boiler capacity represents what spare you have — if any.

If your system was planned economically in the first place, there may be very little spare output indeed. Any remaining normally arises from the fact that installers tend to err on the generous side when the decision as to boiler size is a marginal one.

Metric calculations

If you prefer to work out boiler and radiator outputs in metric, convert Btu/h to kW by dividing the former by a factor of 3,412.

The radiator rating of 430Btu/h per square foot converts to a metric equivalent of 1.36kW per square metre. The rating 730Btu/h per square foot converts to 2.3kW per square metre.

What heat do you need?

System designers use detailed tables to work out the size of radiator needed to heat a room to the required temperature. These tables are too extensive to

quote here, but by following some guidelines based on typical rooms, you should be able to come up with an assessment of your needs.

The following examples of four different situations can be adapted to your requirements by substituting your own room's measurements.

1 Downstairs living room 3.7 by 3.3m (12 by 11ft) with one outside wall, in a Victorian brick two-storey terrace house. Temperature 21°C (70°F).
Heat requirement 5,700Btu/h
Based on 343mm (13½in) solid external wall, 229mm (9in) party walls, suspended board floor, heated bedroom above.

2 Upstairs bedroom 4 by 3.3m (13 by 11ft) with two outside walls, in modern brick two-storey semi-detached house. Temperature 18°C (65°F).
Heat requirement 4,000Btu/h
Based on 279mm (11in) cavity external walls, 114mm (4½in) party walls, suspended board floor, heated room below, insulated roof space above.

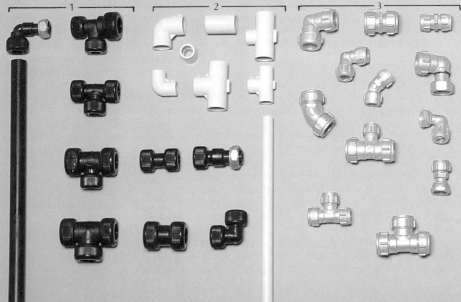

3 Downstairs kitchen 3.7 by 2.4m (12 by 8ft) with two outside walls, in a modern single-storey extension to a brick house. Temperature 18°F (65°F).

Heat requirement 4,600Btu/h
Based on 279mm (11in) cavity external walls, 114mm (4½in) party walls, solid floor, board, felt and bitumen flat roof.

4 Upstairs bathroom 3 by 1.8m (10 by 6ft) with one external wall, in a flat in a Victorian brick multi-storey house. Temperature 21°C (70°F).

Heat requirement 2,700Btu/h
Based on 343mm (13½in) solid external wall, 229mm (9in) party walls, suspended board floor, heated rooms above and below.

Planning the pipework

Having decided the size and position of your intended additional radiators, you should consider the route that the flow and return pipes must take. When you are planning new runs, keep these six factors in mind:

Pipe routes It will simplify the work if the pipes can be routed above the floor — along the tops of skirtings and through walls at skirting height.

Inverted loops Avoid when possible. If it's unavoidable, fit draincocks.

Connecting radiators Extra radiators must be connected directly into the flow and return mains.

Breaking in points The easiest point at which to break into a main is at an elbow joint.

Connector valves While it's possible to use a 'straight' radiator valve to connect a horizontal pipe, it's a simpler fitting task to join the pipe to the radiator by a rising 'angle' valve.

Repositioning pipes If the preferred position of a new radiator means the pipe crossing a doorway, it's best to change the position rather than taking it over or under the door.

Pipe and fittings

1 Polybutylene push-fit fittings and pipe; **3** CPVC plastic solvent-weld fittings; **3** compression fittings; **4** microbore manifold and pliable copper pipe; **5** various pipe clips; **6** Yorkshire capillary fittings; **7** end-feed capillary fittings and small bore copper pipe.

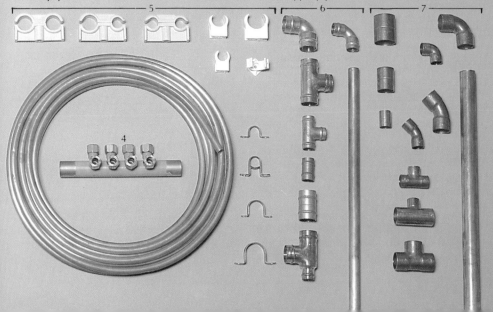

266 Installing a new radiator 1

Having established a practicable pipe route from the existing heating pipes, you're then able to decide on the final position of the new radiator. Before you fix it, however, you must decide at which end of the radiator you want the wheel valve. Split the two halves of each radiator valve, apply PTFE tape to the horizontal connectors and screw them into the radiator inlet and outlet (see page 246). Reassemble the valves to their connectors, with the wheel valve at your chosen end.

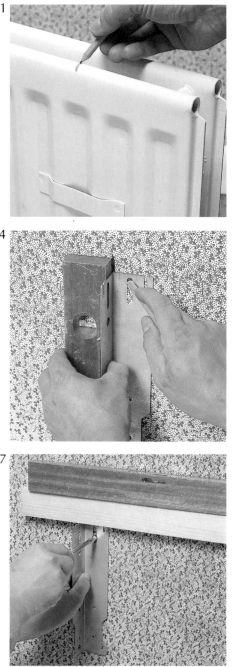

Hanging the radiator
The next job is to hang the radiator. First of all, mark the centre of the wall brackets on top of the radiator in pencil. Stand the radiator against the wall where you want it to be fixed and transfer the pencil marks to the wall to indicate the bracket positions.

Slot the brackets into the hangers and measure the distance from the bottom of the radiator to the top of the brackets. Add the clearance between the radiator and the floor — about 75mm (3in) above the top of the skirting is adequate.

Position the brackets one at a time in line with the marks on the wall and measure the distance from the top of each to the floor: this should equal the distance calculated previously. Check that the bracket is vertical by holding a spirit level against it then mark its screw hole on the wall.

Drill and plug the holes (top only) and screw the brackets to the wall using 38mm (1½in) No 10 round-head screws: the screw should be at the centre of the slot.

Radiators are set with a slight tilt upwards towards the airvent end — about 3mm (⅛in) for a small radiator and 6mm (¼in) for a long one. To do this, you just loosen the screw on the appropriate bracket to slide it up or down the relevant distance. Retighten

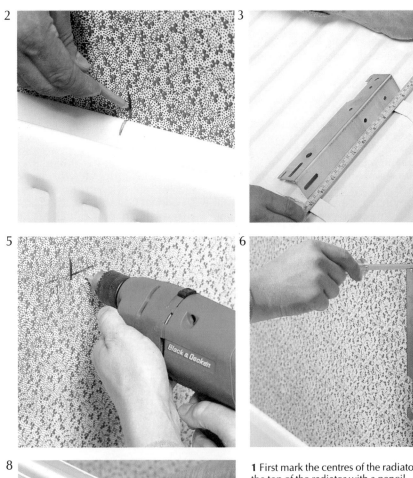

1 First mark the centres of the radiator hangers on the top of the radiator with a pencil.
2 Stand the radiator against the wall and transfer the centreline marks to the wall.
3 Slide a bracket on to the hangers. Measure from the top of the bracket to the bottom of the radiator and add the clearance above the floor.
4 Position the bracket so that its top is at the correct height and it is aligned with the hanger centre. Use a spirit level to make sure that it is vertical and mark the upper screw positions.
5 Drill and plug the holes.
6 Screw one bracket to the wall.
7 Fit the second bracket and align the bracket tops. Mark, drill and plug the bottom screw holes. Insert the screws.
8 Attach the valves to the new radiator.

268 Installing a new radiator 2

the screw when you're satisfied with the slope.

To make the final fixings, ensure the hangers are vertical, and drill through the lower screw hole on each bracket, plug and screw as previously described.

Hang the radiator and check that it's accurately positioned before you link the pipework to it.

Connecting the pipework

With the two break-in tees in position, you can extend the pipework along the chosen route by cutting additional lengths and fitting elbows or bending as necessary. Clips should be at intervals of no more than 1.8m (6ft), and no more than 1.2m (4ft) in vulnerable places such as above skirtings. The pipe must be brought to a point about 70mm (2¾in) below each angle valve of the radiator.

The flow pipe should be brought to the end you decided to fit the wheel valve and the return pipe to the lockshield valve. However, it's also important to ensure that the upper pipe along the wall is the one which has to be

connected to the first valve reached, so that the lower can continue to the far end without crossing the other. Which is on top depends on the choice of wheel valve position and whether the feed pipes come from left or right.

In each case, you should deliberately cut the last pipe slightly too long to allow for final adjustment later. Each pipe end will now be close to the wall and about 70mm (2¾in) below its correct valve and slightly overlength.

The final stage is to fit two elbow joints and two short lengths of pipe to make the connection. If your extension involves more than one radiator, the procedure for subsequent units is exactly the same, except that the fittings taking the short angle pipes from the feed pipes to the first radiator should be tees and the feed pipes continued along the wall to the farther radiator position.

Thermostatic valves

If you intend to fit a thermostatic valve to your new radiator, it may be necessary to adjust the length of the connecting pipe accordingly. Most makes of thermostatic valve are of different

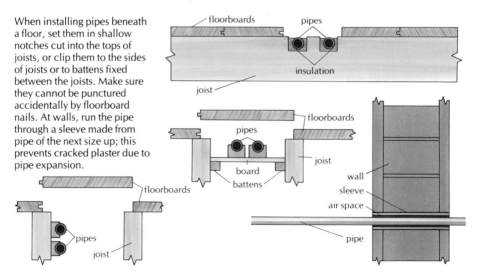

When installing pipes beneath a floor, set them in shallow notches cut into the tops of joists, or clip them to the sides of joists or to battens fixed between the joists. Make sure they cannot be punctured accidentally by floorboard nails. At walls, run the pipe through a sleeve made from pipe of the next size up; this prevents cracked plaster due to pipe expansion.

floorboards
pipes
insulation
joist
floorboards
pipes
joist
board
battens
floorboards
wall
sleeve
air space
pipes
joist
pipe

1 Lift the new radiator on to its brackets, making sure that both top and bottom hangers are properly engaged on the bracket hooks.

2 Decide where you are going to break into the existing central heating system, drain the system, then fit tees to the flow and return pipes as described on page 174. You can use compression fittings, or capillary joints as shown in the photographs here.

3 Insert the branch pipes, adjusting the positions, of the tees as necessary. Here, one branch is bent to clear the neighbouring pipe.

4 Make sure the pipe runs are clipped securely at the recommended intervals, whether below the floor or attached to skirtings or walls.

5 Stop each pipe run just below the appropriate valve position.

270 Installing a new radiator 3

1

2

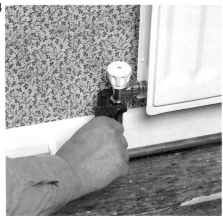

3

4

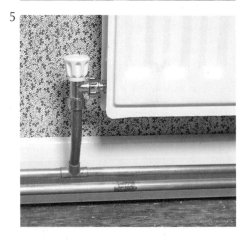

5

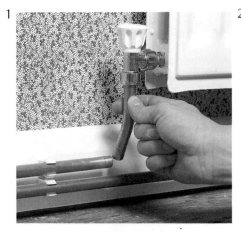

1 Cut and bend short lengths of pipe to connect the valves to the feed and return pipes. Trim the pipe ends as necessary.

2 Slip capillary elbows on to the ends of the circuit pipes and the short pipes to the valves and solder them in place, taking care to protect any nearby woodwork.

3 If the new radiator is situated on an inverted loop circuit, fit a draincock to the end of the lower of the two pipes as shown.

4 Finally, tighten the capnuts to connect the short pipes to the valves.

5 If you are installing more than one new radiator, both feed and return pipes should be taken on to the next radiator position. Consequently, tees are used instead of elbows to connect the short pipes to the circuit pipes.

Commissioning the system 1 271

dimensions to standard hand valves, although all are made to fit on to 15mm pipe and into standard radiator inlets.

Thermostatic valves are fitted in place of hand valves at the flow ends of radiators. Activated by a temperature-reading sensor, the valve opens and closes according to the temperature command preset for the room, thus controlling the radiator's output.

These valves are capable only of maintaining preset temperatures lower than each room's design temperature, as the radiators will have been sized to meet this requirement with the valves fully open.

Nevertheless, this facility is a useful one in a house where some rooms might be wastefully heated — particularly bedrooms in a home where the central heating is running all day. Rooms which receive radiant heat from the sun, for instance, might also require no extra heating. In such a situation, if a roomstat was the only system control and it was fitted in a room receiving no direct sunlight (as is likely), all the rooms might be receiving the full output of their radiators. Individual radiator thermostats fitted in, say, south-facing rooms might produce a useful economy in this situation.

The real benefit of thermostatic radiator valves may only be appreciated when all the radiators in a system are equipped with them. This would preclude the need for a room thermostat (an inaccurate temperature controller at the best of times), overall control being through the boiler thermostat and timer or programmer. These special valves are significantly more expensive than the standard types, but would cost no more to fit, in labour terms, in a new installation.

If thermostatic radiator valves are fitted to all the radiators in a system, a pipe connection (fitted with a lockshield regulating valve) should be made between the flow and return pipes. This will eliminate the risk of the pump operating against a closed circuit if all the thermostatic valves close down at once.

Fitting thermostatic radiator valves to every radiator in an existing system, however, is unlikely to prove a cost-effective measure in terms of fuel economy. Because there's no guarantee that you can buy thermostatic valves that will be interchangeable with your existing hand valves, a certain amount of plumbing work will be unavoidable: expensive if you have a plumber do it; time-consuming if you do it yourself.

Using the plumbing skills described in the preceding pages, you can certainly fit an interchangeable valve — aided by the maker's fitting recommendations, if any are supplied. Where some alteration to pipework is called for (the rising flow pipe may need to be set a little further away from the radiators, for example, to accommodate the new valve's longer body), you should follow the plumbing instructions for cutting and soldering that also appear on the preceding pages.

Because of the marked differences in thermostatic radiator valve design, you should shop around carefully to try and find one that will be interchangeable with your existing hand valves.

Commissioning the extended system
Bringing an extension to your central heating system into use involves filling and checking for leaks, followed by adjusting the new circuit with the lockshield valves.

Refill the system as described on page 258. Check that the lockshield valves as well as the wheel valves are open on the new radiators. Check all soldered joints. There is no likelihood of any leaks if the job has been done carefully but leaks *are* possible at the valve compression joints — on the flow

272 Commissioning the system 2

and return pipes and the cone-faced unions between the vertical and horizontal halves of the valves. In both cases, further tightening with an adjustable spanner should stop a leak. Tighten little by little and avoid overtightening, which can damage the thread and cause a worse leak.

Setting the lockshield valve

Lockshield valves are normally set by an installer using special instruments — which is why you shouldn't normally interfere with them. These instruments are hardly needed for a small extension, however, and setting the lockshield for correct flow can usually be done by trial and error.

A lockshield valve set too far open can 'short-circuit' part of the system, by providing the flow of hot water with too easy a route into the return — thus robbing other radiators of their supply. On the other hand, if the lockshield valve is not open enough, the radiator will hold the same water for longer than it takes the temperature to drop by 11°C (20°F) and it will never reach its rated output.

The first trial, then, is to set the lockshield valve exactly half open, let the system run for an hour or two with its room thermostat (if fitted) at maximum and see whether the extension radiators seem hotter or cooler than others on the same circuit. The wheel valve must be fully open all the time.

Adjust the lockshield half a turn up or down accordingly and leave for another hour.

Radiators near the beginning of a circuit may need their lockshield valves opening by only one turn, while those most distant from the pump may be fully open. However, this isn't a strict rule, and only trial and error will get it right for your particular system.

When the setting seems satisfactory, simply replace the loose cap on the valve.

Balancing the system

If a number of radiators are added to an existing system, you may be forced to 'rebalance' the entire system to ensure that the water will be sufficiently hot throughout. In practical terms, this means that the water returning to the boiler should, in most systems, be 11°C (20°F) cooler than the water leaving the boiler.

At the boiler

To test the temperature you need to position thermometers on the flow and return heating pipes near the boiler. When the system is running, the temperature of the return pipe should be lower than that of the flow by the required amount.

For a reasonably accurate measure of this temperature, you can buy a special thermometer that clips firmly on to the pipe. A heating installer would use a

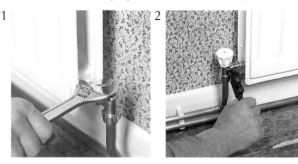

1 Once the system is running, you can balance the flow of water through each radiator by opening or closing the lockshield valve. Do this by turning its square shank with an adjustable wrench. If only one radiator is involved, balancing can be done by 'trial and error', otherwise special thermometers may be needed.
2 Check all joints for tightness.

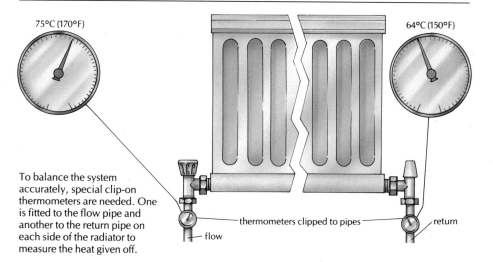

75°C (170°F)

64°C (150°F)

To balance the system accurately, special clip-on thermometers are needed. One is fitted to the flow pipe and another to the return pipe on each side of the radiator to measure the heat given off.

thermometers clipped to pipes

flow

return

pair of such thermometers to take simultaneous readings, but you can make do with one perfectly easily. Before buying it from your plumber's merchant, measure the size of the flow and return pipes — both are likely to be either 22 or 28mm — then buy a thermometer with the appropriate size of clip fitting.

First, attach the thermometer to the flow pipe and leave it for a few minutes to allow an accurate reading. Note down this temperature and then move the thermometer over to the return pipe. Give it ten minutes or so to settle before taking a reading.

If return temperature is more than a degree or two lower than the desired 11°C (20°F), the pump is not pushing water around the system quickly enough. Check that the pump is working properly (see page 254). If it seems to be working normally but not up to the additional load, its 'head' can be adjusted if it's a variable model of pump. A non-variable-head pump will probably need to be replaced with a more powerful version.

To increase the pump output, turn the adjustable knob or lever in the direction indicated (usually clockwise) by one segment or a few degrees. Repeat the temperature readings after about ten minutes. One adjustment of the pump head should be enough if it is in good working order.

At the radiators

Where a number of radiators need balancing — that is, adjusting for an 11°C (20°F) water-temperature drop — it might be worthwhile buying thermometers for the job, rather than balancing each one by the comparatively laborious trial-and-error method.

For this purpose, you'll need a pair of thermometers with fittings to clip firmly on to the 15mm flow and return pipes. When the radiator is fully warmed up, attach each thermometer as close as you can to the valve at either end and allow a few minutes to get an accurate reading.

To adjust for correct temperature drop, open or close the lockshield valve according to whether the original reading at the return shows too much or too little fall. After each adjustment, allow a few minutes before taking the new reading.

274 Reducing heating costs

All the expensive warmth generated by your central heating system ends up by disappearing into the outside air. There's nothing you can do to stop it happening, but by insulating your home to a reasonable extent it's possible to delay the loss of the heat long enough for it to do some good.

Without efficient insulation, a heating system costs a fortune to run, even in the smallest home, and provides little comfort. If the air in your rooms is rapidly sneaking out through gaps in doors and windows or through the roof, the radiators are fighting a losing battle to warm it.

Central heating systems, in fact, are designed on the understanding that the air will 'change', or lose its heat, in rooms at a known rate — ranging from one complete air change every two hours in bedrooms to two every hour in kitchens and bathrooms. Not that you'd wish to prevent these air changes, of course — ventilation is as vital to comfort as insulation is.

So where does the heat escape; and what can you do to reduce the heat loss

Eventually, all the heat produced by your central heating system will escape to the atmosphere, but if you can slow down the rate at which it escapes you can reduce the amount of heat you need to produce and thus cut down your heating bills. This illustration shows where the heat goes from your house. The greatest amount of heat is lost through the walls (A), which can account for up to 35% of the total warmth produced. Another major problem area is the roof, where up to 25% can escape (B). Both areas can benefit from simple insulation procedures. Draughts blowing under and around doors (C) put an extra demand on the heating system, consuming up to 15% of its output. Another 15% can disappear through the floor (D), and up to 10% can be lost because of poorly fitting and single-glazed windows (E). Any unused chimneys can also be a source of lost heat by allowing strong draughts to enter the house (F). All of these problems can be dealt with effectively, most for a relatively low outlay. By insulating with care, you could reduce your heating needs by 50% or more.

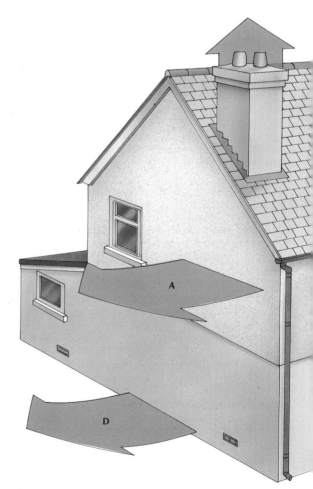

to a level that will enable your heating system to keep you comfortable at an economic rate?

The illustration on these pages shows where the crucial heat loss areas are, and what proportion of the overall loss they represent. The figures apply to a typical semi-detached house.

Clearly, if you live in a terraced house, you'll have less wall space to worry about; in a ground-floor flat you needn't give the roof a thought; on the other hand, in a detached house, you will lose heat in every direction. But whatever kind of home you live in, the reason for insulating it, if you've not already done so, is to reduce the amount of heat you need to maintain a comfortable temperature and a draught-free environment.

If you improve the insulation just enough to enable you to turn down your central heating thermostat by one or two degrees centigrade with no loss of comfort, you could reduce your fuel bill by 10 per cent. In other words, insulation saves not only heat, but also hard cash.

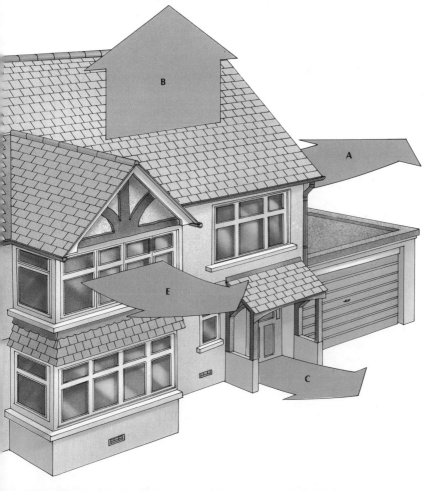

276 Insulating the heating system

Start insulating where it will do the most good — at your heating source. Pipes, hot water cylinder and water tanks can all be protected to great effect. All water pipes that may be vulnerable should be insulated against freezing, too, to prevent the catastrophe of a burst.

As the illustrated guide on these pages shows, pipes carrying hot water through unheated spaces should be covered or 'lagged' with a suitable insulant to minimise heat loss, as should all pipes at any risk of freezing. The hot water cylinder can be fitted with a special insulated jacket that will hold in the heat and reduce the load on the heating system.

Water tank insulation should ideally be movable; it's possible that the heat in the loft during a hot summer could warm the water in the tank and so reduce your water heating costs.

Below Here, thick sheets of rigid polystyrene are cut to size and taped together to form a box around the cistern. A separate sheet is used for the lid. Whatever you do, never put any kind of lagging beneath the cistern.

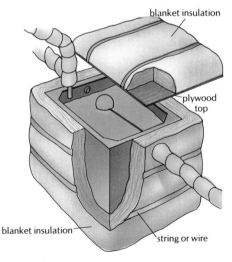

Above A cistern can be insulated effectively by building a box around it from softwood battens and plywood or hardboard, filling the space between this and the cistern with loose-fill insulation material.

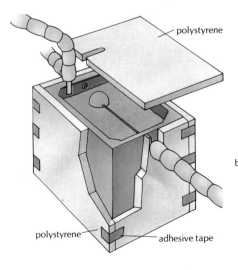

Above Of course, you can use glass fibre blanket insulation to lag the cistern. Simply tie the material round the cistern using wire or string. Make a plywood lid and tie or glue more blanket to the top of this.

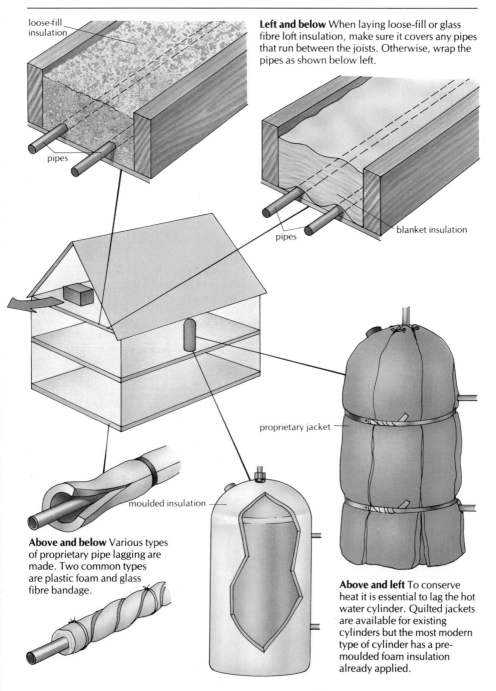

loose-fill insulation

pipes

Left and below When laying loose-fill or glass fibre loft insulation, make sure it covers any pipes that run between the joists. Otherwise, wrap the pipes as shown below left.

pipes

blanket insulation

proprietary jacket

moulded insulation

Above and below Various types of proprietary pipe lagging are made. Two common types are plastic foam and glass fibre bandage.

Above and left To conserve heat it is essential to lag the hot water cylinder. Quilted jackets are available for existing cylinders but the most modern type of cylinder has a pre-moulded foam insulation already applied.

278 Insulating the roof 1

Hot air rises, and if your loft is uninsulated, it will continue to rise — straight through your roof. An average semi can lose 25 per cent of its heat through the roof, but if you live in a terraced house — which has only two exterior walls instead of the semi's three — you may be losing an even higher proportion through the roof.

The Government is so firmly convinced that the nation's limited energy resources are pouring out through uninsulated lofts that special grants are made available through local authorities to subsidise the cost of having the appropriate remedial work done. If your loft awaits such attention, contact your local town hall for information before starting any kind of work.

There are basically three types of loft insulation you can lay yourself: blanket, loose-fill or sheet materials. All three are commonly laid on the loft floor between the joists, both blanket and sheet materials also being suitable for insulating between rafters; where you're converting the loft into a habitable room, for instance.

A fourth loft insulation material, blown fibre, must be installed by a contractor. More costly than other methods, it involves literally 'blowing' mineral fibre, pelleted glass fibre or cellulose fibre on to the loft floor, where it quite successfully covers the nooks and crannies other insulation materials cannot reach.

Safety aloft

Insulating a loft can be a precarious business. Access might be very difficult, especially when carrying bales or sacks full of insulating material. If you're tackling the job yourself, be sure you follow these safety precautions:
● **Safe access to the loft space** — a loft ladder or suitable-sized stepladder is preferable to just a ladder.
● **Adequate lighting** — a powerful light on a long lead will do if you've no fixed lights in the loft, but keep it well clear of water cisterns.
● **Somewhere to stand** — you can't expect continuously to balance on the joists. A panel of 19mm (¾in) thick chipboard makes a secure, portable platform; it should be large enough to span at least three joists — make sure the edges don't overhang the joists in case you should accidentally step on them, with disastrous results.
● **Protection for your lungs** — glass or mineral fibre insulating materials can emit unpleasant dust and fibres that are dangerous to breathe in; buy a proper protective mask with lint filters.
● **Protection for your skin** — insulating materials can cause skin irritations. Always wear rubber gloves when handling them; roll up your sleeves and remove your wristwatch to prevent trapping fibres.

Insulating between rafters

If, for any reason, the floor of your loft has been boarded over without any insulation having been laid previously, it might be more practicable for you to insulate the underside of the roof than to rip up the floor for the purpose.

Here, use 100mm (4in) thick blanket insulation of the appropriate width, or expanded polystyrene sheet, held between the rafters with a polythene 'vapour check' or timber battens nailed across the rafters. Or you can buy paper-wrapped blanket insulation, which you can pin or staple to the rafters.

If you're converting the loft into a habitable room, however, you need a much sturdier form of insulation, such as sheets of insulating plasterboard or fibreboard nailed across the rafters.

Laying blanket insulation

The most commonly used loft insulation material, rolls of glass or mineral fibre mat, is laid on the loft floor between the joists. It comes in two thicknesses: 80mm (3in) and 100mm (4in). You'll certainly benefit in terms of warmth in rooms below by laying the thicker insulation.

Rolls generally measure about 6 to 8m (20 to 26ft) long, and commonly 400mm (16in) wide: the usual joist spacing. Some houses, though, have irregularly-spaced joists — sometimes varying between about 300mm (1ft) and 450mm (18in) — and you may be able to buy glassfibre in 600mm (2ft) wide rolls, which you can cut to fit. For convenience, you'd be wise to cut the roll to width, using a panel saw, before

you remove it from its pack, as it expands when unwrapped and is awkward to contain.

Buy a 'kitemarked' brand of material, which conforms to the British Standard for 'thermal insulation for pitched roof spaces in dwellings' (BS 5803 Part 1).

Whatever type of mat you choose, first measure the width between the joists. The material you use must be wide enough to touch the joists at each side — even curling up the sides — without any gaps, which would allow warm air to escape in great quantities.

To calculate the number of rolls you'll need, multiply the length by the width of your loft to give the area in

1 If the floor of your loft is boarded over, you can insulate the roof by putting glass fibre mat between the rafters. First, nail battens across the rafters.

2 Cut the glass fibre mat into relatively short lengths and carefully push these in between the rafters behind the battens. A mask and gloves are essential.

3 If laying glass fibre mat between the loft joists, clean out all the dust and debris with a vacuum cleaner. Kneel on a sturdy board across the joists.

4 Clip any electrical cables to the top edges of the joist sides. Do not lay the glass fibre insulation over the top of them.

5 Working from one side of the loft to the other, unroll the insulation material, tucking it down between the joists.

6 Cut the mat to fit around any obstructions and use a stick or broom to push it to the eaves, but do not block them up.

280 Insulating the roof 2

square metres, then check the chart below. Buy one roll too many rather than one too few (the extra can.be useful for insulating water tanks and pipework — see page 276).

How many rolls?			
Sq m	Rolls	Sq m	Rolls
1.8	1	10.8	6
3.6	2	12.6	7
5.4	3	14.4	8
7.2	4	16.2	9
9.0	5	18.0	10

To lay blanket insulation, simply clear the loft floor of obstructions and unroll the material between the joists, starting at the eaves, butting lengths together to prevent gaps. Use a long length of wood or a broom to push the insulation into inaccessible parts.

Do not cover any electrical cables with the blanket to prevent overheating: instead clip the cables to the sides of the joists, or lay them over the insulation.

Finally, don't forget to insulate the loft hatch: cut a square of blanket, wrap it in polythene and tack it to the top of the trap door, overlapping the edges by about 50mm (2in) for a better seal against warm air escaping.

Laying loose-fill insulation

Loose-fill insulation tends to be easier to install than the blanket types. It consists of either a granulated mineral called vermiculite, polystyrene granules, mineral wool fibre or cellulose fibre. It's commonly sold in bags containing 110 litres (4cu ft) — sufficient for 1.1sq metres (12sq ft) — and is simply poured on to the loft floor between the joists, being spread out to a depth of 100mm (4in) with a simple home-made T-shaped spreader. It's important, though, to prevent the granules falling into the wall cavity at the eaves with a few bricks or a chipboard panel between the joists.

However, there are disadvantages with this material. To achieve the same insulating effects as 80mm (3in) of glassfibre blanket, you'd need about 130 to 140mm (5 to 5½in) of loose-fill, probably a greater depth than many

1 Pour loose-fill insulation directly from its bag, filling the spaces between the joists. But keep it clear of the eaves.

2 The loose-fill material can be spread out to an even thickness with a T-shaped batten. Aim for a depth of 100mm (4in).

Adequate ventilation is essential in the loft to prevent condensation forming and harming the supporting timbers. Any airbricks in gable ends should be kept clear, and insulation material should be kept away from the eaves. These moves will ensure a free passage through the roof space for any draughts which will then carry away moisture.

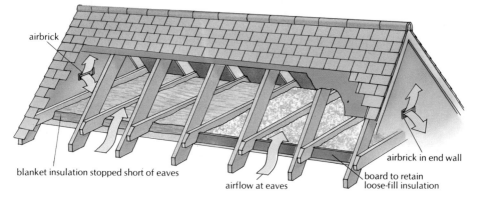

airbrick

airbrick in end wall

blanket insulation stopped short of eaves

airflow at eaves

board to retain loose-fill insulation

roof joists will accommodate. Also, loose-fill, being extremely light, can be blown about in a draughty loft, and may block vital ventilation points or leave gaps.

So, using blanket-type insulation — or even slabs of expanded polystyrene laid between the joists — may be a bit more laborious, but at least you can depend on it staying where it is.

Ventilating the loft
When laying any kind of insulation in the loft, always be sure to leave vital ventilation points free from obstruction to prevent condensation.

Usually, the roof space is ventilated at the eaves. A gap of about 13mm (½in) should always remain between the top of the insulation material and the roof lining.

According to the design of your house and its roof, ventilation of the loft space may be by another method, that of air bricks set into the end walls (gables). There should be at least three air bricks at each end, and you must not block them in any way.

Ventilation is vital in the loft because, without it, the damp that will build up is capable of damaging timbers through rot — and attacking other materials such as pipework, cable and, of course, your new insulation.

Calling in contractors
If the prospect of blundering about in the loft fills you with as much dread as inflated heating bills do, you would be wise to pay a professional installer to do the work for you.

Some contractors use a loose-fill version of the mineral fibre used in blanket-type insulation. This is literally hosed or 'blown' into the loft space (after adequate protection of tanks, ventilation spaces, etc.) to give an even covering to the whole floor area.

You'll find a number of insulation contractors listed in your local *Yellow Pages*. Ask for a free estimate, and enquire about the method of insulation they use.

Using a contractor is obviously going to be much more expensive than doing it yourself, but in terms of comfort and fuel savings, it's better than not having the job done at all. You may still be entitled to a grant towards the cost, so enquire before you do anything else.

282 Insulating the walls

Walls enjoy the dubious honour of being the major contributor to the average home's heat loss. About one third of all heat produced in a semi-detached house passes through them.

It's the walls, of course, that comprise the major part of every home's fabric, so it's hardly surprising that they dispose of so much heat. So it follows, naturally, that the large surface area made up by walls is correspondingly expensive to insulate.

There are three options: to insulate the outside of the walls, or the inside, or in the case of 'cavity' walls to fill the gap in between them.

Outside External wall insulation is usually an integral part of the house, applied during construction and planned by the architect as part of the whole aesthetic, as well as energy-saving, approach to the project.

Familiar methods of external insulation include tile-hung or timber-clad battens between which special weatherproof materials are fixed. Walls can also be rendered with insulating finishes — although to a much greater thickness than purely decorative rendering.

In pure heat-saving terms, it seems highly unlikely that the cost of these types of insulation could ever be recouped; the damage done to the looks

1

1 When dry lining a wall, a supporting framework of battens is nailed up first. Pack it out as necessary to make it truly vertical.

2

2 The sheets of plasterboard, which can be bought with a thermal lining bonded on, are nailed in place with galvanised nails at 150mm (6in) centres.

3

3 Bevel-edged board should be used, as it is easier to conceal the joints between boards. First, apply a narrow layer of filler down the joint.

4

4 Press a length of special joint tape into the filler before it has a chance to set. Make sure there are no air bubbles.

5

5 Apply a wider band of filler over the top of the joint tape, filling the bevelled depression in the board face.

6

6 Finally, carefully feather out the edges of the filler material, using a moist sponge in a circular motion.

of most houses thus treated might be no less easily retrieved!

Inside If there's one thing to be said for externally insulating walls, it's that it does not deprive you of any space within the house. For the only way to improve the insulation of solid external walls is to add somehow to their thickness, using a material with the least possible heat conductivity.

New rooms built as part of extensions or in conversions (e.g. in a loft) and in areas where major replastering is called for, can all be economically improved by using 'dry lining' techniques, which involve cladding the walls with an insulating surface.

Comparatively simple DIY techniques for dry lining include using specially insulated plasterboard sheets fixed to timber battens, or conventional plasterboard fixed to battens over glass or mineral fibre insulation, and incorporating a polythene vapour barrier to prevent condensation affecting the masonry. Thermal wallboard, for example, consists of a standard plasterboard bonded to a thick backing of expanded polystyrene, with a vapour barrier between. It can be fixed to a timber frame or stuck directly to a sound plastered wall using a special adhesive. If using battens, make sure they are treated with preservative.

Plasterboard cladding has an ivory-coloured side for direct decoration with paints or wallcoverings, and tapered long edges which can be filled to make invisible joints. In short, it's a practical wall surface which can reduce the heat loss through a solid wall by as much as two-thirds.

Dry lining internal walls between rooms would serve no useful purpose, incidentally, other than to reduce the size of your rooms.

In-between Cavity-wall construction has become the usual method in modern house building. Brick houses are commonly built with an outer wall of brick round an inner one of cheaper concrete blocks. The space between these two walls, filled with some sort of insulation material, supplies the most useful of all opportunities for cutting down heat loss through the walls of your home.

It's not a do-it-yourself job. For safety and for indemnity against any problem that might arise out of having wall cavities filled, a professional installer must be employed.

Easily the cheapest method of cavity insulation is that using 'UF' or urea-formaldehyde foam. This substance, which is delivered to the site in dry form and processed on the spot for pumping into the cavity, has been the subject of some publicity because of alleged risks to the health of people breathing its gases.

To be on the safe side, only use a cavity insulation specialist registered with the British Standards Institution. The Institution has established criteria for the safety of the foam itself, and a code of practice to cover the procedures and precautions that must be followed when treating various types of cavities.

You should have no trouble finding a BSI registered firm in your area, as there are more than 150 companies around the country who hold the appropriate certificate.

Foam insulation is suitable for cavities no more than 75mm (3in) across. Other materials available include mineral fibre, polystyrene and polyurethane substances, the 'dry' types of which would be suitable for a wider cavity. They are quite expensive.

Cavity wall insulation can cut the heat loss through walls by as much as two-thirds. Given that one third of your overall heat loss is through walls, that might mean a saving on your heating bill of 20 per cent.

284 Insulating the floors and ceilings

Suspended timber floors at ground level can allow uncomfortable draughts to enter your rooms from beneath skirtings or even between the floorboards if there's no floorcovering. Where the space beneath the floor is particularly chilly, even a covered floor may be very cold and allow undesirable quantities of heat to escape.

The simplest way to insulate such floors is to lay sheets of hardboard over them, firmly tacked or pinned down, before laying carpets or other coverings. Hardboard has the additional merit of evening out floors with worn or warped boards.

Of course, this method doesn't help if you wish to make a feature of the floorboards themselves. To prevent dust and draughts entering through the gaps between them, insulate beneath the boards where there's suitable access from the cellar or 'crawlspace'.

You can fit glassfibre or mineral fibre mat under the boards between the joists if you can find a width that will stay in place. You may well need to fix timber battens to the joists to secure the material.

Alternatively, you can tack panels of expanded polystyrene between the joists. Keep electrical cable away from polystyrene, as long-term contact between the two can cause damage to the material covering the cable.

In some cases, access to the space

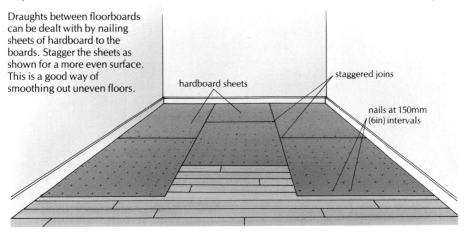

Draughts between floorboards can be dealt with by nailing sheets of hardboard to the boards. Stagger the sheets as shown for a more even surface. This is a good way of smoothing out uneven floors.

hardboard sheets

staggered joins

nails at 150mm (6in) intervals

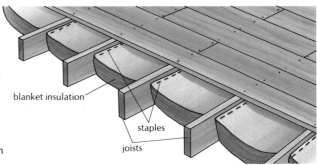

If you can gain access to the joists below the floorboards, the floor can be insulated by stapling glass fibre or mineral mat between the joists. Take care not to block any means of ventilating the space beneath the floor as this could cause rotting of the timber. An alternative to a mat material would be to fit panels of expanded polystyrene between the joists.

blanket insulation

staples

joists

Draughtproofing chimneys 285

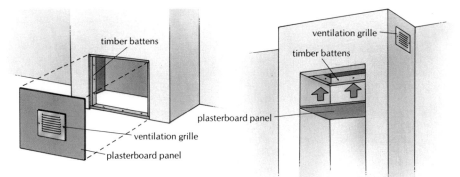

A simple way to block off a disused chimney is to fit a framework of battens around the fire opening and then to nail a panel of plasterboard to the frame, applying filler round the edges. A vent prevents condensation in the chimney.

To make more use of a disused chimney, a lintel could be fitted higher up the chimney breast and the opening extended upwards to form an alcove, which could be lined with shelves. Note the ventilator at the side and the closing panel.

under suspended floors simply isn't possible and short of tearing up the floorboards to attach insulation from above, the best you can do is to unobtrusively fill any wide gaps between the boards themselves.

An often-commended method of doing this is to mix up a concoction of papier mâché, glue (e.g. wallpaper paste) and sawdust. This pasty substance is then carefully squeezed into the gaps' with a putty knife or old kitchen knife and the residue neatly scraped away. Inevitably, it's a lengthy business, but it's cheap, and probably as effective as any other method of insulating uncovered floorboards. You can even stain the filler to blend with the boards.

Whatever you do, don't attempt to reduce the draughtiness of a suspended floor by blocking up the airbricks that allow air circulation in the space beneath. Blocked airbricks are one of the most dependable sources of damp and consequent rot in floor joists. Inspect the airbricks regularly and clear any obstructions immediately.

One more cautionary note. If you do successfully insulate your floors from the space beneath, be sure that all pipework in the now-chillier area is properly protected against freezing by lagging it thoroughly.

Draughtproofing chimneys
A disadvantage of coming home to a real fire can be that you come home to a howling draught from the chimney when the fire is not alight. If your chimney is not fitted with a trap in the flue, there's little you can do about draughtiness if the fire is in regular use. If you only use the fire at certain times of the year, you can block the chimney temporarily by filling a large plastic bag with crumpled newspaper, tying it up and shoving it up the flue. It's a simple and cheap method of cutting out at least some of the draught.

Unused chimneys should be draughtproofed if they haven't been capped at the pots, either by boxing round the fireplace (which can provide a handy space for a small cabinet, shelves or other decorative items) or by boarding up the front. Provide ventilation for the flue by fitting an air grille set in the chimney breast or the fireplace panel.

286 Draughtproofing doors

Doors tend to have the double disadvantage of letting heat out and, at the same time, admitting icy draughts, mainly because of the clearance gap that's necessary if they're to open without binding. The purpose of draughtproofing, then, is to seal these tiny gaps without hindering the operation of the door.

While the most important doors to insulate are the external ones, it may be necessary to draughtproof internal doors as well. Those leading to inevitably draughty utility rooms or cellars should certainly have draughtproofing fixed around their frames, and at floor level if necessary. Rooms which produce steam are often best kept behind well-insulated doors. Kitchens, bathrooms and WCs, for example, should have their own ventilation so that they can be kept safely separate from other rooms. Good door insulation is also vital for keeping steam and smells from spreading throughout the house.

Adhesive foam strips

Basically, there are two areas of a door that need attention: around the rebate into which the door closes, and under the door. The rebate is the easiest part to treat, using draught-resistant strips. The cheapest rebate draughtproofing is plastic-backed, self-adhesive foam strip. Supplied in reels, it's easy to handle, and usually available in various widths to suit different frame sizes. As the door closes on the jamb, the strip is compressed to form an airtight seal.

Foam strip may not be the longest-lasting or most attractive of draughtproofing materials — plan to replace it after a few years — and it does have a tendency to come unstuck.

In this case, a more substantial strip should be used. Of the many types available, sprung metal or plastic strips, which fit in the rebate and press against the door as it closes, are most widely used. Unlike foam strips, they can be painted.

When attaching any kind of draughtstrip, it's important always to work on a clean, dry surface, free from grease and flaking paint. The best time of year to do these jobs is in the summer when having doors and windows open for lengthy periods is no problem.

Threshold draught excluders

Sometimes, the worst draughts admitted by doors blow underneath, and the most effective method of preventing them is to fit threshold strips or excluders. Again, there are numerous types to choose from, but common types include rubber, plastic, felt or nylon-bristle strips, attached to a rigid batten which you screw across the full width of the bottom of the door (on the inside in the case of an exterior door) at a level which keeps the strip in firm contact with the floor when the door is closed. Other, more complex, types incorporate a rise-and-fall feature to clear carpets. Threshold excluders, which consist of a rubber or plastic tubular insert set in an aluminium strip, are designed to press against the underside of the door to form a seal, but can be a trip hazard.

For exterior doors, a combination excluder is most effective. This comes in two parts: one to fix at the threshold, the other on the outside face of the door. The two parts press together or interlock when the door is closed.

Other points at which draughts can enter through doors include letterboxes and keyholes. As a rudimentary measure, you can attach a piece of heavy felt in the form of a flap over the letterbox opening on the inside. More effective, however, is another brush-type of excluder, which is supplied in the shape of a rectangular frame with nylon bristles all round to close the gap. When screwed to the back of the letterbox opening, this device should eliminate blasts of cold air.

Covers for mortise-lock keyholes should be supplied as standard. Failing that, you can either fit a brass cover of your own, or simply attach a small felt flap to do the job.

A common source of howling draughts through back doors is the ubiquitous cat flap. Many makes seem to close up very reluctantly, whether fitted with magnets or not, and the more worn they become, the worse the draughts. Unless you can train your cat to close the door firmly some draught-proofing is needed!

Again, a felt flap can supply some sort of draughtproofing. Fit a fairly large piece to cover the cat door on all sides with a generous overlap. With magnetically operated cat flaps, keeping the metal strips clean will help the device to close itself.

An effective and durable seal for doors is this V-shaped metal or plastic weatherstrip (right). One edge is pinned to the frame and the other bears against the face or edge of the door.

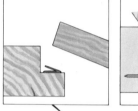

The seal shown on the left has a thin flexible blade in a metal or plastic mounting strip. When screwed or pinned to the door frame, the blade presses tightly against the face of the door.

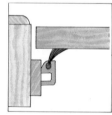

Similar to the flexible blade in principle is this brush type strip. The plastic filaments provide a good seal.

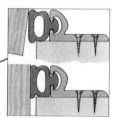

Another door face seal is the device above. It has a soft vinyl sealing bead attached to an aluminium extrusion.

A simple threshold seal for internal doors is this brush type in plastic or aluminium.

Pivotting seals (internal and external) lift to clear floorcoverings as the door is opened.

This unobstrusive flexible moulding is designed to be fitted to the floor.

This threshold strip for an external door has a seal that sits against the door face.

288 Draughtproofing windows

Windows can be just as much to blame as doors for letting in draughts, and glass itself is a poor protection against heat loss. To minimise what is lost through single-glazed windows, they need to be kept in good repair.

Ill-fitting sash windows are particularly prone to letting in draughts. Damaged beadings, broken cords and rotting or warped frames all contribute to the numerous gaps that form around neglected sashes.

Unfortunately for the looks of many houses originally built with sash windows, the common solution to such problems seems to be to rip out the windows and fit aluminium or PVC framed replacements. Though reputed to be maintenance-free, these new non-opening units are still expensive, usually out of character with the house — and most of the time unnecessary.

It *is* possible to repair a sash window fully, to make it largely draughtproof — and for very little cost, as the illustrated guide on these pages shows.

Casement windows (right) can make use of many of the methods used for sealing round doors. However, sliding sash windows present problems when it comes to draughtproofing. An effective solution using flexible blade seals is shown below.

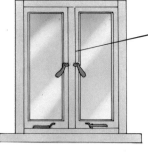

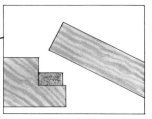

The simplest and cheapest way of draughtproofing casement windows is with self-adhesive foam strip (above), but it is not durable.

On a sliding sash window, fit a blade seal to the outside of each upper window stile so that it seals against the frame (above).

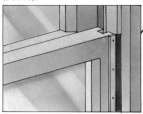

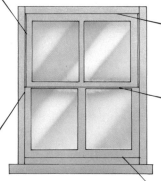

One strip attached to the upper window top rail seals against the frame; another on the bottom rail seals against the lower window.

Inside, fit a seal to each of the lower window stiles so that they seal against the sash stop beading of the window frame as shown above.

The job is completed by attaching a sealing strip across the bottom rail of the lower window so that its blade is compressed against the frame's draught stop beading as shown on the right. The seal fits between those on the stiles.

Casement windows

You can draughtproof casements in the same way as doors, being careful not to put any strain on hinges or fittings by using draughtstrip that is too dense. Plastic-backed self-adhesive foam is usually adequate for all windows except those that are likely to be opened and closed very often, or those which are regularly exposed to steam or penetrating rain.

Sash windows

If a sash window rattles, lets in draughts or won't open or close properly, it's likely that the beading is at fault or that one or both of the cords is broken. It's quite straightforward to adjust or repair a suspect window, although it may mean removing the sashes.

The sashes should run smoothly between their respective beadings without rattling. The 'stop' bead against which the outer sash runs is an integral part of the frame, so only the 'parting' bead, which fits into the channel between the two sashes, can be improved in this case. This parting bead often becomes loose, its channel filling up with dust and debris. The inner 'staff' bead may also be loose or rotten.

To gain access to the sash weights you may have to remove the parting bead if it covers the pockets.

1 To mend a frayed or broken sash cord you must remove the sash frame. Lever off the staff bead carefully from the sides of the frame with an old chisel.

2 Lift out the sash frame and, holding the frayed cord in one hand to stop the weight from dropping, lever off the nails that hold the cord in the grooves.

3 Prise off the central parting bead and remove the sash box cover. Pull out the iron weight and old cord. Untie the cord from the weight.

4 Tie some string to a small nail and to the new cord. Feed it over the pulley and retrieve it from the weight pocket.

5 Attach the weight and holding it just above the bottom of the box, cut the cord to fit in the sash frame's side groove.

6 Nail the new cord to the sash frame, then replace the pocket cover, parting bead, frame, and lastly the staff bead.

290 Double glazing

Certainly the most effective way of cutting both draughts and heat loss at windows, double glazing provides comfort, good sound insulation and even added security to the home. As an economic means of reducing heating bills, however, it's invariably a non-starter. Most double glazing is far too expensive to be a redeemable investment in this sense.

Secondary glazing

However, by fitting your own double glazing in some form, you can reduce the size of this investment without sacrificing too much of the benefit. A number of companies now offer 'secondary' windows, which you can fit inside your existing windows to create your own double-glazed arrangement. The photographs opposite show a typical installation for sliding sash windows.

Made to measure, and supplied either as fixed or opening (casement or sliding) units, these can be quite effective if you carefully follow the recommended method of installation. Not all these secondary windows are glazed — some have plastic panes, which are certainly less intimidating to work with if you have never handled window glass before.

Removable panes

Cheaper versions include kits from which you can assemble and construct secondary windows to fit according to your measurements. They're designed to be unclipped, enabling you still to use the original windows. You'll need to supply glass cut to the right size, of course, unless you're using a kit based on plastic panes.

Condensation problems

Less expensive forms of double glazing such as these cannot be expected to match the heat-saving capabilities (such as they are) of factory-made, sealed window units installed by specialist firms. This might be a minor difference, however, compared to that of relative problems with condensation. A properly sealed unit will be free of condensation, since the air between the panes will have been dehydrated, while secondary double glazing will inevitably be troubled by it.

Any moist air trapped between the panes during installation will deposit its moisture on the outer pane when the temperature drops sufficiently. If the temperature rises, this moisture will be reabsorbed by the air until the glass cools again. If the inner window is not sealed properly to the window reveal, it will allow warm moist air from the house to flow into the space between the panes where water droplets will again be deposited on the cold outer pane as the air cools on contact with it. Similarly, opening inner windows will allow moist air to enter the gap every time they're opened.

Adding ventilation

With do-it-yourself double glazing, the only effective answer to the problem is to ventilate the space between the panes, so that a flow of air passing through will prevent the moisture condensing on the glass. Drill at least one small hole in each side of the frame between the panes, near the bottom of the window.

Obviously, this undoes some of the good that you expect from double glazing, but the difference in heat saving will be marginal. To avoid having to drill holes in the frame, you could try using special silica gel crystals — available from builders' merchants — in the space to absorb the moisture. These may cope with mild condensation problems, but you have to remove them regularly to enable them to dry out.

1 Here, a sliding sash is being fitted with UPVC double glazing. The method is similar for all windows. First, measure up the window opening.

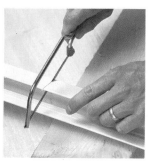

2 Transfer the measurements to the window track sections and cut them to length using a junior hacksaw. You may need to trim the corners to fit.

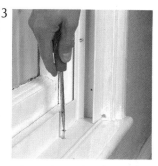

3 Screw the track to the inside of the window opening. The track must be set square, and you may need to pack it out with wood and filler.

4 Measure up for the glass and have a local glazier cut it to size. Stand each pane on a folded cloth or newspapers and tap on the upper glass carriers.

5 Fit the lower glass carrier to each pane. Start at one end and gently tap it into place with a rubber mallet or a block of wood.

6 Complete the sliding glass panes by adding the side glass carriers, which are also tapped into place. The carriers incorporate brush seals.

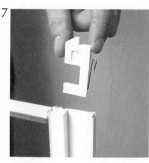

7 The lower glass carrier of each pane is designed to accept a spring catch. One catch is slid into each end.

8 Fit the ratchet sash guides. These clip into the tracks and will hold the windows in any chosen position.

9 Fit each pane, locating one catch in its guide and retracting the other for clearance. Then release the catch.

Central heating and insulation projects are safe for the competent do-it-yourselfer only so long as the correct procedures are followed. This applies not just to the installation or maintenance work, but to the safe use of installations and appliances.

Other than the commonsense guidelines already described, a number of specific recommendations on safety are made by bodies such as the British Standards Institution and the nationalised fuel corporations. Some of the relevant points, along with safety aspects not already touched on, are outlined in the brief guide that follows:

Boilers If you are thinking about installing a new boiler, either as a replacement or as part of a new system, make sure a safe appliance is fitted. Gas boilers should conform to relevant British Standards (BS 5258, and in some cases BS 1250). Many floorstanding gas boilers are approved under the British Standards Safety Mark scheme.

Oil fired boilers should comply with the standards of, and be approved by, the Domestic Oil Burning Equipment Testing Association.

Solid fuel boilers are covered by the Domestic Solid Fuels Association.

The Electricity Council publish a *Supplementary List of Household Electrical Appliances* to cover approved heating appliances.

Convectors Avoid draping cloths over, or in any way obstructing, convector or fan-convector heaters.

Draughtproofing Remember that any room containing a conventionally flued boiler must have permanent ventilation to the outside.

Electrical appliances Motorised valves, pumps and all electrical equipment must be safely wired according to the Institution of Electrical Engineers' regulations. Heating appliances should be among those approved in the Electricity Council's *Supplementary List of Household Electrical Appliances.*

Flues Avoid the use of two flued appliances at one chimney if possible. Never use one chimney for the flues of two appliances burning different fuels.

Gas According to British Gas, 'Customers may not use, or let anyone else use, gas appliances which they know, or suspect, are in a potentially dangerous condition'. Installing and servicing gas systems, they say, 'is no job for the do-it-yourself amateur. Only competent people may install or service appliances or systems. Customers must not attempt such work (unless they are qualified to do so).'

Should you suspect any kind of gas leak, British Gas urge you to shut off the main supply immediately by turning the gas tap through 90 degrees to the off position, the notched mark on the tap's spindle pointing horizontally across the pipe.

Then, contact your local Gas Service Centre's emergency service. They are on 24-hour, 365-days-a-year call.

Pipes Where hot pipes are exposed, along skirtings for instance, they may present a hazard to very young children. At maximum temperature, a pipe could cause painful burns to a child too young to have developed quick-enough reflexes to withdraw from contact in time.

If you do have young children, careful supervision at least is desirable; ideally, the pipes should be insulated as well. The best answer, if you are having a new system installed, is to insist that no pipes are left exposed.

Radiators Again, very young children should be kept away, as radiators can be very hot to the touch.

Second-hand equipment Don't buy used central heating appliances, unless the vendor is willing to have a complete check carried out by a qualified expert, preferably at his own expense.

An explanation of some of the common terms in the language of central heating and insulation.

airbrick A brick cast with a number of air passages, which is a vital source of underfloor and roof space ventilation. Always keep clear.

air change Timed rate of heat loss in a room for which heating is designed to compensate.

balanced flue Combined boiler exhaust and air intake.

balancing the system Adjusting each radiator so that water passing through gives off 11°C (20°F) of heat.

Btu/h British thermal units per hour. Still widely used measure of heat output. 3,412Btu/h equals 1kW (equivalent metric heat output unit).

cavity wall Common external wall construction for 50 years, comprising outer and inner brick or block 'leaves' on each side of a central cavity. Most cavities are about 50mm (2in) wide.

capillary joint A soldered type of plumbing fitting.

compression joint Plumbing fitting with threaded joints.

convector Heater that warms air rather than surfaces — can be combined with a radiator.

cylinder Hot water tank.

draincock Tap for emptying central heating system, located at lowest point.

elbow Right-angled plumbing joint.

feed and expansion tank Water supply for system with an overflow point should water rise through overheating or blockage.

flue liner Metal tube inserted in a conventional flue to prevent condensation damaging the brickwork.

flux Paste or liquid that aids flow and fusion of solder.

forced flow Central heating water circulation by pump action.

gravity check valve Non-electric valve to prevent hot water rising by gravity in the system when the pump is not running.

hand valve Adjustable on/off radiator valve, also known as a 'wheel valve'.

immersion heater Electric heating element used in cylinder to heat tap water. Sometimes used as an alternative water heater in boiler-powered systems during the summer when running the boiler just to provide hot water would be uneconomic.

indirect system Combined central heating and hot water system, where water from the boiler passes through a coil in the hot water cylinder to heat the water it contains.

isolating valve Any valve which, by closing, can seal off part of the system to allow work on it without having to drain down.

lockshield valve Balancing valve at radiator return; needs a special key.

microbore Narrow, flexible pipe used in some systems.

motorised valve Electrically operated diverting valve.

overflow Pipe connecting feed and expansion tank to outside, to drain off excess water if the level rises (usually when ballvalve sticks).

pilot Continuously burning ignition flame. Some systems are now ignited electrically.

primary circuit Pipe carrying heated water from boiler to the cylinder coil and back again.

radiation Emitted heat which warms surfaces.

resistance The 'head' or pressure exerted by the pump to push water round the system, is determined by calculating the total friction encountered by the water in the full length of the pipework and radiators — known as the resistance of the system.

return pipe Pipe carrying cooled radiator water back to the boiler.

sealed system System with a closed expansion vessel rather than an open feed and expansion tank. Works at high pressure so special fittings are needed.

small bore The usual narrow pipe size used for modern domestic central heating systems.

straight coupler Plumbing, fitting, joining one straight length of pipe to another.

tee Plumbing joint used to branch out of a run of pipework.

thermostat Device to sense temperature and trigger heating controls according to setting.

thermostatic valve Individual radiator control activated by an inbuilt temperature sensor.

'U' values Measured rates at which different building materials are known to transfer heat.

vent pipe Open pipe rising from circulating pipe to a high point over the feed and expansion tank. Allows air to escape from flow, and water to escape — back into the tank — in the event of serious overheating.

wheel valve See 'hand valve'.

Index

Acknowledgments

CARPENTRY

The publishers wish to acknowledge the help of Lindsey Edwards and Ron Kidd for constructing the projects, and Ronnie Rustin for demonstrating French polishing.

The following organisations kindly supplied equipment and other materials: Aaronson Brothers; Black and Decker; DIY Timber; General Woodwork Supplies; Rustins; Stanley Tools.

Photography: Chris Linton; Simon de Courcy Wheeler.

Illustrations: Will Giles; Janos Marrfy.

ELECTRICITY

Tools, Equipment & Facilities
The publishers are grateful to the many organisations and individuals who supplied materials, tools and other equipment, or provided locations and/or facilities for photography. Thanks are due especially to the following:
Ashley Accessories Ltd, Ulverston, Cumbria (Mr Alan Brook): Electrical fittings.
B & R Electrical Products Ltd, Harlow, Essex (Mr Peter Barnett): ELCB socket and PowerBreaker plug.
Blomberg (UK) Ltd, Birkenhead, Merseyside (Elizabeth King, Link Communications): Electric cooker.
City Electrical Factors Ltd, Stoke Newington, London (Mr Brian Vince): Electrical fittings, electrician's tools.
Crabtree Electrical Industries Ltd, Walsall, West Midlands (Mr Alan Preston): Electrical fittings.
Econa Appliances Ltd, Solihull, West Midlands (Elizabeth King, Link Communications): Parkamatic Silver waste-disposal unit.
General Woodwork Supplies Ltd, Stoke Newington, London (Mr Geoff Bentley): General purpose tools.
Home Automation Ltd, Hoddesdon, Herts (Mrs Weston): Dimmer switches.
Marlin Lighting Ltd (including CONELIGHT), Feltham, Middlesex (Mr C R Fielding): Light fittings.
Marshall-Tufflex Ltd, Hastings, East Sussex (Mr D E Smart/Mr J C Boles): Electrical conduit and trunking.
Philips Electrical Industries Ltd (Lighting Division), Croydon, Surrey (Mrs Pam Gillett): Lamps.
Rock Electrical Accessories Ltd, Brentford, Middlesex (Mr Brian Godwin): Electrical fittings.
Thorn-Emi Lighting Ltd, Tottenham, London (Mr Cyril Phillips): Lamps.
Tools and equipment co-ordinator: Mike Trier.

Photography: Jon Bouchier 87, 100-150; Simon de Courcy Wheeler 92-97.

Artwork: Chris Forsey 152-153; Brian Watson/Linden Artists 82-150.

PLUMBING

Tools, Equipment & Facilities
The publishers are grateful to the many organisations and individuals who supplied materials, tools and other equipment, or provided locations and/or facilities for photography. Thanks are due especially to the following:
Barking-Grohe Ltd, Barking, Essex (Mr V H King): Thermostatic shower mixer and rose.
Bartol Plastics Ltd, Doncaster, Yorkshire (Trisha Brimblecombe): Plastics push-fit waste and Acorn hot-water systems.
City Electrical Factors Ltd, Stoke Newington, London (Mr Brian Vince): Immersion heater and electric shower unit.
Arthur Collier Ltd, Brixton, London (Mr John Collier): Plumbing tools.
Conex-Sanbra Ltd, Tipton, West Midlands (Mr John Pritchard): Compression fittings, stopcocks and valves.

Delta Capillary Products Ltd, Dundee, Scotland (Mr R McCutcheon): End-feed capillary fittings.
DHC Products (Denton Hat Co), Denton, Manchester (Mr J Greenhough): Pipe-leak repair clamp.
DRG Sellotape Products Ltd, Borehamwood, Herts (Mr J Wallis/Mrs J M Britton): Pipe and hose repair bandage.
Econa Appliances Ltd, Solihull, West Midlands (Elizabeth King, Link Communications): Parkamatic Silver waste-disposal unit.
Footprint Tools Ltd, Hollis Croft, Sheffield (Mr Christopher Jewitt): General purpose tools.
Houseman (Burnham Ltd), Burnham, Slough (Mr Mike Trim): Permutit water softener and installation kit.
Hunter Building Products Ltd, Abbey Wood, London (Mr J P Ward-Turner): Genova solvent-weld hot and cold water system and bib tap.
IAZ International (UK) Ltd, Reading, Berkshire (Lesley Hawthorne/Megan Nixon): Zanussi automatic washing machine.
IMI Range Ltd, Stalybridge, Cheshire (Mr Ken Peacock): Supercal insulated hot-water cylinder.
Key Terrain Ltd, Maidstone, Kent (Mr H W Marden-Ranger): Terrain solvent-weld waste system and fittings.
Kitchen Design and Advice Ltd, Hendon, London and Enfield, Middlesex (Mrs Barbara Ellison/Mr Arlen Whittock): Kitchen base unit and sink top.
Monument Tools Ltd, Balham, London (Mr John Collier): Plumbing tools.
Royal Bathrooms Ltd, Stoke-on-Trent, Staffs (Ruth Francis, Paul Winner Market Communications Ltd/ Mr Martin Morris): Bathroom suite, taps, shower tray and cubicle.
John Sydney Ltd, Walworth, London (Mr B Maizner): Cascade mixer tap.
Yorkshire Imperial Fittings Ltd, Leeds, Yorkshire (Mr Stephen Young): 'Yorkshire' capillary fittings.
Tools and equipment co-ordinator: Mike Trier.

Photography: Jon Bouchier 168-169, 174, 182-183, 185 (above), 187-211, 221, 226; Simon de Courcy Wheeler 166-167, 170-173, 175-181, 187, 215, 217, 224.

Artwork: Trevor Lawrence 172-173, 191, 220; Ian Stephen 185; Brian Watson/Linden Artists 158-165, 178-184, 186-190, 192-219, 222-230.

CENTRAL HEATING AND INSULATION

Tools, Equipment & Facilities
The publishers are grateful to the many organisations and individuals who supplied materials, tools and other equipment, or provided locations and/or facilities for photography. Thanks are due especially to the following:
British Gypsum Ltd, Gravesend, Kent (Mr Gordon McAra): Thermal insulating board and use of their facilities.
Arthur Collier Ltd, Brixton, London (Mr John Collier): Plumbing tools.
Conex-Sanbra Ltd, Tipton, West Midlands (Mr John Pritchard): Compression fittings, gate valves, stopcocks, radiator valves.
Delta Capillary Products Ltd, Dundee, Scotland (Mr R McCutcheon): End-feed capillary fittings.
DHC Products (Denton Hat Co), Denton, Manchester (Mr J Greenhough): Pipe-leak repair clamp.
DRG Sellotape Products Ltd, Borehamwood, Herts (Mr J Wallis/Mrs J M Britton): Pipe and hose repair bandage.
Footprint Tools Ltd, Hollis Croft, Sheffield (Mr Christopher Jewitt): General purpose tools.
Monument Tools Ltd, Balham, London (Mr John Collier): Plumbing tools.
OBC Ltd (Wolseley-Hughes Merchants Ltd), Upper Edmonton, London (Mr Mick Huckle): Programmers, thermostats, thermostatic radiator valves, pump.
Polycell Products Ltd, Welwyn Garden City, Herts (Debbie Sunderland): Vertical sash double glazing system.
Thorn EMI Heating Ltd, Gateshead, Tyne and Wear (Mr Sid Taylor/Sharon Hovells): Panel radiators, programmer.
Wednesbury Tube Co Ltd, Bilston, West Midlands (Mr Geoff Egginton): Microbore tube and manifolds.
Yorkshire Imperial Fittings Ltd, Leeds, Yorkshire (Mr Stephen Young): 'Yorkshire' capillary fittings.
Tools and equipment co-ordinator: Mike Trier.

Photography: Jon Bouchier 254-255, 256, 258-259, 260-261, 262, 264-265, 266-267, 269, 270, 272, 279, 280, 282; Simon de Courcy Wheeler 250-251, 252-253, 289, 291.

Artwork: Dave Allen 241; Mike Saunders 237, 242, 247, 273, 274, 275, 276-277, 281, 287, 288; Ian Stephen 234-235, 236, 238-239, 240, 243, 244-245, 246, 248, 249, 268, 284-285.